Dottie Wiltse Collins

Dottie Wiltse Collins

*Strikeout Queen of the
All-American Girls
Professional Baseball League*

CAROLYN M. TROMBE

McFarland & Company, Inc., Publishers
Jefferson, North Carolina, and London

LIBRARY OF CONGRESS CATALOGUING-IN-PUBLICATION DATA

Trombe, Carolyn M., 1957–
    Dottie Wiltse Collins : strikeout queen of the All-American
Girls Professional Baseball League / Carolyn M. Trombe.
        p.   cm.
    Includes bibliographical references and index.

    ISBN 0-7864-2188-6 (softcover : 50# alkaline paper)

    1. Collins, Dottie Wiltse, 1923–   2. Baseball players—
United States—Biography.   3. Women baseball players—
United States—Biography.   4. All-American Girls
Professional Baseball League—History.   I. Title.
GV865.C65T76   2005
796.357'092—dc22   2005010699

British Library cataloguing data are available

On the cover: Dottie as a member of the Fort Wayne Daisies, 1945
(courtesy Northern Indiana Center for History)

Manufactured in the United States of America

*McFarland & Company, Inc., Publishers
  Box 611, Jefferson, North Carolina 28640
    www.mcfarlandpub.com*

To Dottie Collins and all those like her
who long for the crack of the bat on the ball;
and to the memory of Robert I. Ducas, the first
professional to believe in me as a writer.

Acknowledgments

Numerous people have contributed to the success of this book. Needless to say, this book would not have come about without the input of the women from the AAGPBL: Jacqueline Mattson Baumgart, Jean Geissinger Harding, Frances (Fran) Janssen, Vivian Kellogg, Margaret (Marge) Callaghan Maxwell, Jane Moffett, June Peppas, Mary Rountree, Kathryn (Kate) Vonderau, and Delores (Dolly) Brumfield White. I would also like to thank Jeri Baldwin, Jim Glennie, and Carol Sheldon for sharing with me their experiences concerning women in baseball today. Jim Robertson of the Historical Society of Centinela Valley and Kay Ikuto of the Inglewood Library gave me background information on Dottie's hometown. Dottie's childhood friends, Barbara White Hoffman and Virginia Bruner Larson, gave me some wonderful material about growing up with Dottie in southern California, while Harvey Collins's lifelong friend, Carl "Bud" Offerle, also shared his recollections with me.

Dottie Collins spoke with me at length and endured innumerable questions as we traveled back almost seventy years in time. Dottie's daughter, Patty Tyler, and her grandsons, David and John Gilbert, shared with me stories of their mother and grandmother that added an important dimension to the book. Judy Berg Widen gave me invaluable information about her father, Ernie Berg, business manager of the Daisies, and some wonderful insights about what it meant to be a Daisy fan, while Monica Wehrle talked to me about Daisy ball and the first "Run, Jane, Run" reunion. For sharing their memories of Dottie as a golfer and giving me insight into her character at that time, I am grateful to Pat Wright, the late Gert McAtee, and Sue Langas. My special thanks to Pat Wright for explaining match play to a person who knows little about the game of golf. Any errors are, of course, my own. Rich Sangillo provided me with a heartwarming anecdote involving Dottie Collins and Dottie Schroeder, which fit perfectly into the epilogue.

Claudette Burke, Jeremy Jones, and Tim Wiles of the National Baseball Hall of Fame in Cooperstown, New York, helped me with my research, and Ted Spencer took the time to speak with me about Dottie's role in the opening of the Women In Baseball display at the Hall of Fame. Maki Bauer, Joe Hughes, and Jennifer Johns of the Northern Indiana Center for History in South Bend, Indiana, provided me with photographs and the scrapbooks of Dottie Wiltse Collins. Much of the wealth of material in this book would not have been resent without Marge Graham, my research assistant, whose accurate and lively "digging around" truly made the book come alive. Don Graham's incomparable knowledge of sports in Fort Wayne, Indiana, allowed me to illustrate the Daisies' role in the Fort Wayne sports scene much more clearly. I also give many thanks to Rosemarie (Snooky) Fitzpatrick, who transcribed countless tapes, sometimes against impossible background noise.

I am especially grateful to Merrie Fidler, who blazed the trail for all of us who came after by writing the first history of the AAGPBL, for sharing her invaluable research and insights and serving as a sounding board as we worked together to preserve the history of the League. Sue Macy, another chronicler of the League, offered to read this rather lengthy tome and has served as inspiration for my own development as a writer. Jim Sargent's biographical sketch on Dottie Collins started me on my way. My thanks also go to Douglas Hoyt for providing me with a list of educational and fascinating books relating to World War II.

I owe a great debt to my agent, the late Robert I. Ducas, for guiding me in my growth as a writer, and to his wife, Louise Chinn, who has taken over where Robert left off. I also want to thank all my friends and family for supporting me on my road to publication. Finally, I would like to acknowledge three key people who helped make my dream a reality: My friend of almost thirty years, Thomas F. Martin, who suggested the idea for this book, telling me to look into the women's league because "so many stories waited to be told"; my mentor and friend, Pauline Bartel, whose counsel and encouragement has enabled me to reach the point where I am today; and my husband, Brian A. Hains, without whom none of this would have been possible.

Table of Contents

Preface

Eleanor Roosevelt once said, "We must do what we think we cannot do." During the 1940s and 1950s over six hundred women heeded that call by joining the All-American Girls Professional Baseball League. The first professional women's baseball league, the AAGPBL was immortalized in the movie *A League of Their Own*. However, while the movie's widespread appeal has brought the league considerable recognition, not so well known are the stories of the individuals who played in that league. This is the story of one of those women, Dottie Wiltse Collins, a premier player in the six seasons she pitched professional baseball and a driving force behind the league's rise from obscurity to its rightful place in the history of sports.

To answer a frequently asked question, Dottie Collins was not the Dottie portrayed in the movie by Geena Davis. The film characters were composites of all the women who played in the league. Yet, just as the characters in the movie represented the league in general, Dottie Collins stands as a fine example of what it meant to be part of the All-American Girls Professional Baseball League. With its emphasis on skill, discipline, and an abiding love for the game, the league nurtured a group of women who dared to move beyond society's barriers and to establish new frontiers for talented, ambitious women.

The book begins with Dottie Collins's softball career, which laid the groundwork for her entry into the women's league almost a decade later. Growing up in Southern California, Dottie was introduced to the game came by her father, a semipro baseball player in the National Niteball Baseball League in Inglewood. Dan Wiltse instituted regular practice sessions with his daughter, supplemented by lessons from his teammates, such as Lou Novikoff, who would later play in the outfield for the Chicago Cubs.

By the time she was 12 years old, Dottie was more than ready to move up from bat girl for the Mark C. Bloome women's softball team when the pitcher faltered in the final game of the *Los Angeles Examiner* tournament. Working before a crowd of more than 25,000 spectators, Dottie pitched her team to the Southern California girls' softball championship. That performance turned out to be just the beginning of her stint as one of the top pitchers in the Southern California girls' softball loop. During the seven years she played softball, Dottie's prowess on the mound helped other teams to the championship title and also led to a brush with stardom when Warner Bros. Films named her the Million Dollar Baby of softball in conjunction with their newly released movie of the same name.

Dottie's years with the All-Americans were even more impressive. Her career with the Minneapolis Millerettes and the Fort Wayne Daisies, from 1944–1950, spanned almost the entire duration of the league. Beginning with the Millerettes in 1944, the second year of the league's existence, Dottie posted a 20–16 record, striking out 205 batters and walking 130 in 38 games for an ERA of 1.88. The following year she moved to the Fort Wayne Daisies and led the league in strikeouts with 293, recording a 29–10 record and a stunning 0.83 ERA. In her five seasons with the Daisies she continually added to her list of brilliant performances, beloved of fans and teammates alike. Dottie's career highlights in her years with the Daisies include 17 shutouts and two no-hitters within 17 days in 1945, three extra-innings games in seven days in 1947, and pitching through her fifth month of pregnancy in 1948. After her child was born, she came back for one more season of play in 1950.

Woven throughout the saga of Dottie's athletic achievements is the story of her life outside of baseball. The book looks at her adolescent years growing up near the beautiful beach towns close to Los Angeles, her courtship and marriage to the handsome sailor Harvey Collins, and the birth of Dottie's daughter in the midst of her playing career. All of this is set against the background of the Depression, World War II, and the years immediately following the war when women's roles changed dramatically. While Dottie's life mirrored these different eras in significant ways, her own life choices clearly show her indomitable spirit and that strong sense of self developed early in her softball career and honed more finely in her years with the All-American League.

Dottie's story does not end with her baseball career. Perhaps her most important contributions to the game came more than thirty years after she thought she had left the field forever. After several decades of raising her family and proving herself just as adept on the golf course as she was on the diamond, Dottie rediscovered her love for the game through a local women's sports festival in Fort Wayne, Indiana, where several former leaguers gathered for an exhibition baseball game in 1981. Fueled by a desire to have even more women gather together and to somehow preserve the legacy of the league, Dottie began a quest for recognition of the league that would continue into the new millennium. The determined efforts of Dottie Collins eventually resulted in the All-American Girls Professional Baseball League Players Association, the opening of the first display on women's baseball in the Baseball Hall of Fame in Cooperstown, New York, and the movie *A League of Their Own.*

Extensive use has been made of personal interviews with Dottie Collins and several women who played with her in the league; personal correspondence with other players, Dottie's childhood friends, and people who knew Dottie through her work in the Players Association; the scrapbooks of Dottie Collins from her years playing softball and baseball; and original newspaper accounts of the games in which Dottie featured. All of this material combines to create a picture of a strong, talented woman living in a unique time for all women, and a person who can serve as a role model for us all.

FIRST INNING

Daddy's Little Pitcher: 1936–1939

Dottie's love affair with baseball started when she was just two years old. Twice a week, her mother bundled her into the car to catch her father's baseball games, either at Centinela Park or at one of the other stadiums situated around the Los Angeles area. Dan guarded second base for the semipro National Niteball Baseball League in Inglewood, California, where Dottie spent her formative years. Being quick on his feet, Dan established himself as an excellent fielder, charging for wayward balls on their way to the outfield. Dan also proved to be quite a proficient bunter, helping to advance his teammates in many tight situations. One can picture Dottie as a winsome toddler squirming in her mother's lap as she watched her daddy play ball, not quite sure what was going on but caught up in the excitement nevertheless.

Dan was in his early twenties at the time, playing with the likes of such future major league players as Lou Novikoff, who later played in the outfield for the Chicago Cubs in the 1940s. Dottie remembers her father and the owner of his baseball team going down into Russiantown, a small settlement outside Inglewood where people made pots of borscht in their front yards, to convince the phenomenal youngster they had heard so much about to join their team. Known in the majors as The Mad Russian, Lou became known for his prodigious appetite, especially when it came to high-grade caviar that he supposedly shared with his pet Russian wolfhound.

Although Novikoff turned out to be an inefficient fielder in the majors, he continued the outstanding hitting he had demonstrated in the Niteball League. He won the batting title of four different minor leagues from 1938 to 1941, and he left the majors after the 1946 season with a .282 career batting average. Dottie remembered watching

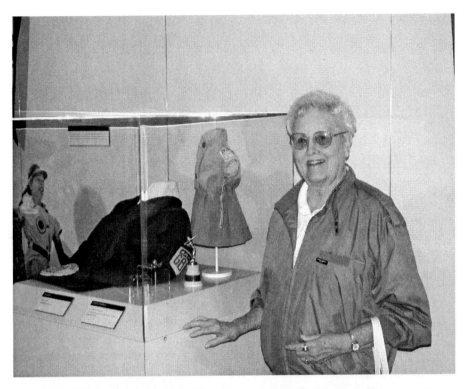

Dottie Wiltse Collins is thrilled to see her daughter's uniform on display at the opening exhibit of "Women in Sports, Breaking Barriers" at the Northern Indiana Center for History in 2002. More than fifty years had passed since Patty donned the uniform, which was identical to the one her mother wore when she pitched for the Fort Wayne Daisies.

him pummel the ball when he played on her father's team. "There was a place up the hill from Centinela Park where you could buy angels and things for cemetery plots," Dottie said. "Louie hit the ball so hard he knocked the wings off I don't know how many angels up there on top."

Lou and another player, Earl Morrell, took a special interest in Dottie and often spent time teaching her the basics of baseball once their games were finished. Both men probably recognized her potential. What started out as games of catch soon evolved into regular instruction sessions. "Lou and Earl showed me what to do," Dottie said, "and then I went out and practiced." Yet while Lou helped Dottie as a hitter, he affected her more as a pitcher. His great hitting ability aside, Lou was known as one of the greatest softball pitchers ever.

He returned to softball after his stint in the majors, let go mainly because of his bumbling plays in the outfield, although Dottie suspected he didn't follow the rules very well, either, being known as something of an eccentric. He superstitiously feared touching the ivy-covered walls at Wrigley Field. Once he resumed softball pitching, however, he played until he was 53, after which he was inducted into the Softball Hall of Fame.

Several parallels exist between Dottie and Novikoff, or Lou Nova as he was called during his softball days. First, Lou was only thirteen years old when he was recruited to play on Dan Wiltse's team, much younger than the rest of the players. This foreshadowed the position in which Dottie would be placed several years later when she debuted as a fast-pitch softball player just shy of her thirteenth birthday. Even more interesting is that Lou got his start in the majors as a war fill-in. Just a few years later that same war opened the door for Dottie and her AAGPBL teammates to break the gender barrier for the first time in the chronology of baseball. Who could have guessed that one man's desire to bring a young girl's aptitude to the fore would have such a far-reaching effect on the history of women in sports?

Still, as much as she was helped by Lou and Earl Morrell, Dottie relied most heavily on her father's expertise. Dan Wiltse's role in his daughter's development as one of the best pitchers both in the softball leagues of Southern California and in the All-American Girls Professional Baseball League cannot be overlooked. Early in her life, he instilled in his daughter the need for discipline and the confidence that would catapult Dottie into the world of professional sports. Dottie's father led her down a different path than the one he followed, encouraging his daughter to pitch rather than establishing herself as a fielder. Perhaps it was the memory of his second cousins that caused him to steer his child as he did.

George Leroy "Hooks" Wiltse played for the New York Giants in the early 1900s and gained his moment of fame when he pitched a no-hitter against Philadelphia on July 4, 1908, before a capacity crowd in the old Polo Grounds in New York City. He walked no one and would have pitched a perfect game if not for a controversial call in the ninth inning. He continued his outstanding performance for the next several years with the Brooklyn TipTops of the now defunct Federal League. Over the course of his twelve-year career in the majors he amassed a win/loss percentage of .607 and an ERA of 2.47. Later, he coached for the New York Yankees.

Lewis DeWitt "Snake" Wiltse, while never achieving the success of his younger brother, still made it to the majors, playing from 1901–1903. Snake pitched for the Pittsburgh Pirates, the Philadelphia Athletics, the Baltimore Orioles, and the New York Highlanders, the precursor to the New York Yankees. He won thirteen games for the A's in 1901, the AL's first year, and was the only hurler at that time to collect four extra-base hits in a game.

A few years prior to receiving instructions from Novikoff and Morrell, Dottie worked out daily at home with her father. Every day at exactly 4:30, Dan returned home from work to find his daughter eagerly awaiting his arrival for their regular game of catch. "I was always sitting there on the back porch with my glove waiting for him to come home," Dottie said, smiling with remembrance even after more than seventy years had passed. "First we started out playing catch, and then later my dad built a backstop in the vacant lot next door."

Dan wasn't just throwing the ball around, though. He was molding a pitcher, specifically a fast-pitch softball pitcher. Fast-pitch softball is a pitcher's game. With slow-pitch softball, the pitcher loops the ball up in the air so it moves slowly and is easier to hit. Fast-pitch softball allows the pitcher to vary the speed and the arc of the ball. The ball can be thrown as hard as the pitcher desires, and the pitcher chooses whether to put a curve on it, a drop, a raised ball or a slow ball. While Dottie's speed and variations on the type of pitch developed over the years, her father began building her pitching repertoire by teaching her the curveball and the slow ball. Dottie took these practice sessions with her father seriously. She may not have realized at such a young age what heights her talent would reach, but she was honing the discipline she would need for a much more rigorous role later on.

It may seem odd during the time period of the late 1920s and the 1930s that a young girl would follow the path her father mapped out. More traditionally, Dottie might have obeyed her mother's wish that she become a dancer. Dottie had taken lessons in dance and appeared in several recitals, but in the end she emulated her father and became what he wanted her to be, a ballplayer. But plenty of girls played in softball leagues in southern California during the time Dottie was growing up, and moreover, by steering Dottie towards the role of an athlete, Dan instilled in his daughter a strong sense of independence. That, coupled with a keen competitive spirit, assured Dan that he had fostered in his only child the attributes she would need to succeed in any of life's endeavors, no matter which direction she chose to follow.

If, as Dottie believes, her father would have liked to have had a son, it is equally clear he was never disappointed having a daughter. "After all," she laughed, "he got to turn me into a tomboy." Dottie and her father shared a close relationship. She asserts that if it were not for her father she would not have developed into the athlete she became. Dan Wiltse made sure that his daughter had the early start he never had, and he gave his daughter every opportunity to achieve a caliber of play that would ensure her a spot in the limelight, a spot that at first perhaps only he could foresee. He controlled the direction she took every step of the way. In turn, she relied on his wisdom and guidance, a reciprocal cycle she still cherishes today.

All of what Dottie remembered of her father paints a picture of a man of strength, vitality, and above all a deep love of family. Dan was born in Hutchinson, Kansas, but he was raised in Hawthorne, California, another suburb of Los Angeles not far from Inglewood. He worked as a lead burner for Standard Oil in El Segundo, California, one of only about three or four throughout the country after World War I. Lead burning was similar to welding but entailed liquefying lead instead of metal. Many times an official from the military would request Dan's services, and he would have to travel to where the job was, often working during the night. But, this meant a steady paycheck for his family, which was especially important during the depression years when many breadwinners were out of work. Not that Dan would let a little thing like being told there was no work get in his way.

"My father was a pretty stern guy," Dottie said. "I remember when they laid a lot of people off and my father found a slip when he went to punch out saying he had been released. He walked back inside and walked over to the head man's office and opened the door and said, 'What in the hell does this mean?' The guy took the slip from him, looked at it, and said, 'I guess they made a mistake, Dan.' I wasn't there, of course, but I heard the story a million times. That was just like my dad."

Then there was the puppy that Dottie wanted when she was a child. Dan really did not like animals very much, but for his little girl he willingly overcame his objection to having one in the house. However, Dad ruled the roost, and the sooner that dog learned that the better. "I remember he had that dog trained," Dottie said, "and that dog did not put half a paw or any kind of paw into the living room. Kitchen was as far as that dog went."

Another good insight into Dan's character comes from Dottie's recollection of his relationship with one of his sisters-in-law. Dan came from a large family of nine children, seven boys and two girls. One of his brothers was married to Margaret Baldwin, part of the family for whom the Baldwin Hills in California were named. According to Dottie, she dripped money when she walked. Dottie remembered her coming over to their house one night to visit. As Margaret was talking to Dottie's parents, she turned to Dan and said, "You know, Dan, I get along with everybody else in this family, but I can't figure you out." Looking directly at her, Dan replied, "And you never will."

Dottie shared a deep bond with her father, but her mother was also a key figure in her life. Eleanor Runswick spent the first few years of her life in San Francisco. Her father was a fishmonger who traveled the streets of San Francisco selling his wares. His marriage to Eleanor's mother ended when Eleanor was still an infant, leaving his wife to cope by herself with the devastating San Francisco fire of 1904. Luckily, Dottie's grandmother managed to escape the fire, fleeing the house with only Eleanor and a pet bird. Shortly thereafter Eleanor's mother remarried, and Eleanor took her stepfather's name of Runswick. The newly assembled family moved to Inglewood, where Eleanor went to school, married Dan Wiltse, and raised her own daughter.

Dottie loved to hear stories about her mother's colorful family back in San Francisco. Eleanor's biological father, the fish peddler, was Italian, and true to his heritage he loved to make his own wine in the basement of his home. One time Dottie's mother went for a visit to celebrate a relative's long awaited job promotion. It used to be that when someone visited one relative, all the other relatives expected a visit as well, generally on the same day. The only problem was that everywhere a visitor went, that person had to partake of some wine. Dottie remembered that even as a little kid she was handed a water glass half full of wine.

Eleanor's family added its own ingredient to Dottie's baseball career. When Eleanor's father remarried, he had another girl and a boy. This boy, Dottie's half-uncle, became friends with the legendary Billy Martin. Years after Dottie had played for the All-American Girls Professional Baseball League, this connection would serve as an introduction to Billy Martin when he was in the major leagues.

Eleanor was a typical wife and mother of that time period, concentrating most of her energy on her family. She did not work outside her home, and she had little interest in sports. As a traditional wife she went along with her husband's wishes, which in this case meant supporting her daughter's athletic calling. She may have wanted her daughter to dress in pretty clothes rather than toss around a ball, but she kept her opinions to herself. And, as Dottie was quick to point out, once she got into sports, "we couldn't keep her home."

One of Dottie's close friends growing up, Barbara White Hoffman, remembered what a fun person "Ellie" was, a person who loved to laugh and have a good time. "She went to all the ballgames," Barbara recalled. "She would be up in the stands with her afghans she always made and sit with a group of parents cheering Dottie and the other girls on." She was so open with Dottie's friends that many, like Barbara, felt comfortable calling her "Mom." "My mother was always 'Momma,' Barbara noted, but Ellie was 'Mom.'"

If Eleanor played the part of cheerleader, Dan took over as manager. It was he who arranged for Dottie to get acquainted with the girls who played in the softball leagues of Southern California, probably having sensed his daughter's talents and not wanting to limit her to backyard heroics. When one of the girls asked Dottie if she would like to come and watch, Dottie eagerly took her up on the invitation. Sometimes she was granted the honor of sitting on the players' bench, and once when the bat girl failed to show up, Dottie voluntarily took over her duties, collecting the bats and keeping them in order. Soon she became the official bat girl for the Mark C. Bloome fast-pitch softball team in the Beverly Hills League. However, Dottie was not meant to hand out equipment for long.

One day neither Mabel Sparlin or Vic Self, the regular starting pitchers for the team, showed up for the game. The manager of the team, John Berry, told Dottie to take the mound. Glad for the chance finally to suit up, Dottie followed his order and proved herself a capable moundswoman. Berry continued to call upon her from time to time until, finally, opportunity knocked much louder than before. The year was 1936, the park was Old Wrigley Field in Los Angeles, the home of the Pacific Coast League Hollywood Stars. At stake was the Southern California girls' softball championship. More than 25,000 people packed the stands for this last game of the tournament. The pitcher was veteran ace Mable Sparlin. Halfway through the game, with the Bloome girls getting trounced by the Beverly Hills Amazons Payneheats, Mable folded. Needing to make a decision fast, Berry walked over to the bat girl, 12-year-old Dottie Wiltse, and said, "Dot, you're going in."

Walking out from the third base side of the field, Dottie heard her teammates and the fans rally behind her, with shouts of, "Come on, Dottie," and "Show 'em, kid, you can do it," echoing around her. Her response to the cheering "was to set her face in a determined grimace and assume the mound," as one newspaper reported. Concentrating on her delivery, Dottie not only retired the side but thereafter yielded only two runs and three hits to the Amazons, overcoming a nine-run deficit to win the game, 12 to 11. "Making a rise that has seldom been approached in the world of sports," to quote the *Los Angeles Examiner,* "the Mark C. Bloome softball team won the Southern California girls' softball championship with an *Examiner* Tournament title behind the pitching of a new star, young Dot Wiltse."

To think of the poise and confidence Dottie must have possessed is amazing, especially considering that the other players on the team were quite a bit older than she, most of them in their late teens and

The Mark C. Bloome Team, which won the 1936 Southern California Girls Softball Championship thanks to the phenomenal pitching of twelve-year-old Dot Wiltse, is pictured here after the deciding game. From left to right are Margaret Stanton, Jean Fuller, Amy Lemon, Gabby Young, Dottie Wiltse, Millie Guess, Jo Lahogue, Ginger Graham, Babe McDonald, Mary Adley, Al Berry, and Wanda Macha. (Courtesy of Dottie Wiltse Collins)

early twenties. Writing about Dottie's performance after the game, the *Examiner* focused as much on these attributes as on her skill as an athlete, stating that "more than her mechanical ability or physical build, what's important is she has nerve, the kind of nerve that won't allow her to get ruffled, even in the tightest spots." Yet Dottie attributed her lack of nervousness to the blitheness of youth. "It didn't make any difference to me," she said. "I was only twelve and I couldn't have cared less."

The local papers, however, made much of the young star's daring debut. One headline on July 7, 1936, proclaimed, "Twelve-Year-Old Girl Hurls to Victory." The story reported "Dot Wiltse, 12-year-old eighth grader from Inglewood, pitched the Mark C. Bloome team to victory before thousands at Wrigley Field. Dot is the youngest girl softball player in the country, and her speed dazzles the other girls." Another newspaper article also concentrated on the astonishing fact of Dottie's age. Describing her entrance onto the field when she was called upon to assume the team's pitching duties, the reporter described Dottie as "a slim, sweet-looking little girl who stood up admirably to the tremendous pressure." The piece concluded by noting that "the capacity crowd took Dottie to their hearts, giving her the biggest cheer of the evening when she received the trophy after the game."

The raw talent Dottie possessed must have been apparent to anyone who watched her pitch. The same reporter who described Dottie in such innocent terms acknowledged by the end of the article that in his opinion and in the minds of many other sports figures she would be the finest moundswoman by the next year. His predictions were repeated at the beginning of the 1937 season when a fellow reporter, comparing Dottie to another promising beginning player, commented that Dottie was the real prize. This reporter went on to say, "Heavier, taller, and more experienced since 1936, she's getting more zip on the ball, throwing a smarter game, and becoming a really polished mound artist. If she isn't overworked in the strain and stress of what's going to be a tough campaign, she'll come out of this year stamped as one of the best."

There was little fear that Dottie could not take the pressure. She had been honing her skills consistently, and her dedication to the sport was starting to show results. She was already a professional before she joined a fast-pitch softball league. No wonder she was able to perform in circumstances under which someone else might have buckled. It was a remarkable commitment in one so young, a commitment that only grew stronger as the years went on.

The foundation of Dottie's achievements was simply that Dottie loved to play ball. That passion in no way negates the hours of hard work, the fierce concentration, and the stamina needed to push beyond ever-expanding boundaries that both Dottie and her father set for her. However, without a deep, abiding love for the game none of the prerequisites for success would have been met. Her love of the game combined with her skill showed other women what was possible as the war opened a major league to them for the first time.

Long before Dottie's skills spread over such a wide area, however, her influence was felt closer to home. Unknown to Dottie or her father, their nightly practice ritual was closely monitored by another little girl longing to play ball. By now, Dottie and Dan had moved to the big athletic field behind the local high school a few blocks from their home, Dan surmising that Dottie had outgrown the confines of the yard. Barbara White, who became one of Dottie's lifelong friends, lived behind the high school. Sitting on her porch as she did most nights, she often noticed Dottie and her father walking by with mitts and softballs in hand. Wondering what they were up to, one night she decided to follow them.

"After that one time, I watched them every night that they practiced," Barbara said. "Dottie never knew that I didn't just happen to show up. I only told her I planned it when we were much older."

Barbara reiterated Dottie's contention that it was through "Pop's" encouragement and training that Dottie got to be one of the greatest softball pitchers in Southern California during those years. "Having been a ballplayer, he really knew what he was talking about," Barbara noted. "A couple of years after I met them, Dottie's dad built a back stop, a home plate, and a pitcher's mound in the vacant lot next door to them for Dottie to work out on. He let me practice, too. It was through Dottie and her dad that I finally got into the big time and became a ballplayer myself in one of the girls' softball leagues."

Dubbed the fastest-growing sport in Southern California, girls' softball was composed of two leagues at that time, the American League and the National League. Dottie was in the faster American League and Barbara played in the National League, so for a few years they only played against each other if both of their teams were in a championship series. The stadiums in which the girls played were not the kind of ballparks found in public parks. They were built exclusively for girls' softball and were nicely laid out and quite spacious. They needed to be, since the leagues were very popular with the public, drawing thousands of people at a time to watch the girls play, especially during the big tournaments.

So well attended were the games that many stadiums had to move to larger quarters or to undergo a complete renovation. Fiedler's Field, named after promoter Colonel Marty Feidler, was located right in Hollywood. After drawing 200,000 paid admissions during 1936, Feidler put $15,000 into a new and larger park on the corner of Fairfax and Fifth, where Columbia Studios now stands. Since many of the games were played in the land of the stars, it was not unusual to see celebrities in the bleachers, big names such as Buster Crabbe, Babe Didrikson, Joe Louis, the heavyweight champion, or Slapsie Maxie Rosenblum, he of the prize-

Dottie and the man behind her rise to pitching glory: her dad, Dan Wiltse. Easter 1938. (Courtesy of Dottie Wiltse Collins)

fighting cauliflower ears. Movie stars such as Ricardo Cortes often threw out the first pitch or presented the trophy to the winning championship team.

Dottie took all this attention in stride, maintaining that in California seeing a movie star was an everyday occurrence. Besides, she had more on her mind than who was watching her from the stands. She needed to prove that her pitching debut was not just a fluke, a brief surge of adrenalin to thrust her into a spurious spotlight. She got her chance quickly enough. Following her pinch pitching performance in the championship game, she continued with Mark C. Bloome for the rest of 1936 as they played teams outside their circuit. As she faced teams such as the San Diego Girls' team, Dottie posted a 12–2 record for the remainder of the season. She began the next season with the same verve she took to the mound on that eventful day almost one year earlier, this time pitching for George Young's Market, composed chiefly of the former Bloome team.

For the opening of the 1937 season at Fiedler Fairfax Field, several major league personalities were in attendance, including Roy Johnson, manager of the Chicago Cubs, and a few of his players and Jimmy Dykes, manager of the Chicago White Sox. Dykes was slated to throw out the first pitch. Having heard so much about the pastime of girls softball, Dykes told Colonel Fiedler he would be on hand to "give the gals the once-over." As one reporter noted, he planned to bring along a few ballplayers, "perhaps to pick up a few pointers on the game." The colonel responded that the White Sox pitchers might "get a slant for a few new curves." These and similar remarks by the press foreshadowed the crude jokes that would be bandied about when women stormed the major leagues in the next decade.

After a very wild opening pitch by Dykes, who perhaps could have learned something about his own curves, Dottie took over. She turned on some spectacular hurling to fan seven of her opponents from Balian Ice Cream, allowing only five batters to reach base safely. For five innings, she pitched no-hit, no-run ball. In the sixth inning, two runs scored on three singles. Dottie once again led her team to victory.

Commenting on her performance, a local sportswriter noted that Dottie was definitely not "a flash in the pan," validating Dottie's effort after her initial start for Mark C. Bloome. In addition, the article credited her work ethic, asserting that "many people no doubt take for granted that she was suddenly inspired with the idea of pitching, acted on said inspirations, and went out to make herself temporarily famous, perhaps with a bit of luck. However, what earned her a first-string hurler berth on one of the strongest female nines were six long years of training." How proud Dan Wiltse must have been to see his efforts so magnificently rewarded.

Dottie's speed sizzled throughout the season as she piled up more wins for the Marketers. In May, fans looked forward to a "Wiltse/Beck duel," as Dottie sought to hand the Amazons another setback as she had done in the 1936 tournament, while attempting to even up the heated American League race. Rated as a veteran pitcher despite her years, she and Mabel Sparlin were credited with giving the Marketers "one of the best fortified pitching staffs in girls' softball." Living up to her reputation, Dottie next handed the Shamrocks a 4-to-2 loss and was expected to halt the Mark C. Bloome girls a few nights later. The Young's Market team, touted as "powerful" and "fast," continued to stifle the league behind Dot Wiltse, "the fourteen-year-old with great control and a fast one that screams over the plate."

Sometimes, though, Dottie's control wavered and her curveball failed to curve. When this happened, rather than berate her as sportswriters are wont to do, the newspapers excused her lapse, more or less passing it off as a freak occurrence. During one game that Dottie lost to Cantlay Tanzola, the papers explained that Dottie "was the victim of her own ability," having hit a triple that scored two runs in the last inning of play. They attributed her wild throwing in the bottom half of the inning to the fact that she was tired out after her mad dash around the bases.

When not on the playing field, Dottie found time to be a fun-loving kid growing up on the West Coast of the United States. Inglewood boasted a rich history dating back to the Spanish-Mexican era. The Centinela Adobe, which was situated on Rancho Aguaje de la Centinela, was built in 1834 by Ignacio Machado, son of one of the soldiers guarding the first settlers of Los Angeles on their way from Mexico. After a series of transactions the ranch was eventually bought by Canadian Robert Freeman, who helped put the town on the map through dry farming, shipping millions of bushels of barley from his wharf at Playa del Rey. In 1888, soon after a railroad station was built nearby, Inglewood was the first settlement to be carved out of the 25,000 acre Centinela Ranch. It was incorporated as a city in 1908.

From 1920–1925, the period of Dottie's birth, on September 23, 1923, Inglewood was the fastest-growing city in the United States, doubling its population of 3300 in 1920 to over 6000 just two years later. A major earthquake in 1920 drew curiosity seekers to the area, but many stayed because of the mild climate. It became well known as the Chinchilla Capital of the world after 1923, when M.F. Chapman brought the animals there from the Peruvian Andes, and later was renowned for the Air Age, beginning in 1927 when the Andrew Bennett Ranch was leased by Los Angles and converted to the Mines Field. Charles Lindbergh flew the first passenger plane into Inglewood with none other than Will Rogers as his passenger. In 1932 the Olympic marathon passed through Inglewood, and later three alumni of Inglewood High School became Olympic winners.

At the time Dottie was born and up to the middle of her high school years, Inglewood was an agricultural community. Oats, barley, cattle, and sheep dotted the wide-open fields. An advertisement for lots in Inglewood in an 1888 newspaper proclaimed Inglewood as the most attractive town between Los Angeles and the ocean, touting its shaded avenues and its thriving orange trees. The year of Dottie's birth saw rapid development in the town of Inglewood. The cornerstone was laid for a new city hall; the High School District bought all the homes along one side of a residential street to use as classrooms until the new high school could be built; and both an American Legion Post and Rotary Club were incorporated.

Dottie's home at 1212 Rosewood Avenue reflected both the town's boom of new homes and its more rural character. Dottie and her parents lived in a bungalow, similar to a Cape Cod but smaller, with two bedrooms, a bath, a kitchen, a dining room, and a living room. The front and back yards were beautifully landscaped, for in addition to his prowess in sports Dan Wiltse was also a gardener. The entire area around the house was filled with flowers. Bourganvilla crept up latticework at the end of the yard, with carefully laid out gardens curving from the front yard to the back, all of Dan's handiwork regularly watered by an underground sprinkler system that he installed himself. In the middle of the back yard a big cement pond filled with goldfish served as the centerpiece to this magnificent scenery. All of this fit in nicely with the character of the neat, quiet neighborhood where Dottie was raised.

Much of the activity revolving around Dottie and her circle of friends took place at the house on Rosewood Avenue. One of Dottie's favorite memories concerned the dinners her parents prepared for Dottie's softball teammates at the end of each season, one of whom, Alma Ziegler, went on to play for the AAGPBL with Dottie. Dottie's dad would set several long picnic tables in the driveway of their home, and her mom would carry platefuls of food to the hungry mob. These dinners, known as bean dinners since beans served as the staple of the meal, were a perfect opportunity for Dottie and her friends to relax and have fun without the competitive edge that constantly pushed them on the ball field. Her parents, too, delighted in the enjoyment of their daughter and her friends. This was the time of the Depression, and while Dan never lost his job, times were still hard for everyone.

When Dottie turned thirteen, her mother decided to celebrate with a splash. An announcement in the local paper stated that "Mrs. D. Wiltse entertained last evening in honor of her daughter Dorothy Wiltse, who was celebrating her thirteenth birthday." All of the Mark C. Bloome team, with whom she had just helped win the Southern

California softball championship, were there, as well as John Berry, the manager of the team, the parents of the catcher, Millie Guess, and several family friends. The cake Dottie's mother served displayed no lacy ballerina on top or any other typical feminine ornament of the day. Rather, crossed baseball bats and a ball made of icing, which reflected the blue and white colors of the team, adorned the cake. The decorations for the party similarly carried out the team's colors. It is obvious that despite some initial reluctance about Dottie's playing career, her mother knew how to get into the spirit of the thing.

After the entertainment of cards and games, the members of the team presented Dottie with a lovely coat sweater. This personal gift, probably rather pricey for the time, shows how highly regarded Dottie was by her fellow athletes. They had to take the time to choose something in the appropriate size and in a color Dottie would like. Something less personal would have been easier to buy. In addition, considering the age difference between Dottie and the other girls, it was telling that they chose to come to her party at all. With just a few months left of the season when Dottie changed her role from bat girl to pitcher, she had made her mark on the team. No matter her chronological age; the poise and confidence she exhibited both on and off the field ensured her a place at any table. That party signified an auspicious start to her teenage years.

Although a good part of Dottie's leisure time revolved around softball, she still found time to enjoy other activities that captivated most young girls of her time. Living in Inglewood, Dottie and her friends particularly savored their time at the beach. The town was only seven miles from the ocean, and several cities on the shore were not that far away, including Redondo Beach, Manhattan Beach, and Hermosa Beach. However, the favorite haunt of Dottie and her friends was the beach city of Balboa. Every summer during most of her high school years, Dottie and a few of her friends rented a house for a week or two on Balboa Beach. Dottie's mother served as housemother, since at that time it would have been improper for young girls to go away unescorted. However, Ellie probably enjoyed the vacation as much as her daughter and her friends. Virginia Larson, who was part of the party, remembered that Dottie's mom was always right in with the kids, laughing and joking and generally having a good time. "She had the most wonderful giggle," recalled Barbara White, who also made up part of the group.

These trips took place in the late 1930s, up to 1940 or 1941. The changes the war would bring to that part of California, as well as to

Dottie and her best friend, Barbara, brave the waves of Balboa Beach. 1940. (Courtesy of Dottie Wiltse Collins)

the rest of the country, had not yet occurred, so the beach at Balboa was a peaceful place to get away from the everyday hustle and bustle for a while. On one side of the house was a bay where the girls would go swimming, diving, surfboarding, or just spend time splashing around. Dottie could not really swim, but she could dog-paddle quite well. On the other side was the ocean. Each year the girls staged a competition, trying to get tanner than the year before. To counteract the effects of the sun, Dottie's mother slathered vinegar on the girls each night, a ritual stoically endured in order to achieve the image of bronzed goddess.

At night, the girls often went to the penny arcade, mingling with the other vacationers and trying their luck at the games of chance. A bowling alley and a movie theater offered other diversions. Barbara White Hoffman remembered that their favorite place, though, was the pavilion about a mile from the beach house. Inside was a huge ballroom where big name bands used to perform, with favorite players such as Stan Canton. Dancing to all hours of the morning took so much out of the girls that no wonder they needed to collapse on the sand the next day.

When Dottie got a little older, her parents bought her a 1930 Model A Ford. The car could officially only hold a few people, but that didn't stop a group of girls from cramming into the car and heading out to the beach for the day. Three girls would climb in front, and two more would pile into the trunk. "We had a ball in that car," Barbara Hoffman related. "Just about every Saturday morning we would all get ready and head for Balboa in Dottie's little old 'Lizzie.'" Dottie's having a car may seem unusual for that time period, but that fact, too, reflects on her character overall. As Ginny Larson commented, "It seemed Dottie should have a car. She was so efficient and competent, even as a young girl."

When Dottie was home in Inglewood, she and her friends drove uptown to Sally's, where they gobbled up hamburgers, shakes, and fries. Pulling up in the Model A on a Saturday afternoon, the girls parked the car and visited with all the other young men and women who came by as they waited for the waitress to take their order. "Times have changed, I'll tell you," said Barbara Hoffman. "We just never had any alcohol or drugs or any of this stuff that is going on now. Then, it was just fun, clean living."

Barbara also fondly remembered going to Dottie's house when her mother was not home and doing all the things they could not do with a parent looking over their shoulders. "We'd go in the kitchen and make these peanut butter sandwiches," Barbara said. "And in between the two pieces of bread and peanut butter, we'd take a handful of potato chips and we'd smash them together and that would be our lunch, along with a pint of ice cream. And we'd sit in the front room, with her mother not knowing that, because usually we weren't allowed to eat in the front room," she finished.

Those were the times that cemented the friendship between Dottie and Barbara. They sat in the forbidden parlor with their cleverly improvised meal and exchanged confidences about boys and sports and whatever else was close to their hearts at the time. "Dottie being the only child, her parents kind of adopted me, and whenever they would go out of town I would go there and spend the night with Dot so she wasn't alone," Barbara said. "We did so much together."

At that time Dottie and Barbara also belonged to their high school's GAA, or Girls Athletic Association. Along with their friend, Virginia Larson, they played tennis and other sports after school for recreation, keeping in shape and forming the bonds that such activities nurture.

Through the GAA, Dottie diversified into other areas besides soft-ball, which ultimately helped her development in her chosen sport. However, Dottie's high school barred her from playing school sports. Dottie was dismissed from the school tennis team after a week and was excluded from Inglewood High's girls' softball club. "They didn't allow me to play anything, even basketball," Dottie said. "Of course, I didn't like the game of basketball at the time because for the women or kids it was three court basketball. And I hated that."

The school's reasoning was that since each team in the Girls' Softball League had its own sponsor who was responsible for outfitting the girls and paying for all the transportation costs, the girls who played in the League had become professionals because they were taking travel money. In addition, spectators paid to see the games. As Dottie commented about the situation, "Someone asked me if I made a lot of money playing in one of the fields in Holly-wood. And I said, 'Yeah, lots. We got a big bag of peanuts as we walked out the door. A lousy bag of peanuts.'"

Grade school was much kinder to Dottie than high school as far as sports went. In the seventh grade, her accomplishments allowed her to pitch for the boys' team at school. She hadn't yet reached the age when girls are discouraged from certain activities that were per-fectly acceptable when they were younger. Naturally, Dottie was able to hold her own with her male cohorts. She was just another skilled athlete equal to whatever came at her on the field, as evidenced by the victories she handed to her team. Dottie laughed about the pho-tograph she has of herself with the boys' team. "Yeah, I've got a pic-ture of the guys in a pyramid, and I'm up on top." Somehow this does not seem surprising in the least.

Whether she was playing against the boys in grade school or as a professional later on, sports always took top priority in Dottie's life. She did take school seriously, however. An amusing paragraph in a newspaper article has Dottie taking offense that her age was given incorrectly in a previous write-up about an upcoming pitching bat-tle. The reporter noted, "Miss Wiltse wrote in to correct the impres-sion regarding her age, naively remarking that she will start high school next fall 'so if people read that I am 14 they will think I am not so smart.'" School, however, was there to be gotten through so Dottie could concentrate on what mattered most: pursuing the game that suited her so well. She did fine in her all her subjects, or as Dot-tie would say, "I got by," but she always wanted to be somewhere else, preferably out on the mound, winding up for a pitch. "I never found school exciting," Dottie noted, thinking back. Compared to the action on the softball field, schoolwork must have seemed very dull indeed.

Dottie continued to smoke the ball during her high school years, playing for several different teams as the thirties wound to a close. Due to its popularity in Southern California, girls' softball never had a problem finding backers, so there were always plenty of teams. Coca Cola, Goodrich Silvertown Tires, Eastside Beer, Cantlay-Tanzola Heating, Columbia Pictures, and Bank of America were just some of the corporate sponsors for the girls' teams. The success of the league and its continuation depended upon the public spirit of these large companies and also of smaller ones like Bloome's Service Station and Young's Market. It was because of support like this that some of the finest female ballplayers were groomed to play in the only major baseball league for women.

Dottie started out the 1938 season, her sophomore year in high school, playing for Cantlay-Tanzola, transporters of bulk petroleum products. Accolades kept pouring in. Much was made of the fact that Dottie was still so young. With a birthday in September, Dottie was only fourteen when she began her third year of play in the girls' softball league, the youngest regular player in the league and one of the best pitchers. Yet her arm was that of a master. Sportswriters described her as "prepared to give back an argument" and "stifling the opposing team in her last start." In May of 1938, Dottie was chosen as one of the four best pitchers in the American League to pitch for the National League to even the sides in an exhibition game at Fiedler's Fairfax Field. Considering the hundreds of girls who played softball, many of whom had played longer than Dottie, the invitation to appear in the exhibition game was not only an honor but an important indication of more good things to come.

Dottie was not the only young lady whose star was on the rise. Her teammate, Kay Rohrer, was Dottie's catcher for Cantlay-Tanzola, and together they made quite a team. Kay's father, William, more commonly known as "Daddy Rohrer," managed the team. William Rohrer really knew his baseball. He was a catcher for the Pacific Coast League, the same league in which Joe DiMaggio got his start, and he later played for the Chicago White Sox. After managing in the Southern California girls' softball league, he skippered Dottie's Fort Wayne Daisies in the AAGPBL.

Due in a large part to his influence, Kay and Dottie were key components of the Cantlay-Tanzola team, or perhaps one should say *a* key component since they operated together as one well-oiled machine. Such headlines as "Kid Battery Opposes Vets" and "Kid Battery Performs Tonight" raced across the sports pages in the Los Angeles papers. One write-up noted, "The 'baby battery' swings into action tonight. Dot Wiltse and Kay Rohrer, pitcher and catcher who form the battery for Cantlay-Tanzola, are but fourteen years old but figure to give Bank of America a run for its money in their softball clash at Fiedler Sunset Field."

Dottie recalled that Kay "would sit on her haunches without moving and just take her arm and, whoo, throw out people at second base just like that." Her dexterity brings to mind the great catchers of men's major league baseball, such as Johnny Bench, Carlton Fisk, and more recently the incomparable Ivan Rodriguez. Other teams learned to dread facing the indomitable duo, as testified by the comments in another newspaper article. "Fresh from a conquest of Columbia's fast nine, the 'kid battery' of Cantlay-Tanzola, two precocious fourteen-year-olds in pitcher Dot Wiltse and catcher Kay Rohrer, wing into action at Fairfax Park tonight against Lois Terry and her Orange Lionettes. The 'kids' bested the stellar battery of Columbia by a 3 to 0 count the other night, and they are out to add Terry and her mates to their list of victims."

Kay Rohrer, like Dottie, went on to play in the All-American Girls Professional Baseball League, serving as catcher and shortstop for the Rockford Peaches in 1945. However, Kay was not just talented. She was also very beautiful. Wanting to make Kay a star, Harry Cohn, president of Columbia Studios, invited Kay to the studio and interviewed her. To groom her for the stardom that never came, Kay was featured in a variety of movie magazines. Dottie remembered some pictures of her lying on a bearskin rug, posing for the cameras. "That wasn't her life, though," Dottie said. "She wanted to play ball."

Later in that same season, Dottie switched teams and went with the Beverly Hills Amazons, called the Payneheats, in the annual *Examiner* tournament. The strategy of moving players around like chess pieces on a board said much about the competitive nature of girls' softball in Southern California at the time. Like Major League Baseball today, each team wanted to have every advantage as they moved their way up through the different rounds of play. Both her skill and her winning attitude ensured Dottie would be an excellent acquisition for any team. The previous year Dottie had pitched Young's Market into the semifinals. Although her team did not win the big prize, she grabbed at the chance to try for another *Examiner* title this year with Payneheats. "There is nothing as thrilling as the *Examiner* tournament, and I think it's the finest thing that ever happened to softball. I didn't get nervous when I was pitching two years ago; maybe I can keep calm and win the 'World Series' of softball for the second time," Dottie told a local reporter.

The press thought she had a good chance to do just that. The headline alerting readers to the second and deciding round of the competition on September 8 announced that "Little fourteen-year-old Dot Wiltse slips back into the spotlight at Fiedler Fairfax Field...It will be Miss Wiltse's second start in the tournament. She bowled over the Berk Tire Cuties 19 to 0 in her first start Monday night." The largest crowd of the season was expected at Marty Fiedler's sprawling field at Fifth and Fairfax to see the "slender Dot Wiltse face the girls from Kern County." Dottie came through brilliantly. She led the Payneheats to another Southern California girls' softball championship and on to the Western States Championship game, where Dottie downed the Salt Lake Shamrocks one week later, on September 15. Commenting on her pitching performance during the game in Fiedler Field, sportswriter Allan Dale described Dottie as "the personification of poetry in motion."

All of this from a girl who was born with a broken collarbone and whose father used to hang her over the crib and swing her by his thumbs to help her to heal. Dan performed this ritual faithfully every night until, finally, his daughter was whole. "That's what they claimed strengthened me, you know," Dottie said. "My father rocking me back and forth like that." Obviously, Daddy knew best all along.

The Million Dollar Baby: 1940–1943

A new decade beckoned as Dottie entered her junior year of high school, a decade that at first seemed to promise only the expected pattern for a young girl growing up at that time. Now halfway through the final phase of her formal education, Dottie eagerly looked ahead to graduation, the start of her working years, and ultimately raising a family of her own not far from where she herself had grown up. Yet unknown to her, events around the world were building to a climax that would alter the course of history irrevocably. The changes wrought by these events would lead Dottie into a world previously unimagined for a woman and would pave a path that wound its way many miles from the place she had always called home.

In 1937, Mussolini's dreams of expanding the Roman Empire had led to Italy's invasion of Ethiopia. By 1939, Hitler had begun his march through Europe, systematically seizing Austria, Hungary, Czechoslovakia, and Poland, as well as parts of France. Aided in part by the refusal of other European nations to recognize the enormity of his plan, he continued unabated in his quest to avenge Germany's loss of power at the end of World War I. Great Britain vainly tried to check Hitler's crusade by any peaceable means. On September 3, 1939, after the German invasion of Poland, Great Britain finally declared war on Germany, with Paris officially announcing a similar resolution a few hours later.

On the other side of the world, Japan's bid for power pursued its own relentless cause. First setting her sights on China, Japan now occupied Manchuria and had taken over the capital at Nanking, committing countless atrocities against Chinese citizens and sinking a United States gunboat in the process. Now plans were under way to expand the Japanese empire even further, with an eye on British,

French, and Dutch possessions in the South Pacific. While the United States attempted to maintain a neutral position, forces were combining in such a way that would soon make such a stance impossible.

Dottie and her fellow Americans had little inkling that their country was on the brink of war, despite the news from Europe and the Pacific. Indeed, the headlines in the *New York Times* on January 1, 1940, proclaimed "Good Year for Nation Seen." Americans clung to this prediction as desperately as they had disassociated themselves from world affairs. Having struggled to emerge from world war and the throes of a depression, the United States was determined to maintain its perilous peace. Not until the country took a direct hit on its own soil did Americans fully realize the sacrifices that would be required of them and respond accordingly.

In the meantime, Dottie threw herself into her usual round of activities, gathering with friends at the drive-in, relaxing at the beach, and playing games of tennis and pickup softball with Ginny and Barbara. Otherwise, most days found Dottie on the playing field, either participating in league games or engaging in practice sessions with her coach and teammates, a more formalized version of the training workouts with her father. The perfect climate in Southern California lent itself to almost year-round play, so Dottie's progress as she developed into a first-rate pitcher never slowed. Her years just prior to joining the All-American Girls Professional Baseball League demonstrated this well.

Dottie grew to be more of a challenge for the batters she faced with the wide array of pitches she accumulated over the years. Girls in the batter's box never knew what would come whizzing over the plate towards them, but whatever it was they never managed to connect with it easily. Sportswriter Alan Dale commented in a 1939 article in the *Los Angeles Examiner* that "her fast ball has become so proficient that hitters have a difficult time even seeing the ball." That same year another reporter noted, "Adding to her repertoire of pitches, she has been mowing down her foes with a sizzling fastball cleverly mixed up with a baffling change of pace."

Using a full-body spring, Dottie could project the ball with amazing speed. She led the league in strikeouts by a wide margin for several years, this in a league touted as one of the strongest girls' softball loops in the world. Add to this the fact that Dottie was still the youngest girl in the league. Her prowess on the mound brings to mind a wonderful anecdote involving Walter Johnson, "The Big Train," a pitcher for the Washington Senators in the early 1900s. As related in Geoffrey

Ward's and Ken Burns's riveting book, *Baseball, an Illustrated History*, when an umpire informed a batter that he had one more hit left from Johnson's battery of pitches, the batter responded, "I know, and *you* can have the next one. It sure won't do me any good."

Since Dottie played in a fast-pitch softball league, which is more of a pitcher's game than slow-pitch, she had the advantage of really concentrating on her pitching style. For all her multitude of pitches, though, her favorite throw was the curveball. "I always knew how to throw a curve," she said. "You just snap your wrist and things like that. And then I threw what I call a backup curve by twisting it one way and making it go another." No wonder Dottie continually kept the girls at the plate guessing.

Dottie sees a change in fast-pitch softball today that she does not care for very much. "Now they're playing fast-pitch windmill, and that gripes me for a couple of reasons," she said. "First, it's bound to be hard on the girls. I was watching a game the other day and this girl got her whole upper body out of shape throwing that thing." Dottie's pitching style was to go straight forward and then straight back before releasing the ball. She never incorporated the windmill style into her repertoire of pitches.

Even more than the awkward nature of the windmill pitch, though, what bothers Dottie is the limited opportunity it offers for a pitcher to reach her full potential. "Actually," she noted, "you could train the girl to pitch underhand and do a lot more things with it than just the windmill game." Dottie admitted the pitch must have something going for it since it is all she sees on television, but windmill pitching just does not allow the depth her pitching reached. By taking advantage of the various possibilities open to her, Dottie was able to explore different strategies, which is really what baseball is all about. As Thomas Boswell noted in his essay, "The Church of Baseball," "The opportunity to change, to try different approaches, is encouraged. A new pitch. A new stance. A new self can perpetually grow out of the old self." That Dottie lived by this creed is the reason she became one of the greatest softball pitchers in her league and in the world of professional women's baseball as well.

Through Dottie's evolution as a player, or most likely because of it, her confidence also continued to soar. Sports columnist Alan Dale once wrote, "Dottie takes the mound before an important game as if she were sitting down to a chicken dinner," in reference to a tournament at the end of the '39 season. The schedule Dottie adhered to nurtured this poise. Softball teams carried only one pitcher in those days because games were played only once or twice a week, three times at most. Therefore, softball pitchers usually threw complete games with little rest in between. For example, when Dottie played for Young's Market in 1937, she took the mound on July 22, July 25, and July 31. She would have pitched one more game if it had not been called off at the last minute.

Compared to Major League Baseball today, where it is rare for a pitcher to complete an entire game and where the starting ace often goes only four or five innings, the difference is remarkable. Of course, at the time Dottie was playing softball, major league players pitched complete games also. While relief pitchers were not unheard of in the beginning years of Major League Baseball, the rise of the relief pitcher did not come about until the 1950s, when the Phillies' Jim Konstanty became the first relief pitcher to win an MVP award in 1951. Stars prior to that, such as "Lefty" Grove and "Dizzy" Dean, often threw complete games. Dottie and her teammates stood in good company.

"Yes," Dottie proudly related, "we mostly pitched complete games. Unless I was hurt, or unless they were batting me all over the place—you know, if I was having a bad night and not throwing the ball, I got yanked. But now, they treat 'em like babies. They've got excuses not to pitch—some of them I never heard of before."

Her other beef is the batting gloves the ballplayers use today. She feels they interfere with the caliber of play. "If I see some guy that's not hitting well, my thought is: Take the damn gloves off their hands and maybe they could hit the ball. I think that's stupid. I never saw DiMaggio do that, or Mantle, or any of those big hitters. They didn't need those gloves, for God's sake."

Neither did Dottie when it was her turn to hit—not that being gloveless helped much, as she would be the first to admit. She remembered playing for one of Bill Allington's softball teams and both of them were ecstatic because Dottie actually hit a triple. "The only problem was," she laughed, "was that I was so excited I stepped off the bag and got tagged out. I will never forget that."

However, for all her bumbling at the plate, she still rejects the idea of the designated hitter. "I don't like those guys coming in for the pitchers," she said. "I mean, you can always bunt or something. I was a pretty good bunter, but I couldn't run," she recalled with a chuckle. "But at least I got the other girl down to the next base and stuff like that." Dottie's softball years fostered that mindset of the team as top priority and transitioned well into her time with the All-American League several years later.

Dottie continued her team efforts for the Goodrich Silvertown Sweeties in 1939, a group composed of almost the entire Payneheats group from the previous year. She welcomed the season with a 4–2 victory over the Bank of America ladies in the first exhibition game of the softball year. For the second exhibition game, she faced the Pepsi-Cola Club in the feature game of a softball doubleheader. A few days later, she fulfilled the expectations of sportswriters by drawing one of the biggest crowds of the two-week exhibition series during her battle with Thrifty Drugs at Fiedler Fairfax Field. Once regular games got under way, she maintained her brilliant start.

As a first-string hurler for the Goodrich Silvertown Sweeties, her fastball continued to baffle the best of the female sluggers. She pitched several shutouts during the season. The terms used to describe Dottie physically, such as "cute" and "little," belied the strength of her arm and offered a direct contrast to the words used to describe her pitching performances, with expressions such as "hurling phenom" "clever" and "mound star" as just a few examples. Most likely, the diminutive adjectives the press tossed around had more to do with Dottie's youth than her physical appearance, since she was slightly above average height for a female, at five feet, seven inches. Her age, however, was anything but average for the Southern California girls softball league, earning her the title "The Cinderella of Softball."

Perhaps this is what drew the press to her. From her start at age 12 and throughout her teenage years, Dottie's innocent appearance, coupled with her innate ability and the maturity she displayed on the field, ensured that not only the newspapers would find her alluring, but so would a host of fans as well. Some of these fans were average citizens. Others were not.

Barbara White remembered when a very wealthy admirer of the girls' softball league invited her and Dottie to be his guests at the Santa Monica Swim Club. The girls were treated like royalty, which perhaps their host thought was apt considering their feats on the field. Dottie and Barbara were given bathing suits and towels and told to enjoy a swim in the ocean. Later, they showered and were taken to lunch. "We had these beautiful big tuna salads. I can remember them to this day," Barbara reminisced. "They gave us a glass of beer with this, and it was the first time we ever tasted beer. All in all it was a real fun day." A member of the club who was there that day turned out to be the future husband of golf great Babe Didrikson.

Another supporter Dottie remembered particularly well never wined and dined her, but she appreciated him nevertheless. "We called him Daddy Ryan," she said. "Seems we called everybody Daddy back then. He was something else. He would come to all the games, just one of those guys who hung around the ball diamond. He knew everybody on the team and he'd always stay and talk to all of us afterwards." Probably the reason Dottie recalled someone like Daddy Ryan so vividly is because fans like Ryan give sports teams a competitive edge as they face their contenders, pumping them up and adding purpose to their drive for victory. The league recognized the value of these fans by hosting periodic fan award nights. One such event on May 31 promised a hot contest between the second-place Goodrich team and the hustling Dr. Pepper nine.

As the 1939 American league pennant race heated up, Goodrich fans really had something to cheer about. Backed by a "million dollar" infield, which included future AAGPBL star Alma Ziegler, Dottie's pitching moved the Sweeties from the cellar to a commanding position by the beginning of May, tumbling the Pepsi-Cola girls from the lead spot in the process. As they rode the crest of a four-game winning streak, the press wondered, "Who will to stop the Goodrich girls?" in the "furious feminine softball scramble" taking place in the American League. Sportswriters and other pundits of the game consistently credited Dottie's pitching for the sizzling pace Goodrich was setting as her determination drove the Sweeties steadily upward in the standings.

Several teams tried to thwart the Goodrich nine as they battled their way through the fast-paced league. By the middle of May they shared second place with the Optimistic Doughnuts, who had fallen from first due to Dottie's fastball early in the season. The papers had predicted such a result, nothing that the Doughnuts' Laura Rowlette "would face a tough problem keeping her team on top when she pitches against 15-year-old Dot Wiltse of the Goodrich Silvertowns at Fiedler Fairfax Field."

When the Doughnuts fell, Thrifty Drug took over first place, but not by a huge margin. With Thrifty's 10–5 record opposed to Goodrich's 9–6, the games between the two teams guaranteed some dynamic rivalry. For a match between Thrifty Drugs and Goodrich on May 19, *The Examiner* proclaimed, "Two of the fastest feminine softball clubs hook up in a battle for the leadership of the fast American League tonight." That game pitted Dottie against her former teammate Mable Sparlin, the pitcher Dottie had stepped in for in the 1936 championship game. Billed as a Sparlin-Wiltse duel, the thrill was heightened not only by the close numbers in the standings but by the caliber of pitching on both teams. The excitement continued unabated as just one week later the Doughnuts surged back into the lead, only to have Goodrich beat them to force a first-place tie, dropping Thrifty Drugs down to second place.

Dottie faced some tough competition in her quest for the crown, with rivals such as pitcher Laura Rowlette of the Optimistic Doughnuts, hurler Lois Terry of the Orange Lionettes, whom Dottie considered one of her most formidable opponents with one of the fastest "smokers," in the league, and third basewoman Dottie Doerr of powerful Thrifty Drugs. Dottie was the sister of Hall of Famer Bobby Doerr, who played for the Boston Red Sox from 1937–1951. A second baseman like Dan Wiltse, Bobby Doerr had a career batting average of .288 and a career fielding percentage of .980. A nine-time All-Star, he played with teammates such as Jimmy Foxx, who collected 160-plus RBIs in 1938 and went on to manage in the AAGPBL. Although Dottie Doerr was never called up to the majors like Dottie Wiltse, the strong infielder still kept pitcher Wiltse in top form as both teams struggled for the coveted position of first in the league.

Continuing to battle through the first half of the season, Goodrich finished only one game behind the Doughnuts when that half ended. They regained the lead behind Dottie's two-hit shutout against Thrifty Drugs as the second half of the season began in mid–June. Both Goodrich and the Doughnuts started the second half with a 15–8 record. Throughout the season, the two teams battled back and forth, with Pepsi-Cola and Thrifty Drugs thrown into the mix. The season neared its end with Goodrich, Optimistic Doughnuts, and Thrifty Drugs neck and neck for the lead spot.

By mid–August, a reversal of the first half occurred, with the Goodrich nine on top over the Optimistic squad by a scant margin. The press promised a pitching match between Dottie and Grace Bauer of the Doughnuts on August 22 "that would stand the fans on their ears" as they bid for the lead position. Goodrich fans were especially invigorated as once again Dottie led her team to the Southern California softball championship series. Sportswriter Alan Dale predicted she would be one of the prime drawing cards when the tournament took place in mid–September, 1939. Never one to become flustered by such high expectations, Dottie distinguished herself throughout the series and led her team to victory.

At the annual Goodrich Silvertown Softball banquet on November 25, hosted that year by the Melody Lane Café on Wiltshire Boulevard in Los Angeles, Dottie had much to celebrate. She posted a 20–9 win/loss record and chalked up 151 strikeouts for 1939. Plus, for the third time in four seasons of play she had pitched her team to an *Examiner* title for the Southern California girls softball championship. She was helped in her bid for the title by teammates such as Charlene "Shorty" Pryer and Louella Daetweiler, who along with Alma Ziegler and Dottie moved on to the All-Americans. Dottie received a framed certificate from the B.F. Goodrich Company for her efforts, which read "In Recognition of Outstanding Pitching Achievement, 1939." That and the program with her name engraved upon it serve as fitting reminders of another outstanding year as an emerging woman softball pitcher.

The next season, Dottie, along with most of her teammates, followed manager Bill Allington to the Mark C. Bloome team when he switched from Goodrich Silvertown. Touted as the piece de resistance, Dottie welcomed her fifth year of play by stacking up more wins right from the start. Fighting to keep her team in contention, Dottie and Bloome's Bloomer Girls trounced the Bank of America nine, 6–0 and 7–1, early in the season and turned back the Dr. Pepper nine with a score of 3–2. Dottie more than fulfilled the expectations of local sportswriters, who predicted the brilliant pitcher would allow manager Bill Allington to depend on his ace for more than her share of wins. Just one week later, when Mark C. Bloome was tied for the American league championship with John (Pop) Berry's All-Stars, Dottie was again expected to pitch at the top of her form. As a matter of fact, in anticipation of the duel between Dottie and Berry's ace, Laura Rowlette, formerly with the Optimistic Doughnuts, a capacity crowd was expected to fill Fiedler's Field.

Part of Dottie's success came from knowing how to lose. Rather than allowing defeats to get her down, like a true professional Dottie focused on how best to improve her game. After a string of wins in June, 1940, including an impressive 4–1 win over Balian Ice Cream's formidable Elsie Patridge, Dottie's Bloomers were trounced first by the Payneheats, with a 3–1 loss, and then by the up-and-coming Bank of America, with a score of 5–1 on ten hits. Again, the local sportswriters stood behind their ace. Referring to the loss against Bank of America, one article stated, "This is one of the few games this season in which the versatile Ms. Wiltse has been ineffective." Furthermore, the columnist also asserted that Dottie was expected to snap back with her very next game and "redeem herself for the letdown suffered in her last game." Sure enough, shortly thereafter "clever Dot Wiltse" stopped Karl's Shoes with just five hits over nine innings.

Headline after headline proclaimed Dottie as key to the success of her team, with banners such as "Bloomers Rely on Wiltse," "Dot Wiltse on Hill for Bloomers," and "Girl Big Star," under which the subheading read "Dottie Wiltse Steals Show in Prelim Softball Exhibition Tilt." This last referred to an exhibition game played between Mark C. Bloome and Cantlay-Tanzola, in which Dottie scattered just three hits in seven innings. Dottie also took the mound for a pickup game scheduled as a fill-in before the second game of a doubleheader, a game in which the girls played against the boys. As strike after strike went over the plate, a wonderful write-up in *The Examiner* compared her pitching to that of Earl Morrell, who had played baseball with Dan Wiltse and who was Dottie's first coach, along with Lou Novikoff. Hopefully the high praise made up for the fact that Dottie was referred to as "Dolly" and "Little Do Do" throughout the article. The writer's inference that the umpire gave Dottie a slight edge in naming the calls reinforced the idea that women cannot possibly excel on their own merits in an area typically reserved for men.

As the season wound down, Dottie was expected to put the "hex on the opposing team," the Dr. Pepper nine, as she had done the last time when she blanked them for a 2–0 win. Dottie also helped to put the Bloomers back in first place with a 4–1 win over Karl's Shoes on August 28. Once the championship series was under way, Dottie's star rose even higher. Sport pages proclaimed, "With Dot Wiltse and Flavilla Hagen ready to serve up curves, the Bloomer girls reign as the slight favorite," this regarding a game between Mark C. Bloome and Karl's Shoes on September 7. Both teams had tied at the end of the regular season, necessitating a playoff game to determine who would open the Shaughnessy playoffs. The mound duel of Dottie Wiltse for Mark Bloome and Laura Rowlette for Karl's Shoes was so popular that the playoff game had to be moved from Fiedler to Gilmore Field to accommodate the crowd. Gilmore Field was right in the middle of Hollywood and was home to the Hollywood All-Stars Baseball League, owned by Barbara Stanwyck, Bing Crosby, and Cecil B. DeMille.

Unfortunately, Dottie lost that decision to Laura Rowlette with a hard luck score of 9–8, depriving her team of the title of Fiedler Field Champions. While this meant the Bloomers were unable to open the first game of the Shaughnessy playoffs against Bank of America, they faced the Marshall and Clampett team in the second game. Dottie was referred to by the press at the end of the 1940 season as "one of the greatest performers in girls' softball" and "as one of softball's brightest lights." Considering her posting of 21 wins and 9 losses and her 250 strikeouts for that year, the assessment was accurate. Dottie's childhood friend, Ginny Larson, added her own viewpoint, which related closely to that of the press. "I was always in awe of her," Ginny said, as she thought back to watching Dottie play at Gilmore Field and other venues in Southern California. "Everyone just expected she would always play ball."

Among those people who believed that Dottie's rightful place was on the mound was Bill Allington, whom Dottie would once again follow when he moved to a different team in 1941, and through whose encouragement she would travel to Chicago to try out for the women's professional baseball league in 1944. Dottie respected him as a manager and credits him with much of what she learned about baseball. "I wouldn't play for anyone else, if I had the choice," Dottie asserted. "In fact, I felt bad because I didn't play for him in the AAGPBL, but he was with Rockford then and they were pretty well set, and I wasn't needed there, you might say."

Allington really knew his baseball, and he lived for the game. One rumor that still goes around about him is that if someone cracked open his head, baseballs would fall out. While he never made it to the majors because of an arm injury, he still made his mark on the sport as one of the finest managers in girls' softball in Southern California and also in the AAGPBL, his Rockford Peaches winning more championships than any other team in the history of the League. Allington's success as a manager was twofold. In part it came from his ability to recognize potential when he saw it; in addition, he knew exactly how to tap into it.

One way Allington did this was by focusing on the strategy of the game and demanding that his girls do the same. "A lot of the girls wouldn't play for him because he was so strict," Dottie said. "He really made you study everything. And he gave you tests to take home, too. Some of the girls didn't like that very much," she chuckled, "but I didn't mind." If Dottie never resented her manager's tactics it was because she knew what he was after. Without a sure knowledge of the techniques of the game, and the discipline necessary to attain that knowledge, the pinnacle of success remains an illusion, no matter how talented a player proves to be. No wonder Bill Allington had the most wins of any manager in the AAGPBL.

Allington also believed in frequent workout sessions. One of his favorite places to practice was Catalina Island. Located twenty-two miles off the coast of Los Angeles, the island offers a unique array of plant and animal life, as well as abundant aquatic life along its shores. Catalina Island has been home to various native American groups and also possesses its own ties to baseball lore. In 1919, William Wrigley, the chewing gum magnate and owner of the Chicago Cubs, bought the island for three million dollars, sight unseen, after the previous landholder defaulted on his mortgage payments. Wrigley's most prized accomplishment on the island was the construction of the famed Casino, which while never used for gambling was famous nevertheless for the live entertainment it offered. Big bands such as Benny Goodman, Jimmy Dorsey, and Harry James often played in the art deco ballroom, which could accommodate up to 5000 dancers.

However, in 1921 Wrigley decided to use the island for an entirely different purpose. In the winter of that year, his first season as principal owner of the Cubs, he brought his ballplayers from all over the country for spring training on Catalina Island, a tradition that would continue for thirty years. The team usually stopped first in Los Angles to play pickup games against the Los Angeles Angels, Wrigley's team in the Pacific Coast League. Those games took place at L.A.'s Wrigley Field, where Dottie pitched in many a championship game for the girls' softball league. Once the team arrived on the island, they found a diamond and a practice field in Avalon, the island's only city, which Wrigley had built in anticipation of their arrival. The dimensions of the ballfield were identical to those of Wrigley Field in Chicago. Perched just above the field, Wrigley's mountainside country club offered a perfect view of the games being played below. It was to this picturesque ball park, lined with eucalyptus trees, that Bill Allington brought his softball team for exhibition games and general practice sessions.

Whether he chose Catalina Island for its rich baseball association, or simply because it offered a first-class ballfield amidst a beautiful setting of rugged terrain, is anyone's guess. However, his choice made sense, as a precedent had already been set for ball clubs to visit there. The Pacific Coast League Angels were frequent fixtures on the island, giving the Cubs a break from the inter-squad games they played in the first few weeks of training. In addition, comedian Joe E. Brown, who once played semipro baseball and whom Dottie often saw in the stands cheering on the softball girls, put together various teams of movie stars to take on the Cubs during the winter months. Whyever Allington decided on Catalina Island, he could not know that a certain person connected with the island would not only change the face of baseball history but would also profoundly affect his life and that of several of his players as well.

That person was Phillip K. Wrigley, the man whose idea it was to form a professional women's baseball league as a contingency measure during World War II. By the time Allington brought his softball teams for practice sessions to Catalina, Phillip Wrigley had assumed control of the island, William Wrigley having been dead for almost a decade. Although not as passionate about baseball as his father, P.K. had kept on as owner of his father's beloved Cubs and maintained an interest in baseball overall. Because of this interest, perhaps it is not too farfetched to wonder if Wrigley ever wandered over to watch one of the girls' softball games while vacationing at the home his father had built on a bluff overlooking the city of Avalon. Perhaps, too, it is not impossible to believe that the seed of women's baseball was sown here, on this island lush with growth, waiting to blossom under just the right conditions.

Those conditions were drawing nearer as 1940 rolled relentlessly towards 1941. The year 1940 marked Germany's overthrow of Denmark, Norway, and the Low Countries during April and May, followed by the capitulation of France on June 22. During that tumultuous time, British forces had managed to rescue some 338,000 troops, including an evacuation from Dunkirk which left behind ninety thousand rifles, seven thousand tons of ammunition, and one hundred and twenty thousand vehicles. While the United States had managed to stay neutral up to this point, moral sympathy for the Allied cause was clearly escalating, and arms support would shortly follow. Responding to a plea from Winston Churchill on May 15, President Roosevelt arranged for aircraft, antiaircraft equipment, and ammunition to be sent to Great Britain, having presciently revised the Neutrality Act of 1937 the previous November. By the time President Roosevelt was reelected for an unparalleled third term in November of 1940, the majority of Americans believed the country would soon be at war.

In the spring of 1941 a new season of girls' softball began in Southern California, this time against the backdrop of booming production. In Los Angeles Harbor, shipbuilding was proceeding at a furious pace, with camouflage netting used so neither Japanese nor German planes could detect the heightened activity. Aircraft plants were also gearing up throughout the Los Angeles area, including in Dottie's hometown of Inglewood, all to aid the beleaguered European cause. In time, factories such as Douglas Aircraft and North American Aviation would employ over 100,000 workers, creating new communities and recasting the character of Inglewood entirely. And while the bats still cracked in the ballparks of L.A., soon this, too, would change, as blackout restrictions silenced the familiar sounds for the duration of the war.

Dottie made the most of her last full season of play. She could not know, of course, that when she started the 1942 season with Allington's Dodgers the season would be shortened considerably. Playing now for Bill Allington's Knobby Knits, sponsored by the Knobby Knits sweater shop located on celebrated Hollywood Boulevard, Dottie soon demonstrated that her momentum never slackened from year to year. By the beginning of June, she had won seven straight games and pitched her team into the league-leading spot. A newspaper headline on June 4, 1941 proclaimed "Girl Star" in bold print, with "Wiltse Hurls" underneath. The ensuing article referred to Dottie as the feminine Bob Feller, comparing her to the Cleveland Indian pitcher who had a career 3.25 ERA over his twenty years with the team. Another correlation between them, aside from their pitching ability, was their respective ages at the beginning of their pitching careers. Bob Feller was only 17 years old when he started with the Indians, had won 24 games by the age of 20 in 1939, and had three twenty-plus seasons by the time he was 24. Dottie Wiltse began her ball career at the age of 12, never dropped below twenty wins from the time she was 16 in 1939 to the end of her softball career, and had won three championship series by the time she was 16.

At the beginning of the foreshortened 1942 season, more praise would come Dottie's way when columnist Morton Moss of *The Examiner* began a piece by observing, "Here we were under the foolish impression the Christy Mathewson, Lefty Grove, Johnny Vander Meer and Charley Root, plus a flock of other male citizens, were the most eminent pitchers extant, when along happens Dottie Wiltse ... Naturally we know better now." Ironically, he ended the column with the suggestion that since a women's army was being formed perhaps the commissioner of baseball and the presidents of the American and National leagues should take heed. Who could have guessed that a year later someone would do just that?

Accolades one after another continued to pile up for Dottie. On July 13, 1941, she started for her team when the newly renovated Beverly Stadium, formerly Fielder's Field, hosted an opening-night doubleheader. The Knobby Knits, who led the league at the end of the first half of play, faced the Dr. Pepper nine in the newly repainted and redecorated field. Less than a week later, in another game billed as a "Wiltse/Hagen Duel" in a match between the Knobby Knits and

Karl's Shoes, sportscasters favored Dottie over her rival "if she could keep her control in the pinches." A later write-up referring to her as "the leading pitching star of the All-American Softball League" left little doubt that Dottie could handle herself on the mound no matter what the situation.

Nor did the exhibition games that the California teams played against girls' softball teams in Arizona leave any question. In particular, the games the Knobby Knits played that year against the Phoenix Ramblers truly showcased Dottie's talents. Dottie credited the Ramblers as a good team, but in August of 1941 they were no match for her and her teammates. In the first two games on the coast when the Knobby Knits hosted the Phoenix Ramblers in Los Angeles, Dottie blanked the world champion team in the first game, allowing four hits and no runs and pitching a no-hit, no-run game in the second match. Her best pitch, the one that had the Ramblers hitting nothing but fouls in the last game, was her submarine pitch. That pitch came whistling up to the plate like "a limited express" and could be stopped about as easily as a fast-moving train. That these performances were against a Phoenix team that had won 42 out of 45 exhibition games playing against the best teams in Arizona, Utah, Washington, Oregon, and California made Dottie's totals even more impressive.

Coming into Phoenix the following week with the title of world's champion girl softball pitcher, Dottie had her work cut out for her. She was to start the first game against Ameline Peralta, billed as one of the sport's finest all-around players after she pitched her team to a world title against Detroit in 1940. Furthermore, the Ramblers were dying to make up for the trouncing they had taken from the Hollywood team, and the Phoenix papers warned the Knobby Knits that "the Ramblers were aching to wipe out the only serious splotch on their championship prestige." Reporter Bob Allison remarked that the Ramblers were not convinced that even Miss Wiltse's pitching, backed by her airtight infield, could stop the stars on the Arizona team. He further intimated that California rules had given the Knobby Knits an advantage in winning the two games in Los Angeles and implied that the Arizona rules would give the Ramblers a distinct edge. His prognosis, however, failed to take into account Dottie Wiltse's pitching prowess.

In a thirteen-inning game, six innings beyond the regulation contest, the Knobby Knits won a third straight game over the Arizona Ramblers by a score of 2–0. Both Wiltse and Peralta went the full thirteen innings, with Peralta giving up six hits, walking one, and striking out twelve. However, despite the good play by both girls, one local newspaper declared that Dottie deserved to win. After giving up three base hits in seven innings, she allowed only two more hits through the thirteenth and "pitched herself time after time out of a hole into which her mates placed her with errors, seven in all." She walked only three batters and struck out sixteen, a feat second only to her near-perfect strikeout performance of nineteen batters in seven innings.

With numbers like these, it is easy to see why Dottie was such a draw for the thousands of fans who turned out to watch the girls' softball games. Her extraordinary pitching maneuvers, coupled with the grittiness she displayed on the mound, all added up to an exhibition well worth watching, providing as it did that edge-of-the-seat drama that adds a thrill to any sport. During one game early in 1941, her accomplishments did more than energize the fans, however. They led her beyond the dirt of the diamond to the glittering corridor of Hollywood stars.

Among those in the stands that day were several movie executives from Warner Brothers Studios. They were looking for a way to promote their newly released movie, *Million Dollar Baby*, and they had an idea for publicizing the movie involving a female softball player. They had traveled to numerous games throughout the league, trying to decide which girl would best fit their needs. Finally, as they watched Dottie's command of the mound as she pitched the Knobby Knits to another victory, they realized their problem was solved. Out of the hundreds of gifted women softball players in Southern California, Warner Brothers Studio chose Dottie Wiltse as the "Million Dollar Baby of Softball" in conjunction with the motion picture of the same name.

Million Dollar Baby, released in the United States on May 31, 1941, is a lighthearted drama involving a European heiress who is dismayed to discover that her father made his fortune by cheating his partner. The heiress hurries off to America to present the granddaughter of her father's partner with a staggering one million dollars. However, the money causes the young girl untold problems, as her boyfriend refuses to marry a girl with more money than he. The movie stars May Robson as the crotchety heiress, Priscilla Lane as the recipient of Robson's goodwill, Jeffrey Lynn as Robson's lawyer, and Ronald Reagan as Lane's proud boyfriend.

Interestingly, future President Reagan, like Dottie, had reached Hollywood by way of baseball. When he was a young man working for radio, Reagan was invited to Catalina Island in the winter of 1937 to observe the Cubs prior to his broadcasting their games in the upcoming season. Taking a break from his duties one day, Reagan visited a Hollywood studio and ended up auditioning for his first screen test. There, his career path was altered forever. The Cubs were forced to find another voice, and Hollywood inherited another star.

Dottie's role as the "Million Dollar Baby of Softball" was to pose for a publicity photo with one of the film's stars, Jeffrey Lynn. A headline in a local newspaper announced "Dorothy Wiltse Wins Title" and informed its readers that Miss Wiltse, a senior at Inglewood High School, would be a guest at a luncheon given by the studio for the cast of the newly released motion picture *Million Dollar Baby*. For her brush with stardom, Dottie wore a pin-striped suit that fell just below the knee, complemented by a high-collared blouse and open-toe mid-heel pumps with bows on them. She remembered how excited she was about her adventure and how she and Jeffrey Lynn talked quite a bit as they sat for the camera. In the resulting photograph, both Lynn and Dottie are smiling as Lynn spreads his hands as if making a point. Dottie still laughs when she looks at the print, since what is most noticeable are her long shapely legs, demurely tucked sideways and seeming to wind their way to the back of the chair. "All legs," she said. "Oh boy."

Once the formal part of the proceedings was over, Lynn took Dottie and her friend, Ginny, to the studio commissary for lunch. Ginny had come with Dottie for moral support. "She was so nervous about going by herself that she asked me if I would go with her," Ginny said. The studio graciously complied with Dottie's request. Neither Ginny nor Dottie could remember what they ate, most likely because they were so in awe of their surroundings that the food was the least of their concerns. To add to the excitement, JeffreyLynn introduced the girls to Priscilla Lane and some of the other cast during the course of their meal, putting them at ease and adding to their sense of importance. The question posed by the movie's original score, Frederick Hollander's "Who Is In Your Dreams Tonight?" was probably easily answered by both Ginny and Dottie as they finally closed their eyes against their event-filled day.

Million Dollar Baby was not Dottie's first brush with movie fame. In 1937, while playing softball for Young's Market, Dottie and some of her teammates were used as stand-ins for the little known murder mystery called *Girls Can Play*, starring Rita Hayworth and Guinn "Big Boy" Williams. The plot revolves around a beautiful woman who mysteriously dies while a crowd of people watch a baseball game. The baseball scenes were where Dottie and the Marketers came in. "Well, we did the work of the stars, you might say," Dottie related, "which was very comical in that day and age, because Rita Hayworth had to catch a ball and then she didn't know what the hell to do with it." Dottie recalled that the director asked the shortstop on her team, who was a particularly good slider, to slide on some dirt, after which they brought in what Dottie thought looked like a big mattress that they put at home plate for Rita Hayworth to slide into.

Naturally, Dottie played the part of the pitcher. She had the most fun, though, throwing baseballs around off-camera. "I think they lost money because we broke everything on the set," Dottie laughed, thinking back on it. "They had these big reflectors; I don't even think they use them any more. We must have smashed fifteen or twenty of those things. They almost threw us out of the studio because we made so much noise," she said. All in all, Dottie thought being on the set was great. She had a perfect excuse to miss school, and even better, she got paid, a good preview of the time she would earn much more money playing professional ball.

Before that time came, though, Dottie found employment that conveyed her down another avenue to the stars. Dottie's first job after graduating from Inglewood High School in June, 1941 was with Payne Furnace Company in Beverly Hills. One of the women who served in a capacity similar to a chaperone in the girls' softball league had mentioned the job to Dottie. Mainly, Dottie answered telephones in the daytime, making appointments for customers to have their furnaces repaired. Many of these clients were movie stars. "They used to call in, because everyone had a Payne Furnace," Dottie said. Fielding celebrity calls and juggling their schedules must have been pretty heady work for an eighteen-year-old right out of high school. Once Dottie even saw Helen Keller and her seeing-eye dog, when Keller was visiting the plant.

When Dottie's friend Barbara went to work for Payne Furnace the next year, after Dottie recommended she apply for a job there, she and Dottie enjoyed themselves immensely on their lunch hour. Hopping in the Model A, they sometimes drove over to the exclusive Farmers' Market to watch the maids of the stars do the shopping for their distinguished employers. The two of them sat at their table eating lunch, speculating on who was buying what for whom and hoping they could pick up some juicy gossip. Sometimes after work they would treat themselves to a nice dinner in one of the ritzier restaurants in

Beverly Hills, no doubt hoping to catch a glimpse of a famous face, perhaps one whose voice they recognized from the telephone. Dottie and Barbara also belonged to Payne Furnace's bowling league, also located in Beverly Hills. On bowling nights, they grabbed a quick bite to eat after work, bowled a few games, and then drove the twenty or so miles back to their homes in Inglewood through the legendary Baldwin Hills.

Soon, however, the comfortable routine of work, sports, and budding friendships took an abrupt turn. All too soon the events of December 7, 1941, events more horrific than any the United States would see until the terrorist attacks of 9/11 almost sixty years later, shattered any illusion of peace and neutrality the United States harbored, pushing the country from the brink of war into its very center. When Dottie arrived at the ballpark on the evening of December 7, 1941, officials delayed the game for several moments to play the *Star-Spangled Banner.* The strains of the national anthem reverberated over the grassy field, further fueling the patriotic mood that had blanketed those assembled there so suddenly and so forcibly earlier that morning.

The next day, December 8, 1941, saw an onrush of citizens flooding local recruiting offices wanting to enlist. People lined up outside the army recruiting center in New York City by 7 A.M., eager to defend the Allied cause. No doubt President Roosevelt's noontime message to Congress, heard by a record 60,000,000 radio listeners, also spurred people to take action to avenge the "day that will live in infamy." By nighttime, the number of enlistments totaled three times more than the number for April 6, 1917, when the first World War started. The marines logged in over five hundred men by midafternoon, the navy over seven hundred. One of those raw navy recruits was seventeen-year-old Harvey Collins from Fort Wayne, Indiana, the man with whom Dottie Wiltse would share more than fifty years of marriage.

Meanwhile, at 8:15 that night in the Los Angeles area, Dottie and her neighbors experienced their first alert of possible enemy planes overhead. They had only five minutes to respond to the police and fire engine sirens, the city having no air raid alarms, but the people cooperated with the police force, firemen, air raid wardens, and Boy Scouts who went around turning out lights and urging people to seek shelter. Earlier in the day, they had experienced a partial blackout and two radio silences, so they were prepared. Dottie remembered that time very clearly. "Everybody was standing in their back yard, peering up in the sky to see if we could locate any Japanese planes. We probably looked pretty silly," she said from a comfortable distance. At the time, though, it was not all that absurd. Immediately after December 7, false reports of enemy planes flew through the air as numerous as the supposed planes themselves. The previous night in San Francisco, sirens had sounded three times, and by the third time one citizen demanded to know why there were no bombs dropping if Japanese planes were in the air. In truth, there were no enemy planes, but the fear was real enough, especially since no one knew what was going on. Dottie remembered another instance when sirens wailed continuously and antiaircraft guns went off all over Southern California, the reason for which no one ever ascertained.

Dottie's response to the war, like that of her future husband's, was to take action. In addition to her daytime job, at night she joined the millions of women who worked in war industries, helping to push American war production to its height by 1943. Fortunately, Dottie did not have to travel far to fulfill her patriotic duties—merely from the offices of Payne Furnace Company to their factory. "Mr. Payne's secretary, who ran the company, really, would bring us supper and we'd eat at the desk, and then we'd go out to the factory and use the drill to make airplane parts," Dottie said, as she recounts her personal Rosie the Riveter role. As was common at the time, the smaller parts she fashioned for the planes would be sent to other larger factories around Southern California where all of the parts were then assembled for the final product.

To take a break from her exhausting schedule, Dottie still bowled with the Payne Furnace League. One of her more harrowing driving experiences came about after she and Barbara, who also did double duty in the office and the factory, left the lanes after they finished bowling. As Barbara told it, just when they were about to leave, the area had another blackout. During blackouts, no one was allowed to drive with their headlights on, and Dottie and Barbara had quite a long trek home. "We got to laughing so hard," Barbara recalled, "because Dottie couldn't see where she was going. So I got out and sat on the front fender and was giving Dottie hand signals going through the hills. It's a wonder we weren't killed, but being young it didn't bother us at all. But when I think back on it, we were crazy." Needless to say, that was one incident they never shared with their parents.

The war touched both of them in a personal way, also. Both of their boyfriends had been drafted, so they were busy writing air mail letters to them, as well as to boys they had grown up with who were also in the service. Barbara's boyfriend was in the air force, while Dottie's beau was in the navy, demonstrating early on her penchant for sailors that would culminate in her marrying one several years later. Dottie also kept in touch with a childhood friend, Steve Barrett, whose parents were good friends with Dottie's. Steve's dad had played shortstop on the same team as Dan Wiltse, so Dottie and Steve were often together at ballgames. "Our parents would take us to ballgames," Dottie said, "and these ballgames were at night. And we'd end up in the back seat asleep together and our parents always kidded us about that when we got older." Aside from the families seeing each other at the ballpark, Steve's parents had a vacation place at Big Bear where Dottie and her parents often visited. Later, Dottie and Steve ended up in the same high school, although Steve was a year older than Dottie. "His mother, who we called Bubbles, was really upset that we didn't get married," Dottie said. "And I'll never forget when he told her, 'Mom, I can't marry her. She's my friend.'"

Steve ended up in the Marine Corps with Carlston's Raiders during World War II, responsible for evacuating beachheads and other perilous missions. Few came out alive after many of these maneuvers. While Steve survived his many ordeals, he was once lost for almost three months before being found and sent home for a much needed rest. "His mother didn't want him to go back," Dottie said, "so we figured out what to do. We hid him in the park across from a cemetery near where we lived, in a place like a cave. We hid him for a few weeks before anybody found out where he was." Naturally he couldn't stay hidden forever, but once the marines located him they gave him a desk job after what he had been through.

Dottie also thinks back upon the difficulties her many Japanese friends endured, people she met through school and through playing softball. "They were nice people," she said, "but they weren't treated too good at that time. But, anyway..." she trailed off. That was the time period, her unspoken words imply. No matter anyone's personal feelings, what needed to be done to champion democracy's cause would be done, without fanfare or excess emotion. In the end, not only would the effort be worth the cause, but as is usual when personal needs are disciplined for the sake of the greater good, such selflessness would serve as its own reward.

THIRD INNING

Off to the Big Time: The Minneapolis Millerettes, 1944

While Dottie juggled jobs to aid the war movement on the West Coast, another effort was under way in the Midwest that would not only benefit the country as a whole but would change Dottie's life and that of almost six hundred other women as well. The proposed idea, however, relied not on individual sacrifices but on a latent source of untapped talent. Little did Dottie realize that these extraordinary times in which she lived would soon thrust her from the familiar sphere of girls' softball to the Elysian fields of Major League Baseball. What awaited her was an experiment, one that offered untold opportunities and a chance to fulfill a dream.

The birth of this singular notion took place in Chicago, Illinois, where Philip J. Wrigley, still at the helm of the Cubs, was mulling over the fate of America's favorite pastime. That P.K. was about to propound a unique solution to a seemingly unsolvable problem is not supported. Wrigley Senior was one of the first to allow local radio stations to air not just World Series games but regular-season games as well. Since these games were played during the afternoons, many of the newly converted fans were housewives, not the traditional sports supporters of the day.

To capitalize on what his father had initiated, Philip Wrigley declared Fridays Ladies' Day at Wrigley Field during the late '30s, sensing an opportunity to increase attendance at the stadium. One such day drew over 3000 women to just 3800 seats, creating consternation in the minds of some regular attendees. Wrigley also instituted half-price days for children, a good ploy to draw future fans of the game. Now, though, he feared the tide was turning away from his efforts.

The cause of his concern was the war. When the Japanese attacked Pearl Harbor, thus escalating the United States' involvement in the war, attendance at major league ballparks dropped the following season. Even before that, when the country's commitment was less intense, attendance had fallen somewhat in 1941. The future looked even bleaker for 1943. Millions of men had either volunteered for the war or were drafted, including a large number of major league ballplayers such as Ted Williams and Joe DiMaggio. In addition, the number of men fighting overseas meant a depletion in the minor league system. Twenty-six farm teams had dropped to nine. Rumors circulated that the 1943 season could be canceled altogether.

As it turned out, Wrigley's fears about the season being eliminated were unfounded. Looking for guidance to President Franklin Delano Roosevelt, then baseball commissioner Judge Kenesaw Mountain Landis received a letter with these words from the President:

> As you will, of course, realize, the final decision about the baseball season must rest with you and the baseball club owners. So, what I am going to say is solely a personal and not an official point of view.
>
> I honestly feel that it would be best for the country to keep baseball going. There will be fewer people unemployed and everybody will work longer hours and harder than ever before. And that means that they ought to have a chance for recreation and for taking their minds off of their work even more than before. Baseball provides a recreation which does not last over two hours or two hours and a half and which can be got for very little cost.

However, Wrigley harbored other misgivings. He knew that with the strongest and most vigorous players gone to fight, they would be replaced by rookies and others of less than optimal athletic skill. The quality of the game would not be what it had been before the war. Plus, the rationing of gasoline bred the possibly of teams being unable to travel for road games at times. Either scenario meant lowered attendance with a resultant loss of income. To combat this dilemma, Wrigley, ever the entrepreneur, decided to offer something different as a crowd pleaser: a professional women's softball league as a substitute for men's Major League Baseball.

Wrigley happened upon softball because so many women's teams abounded throughout the country. Although he anticipated a game slightly different from softball, Wrigley recognized that in these clubs he would find the talent for his league. He also knew a certain allure attached itself to women playing ball. In the Chicago area alone, a large number of teams had banded together to form several softball leagues, which attracted hundreds of thousands of fans in 1942.

Nor was the idea of women ballplayers a new one. Female "baseball clubs" had successfully barnstormed around the country from the late 1800s to 1920. Called Bloomer Girl teams because of the heavy stockings and striped, shortened dresses they wore, these teams traveled from town to town, playing against men's city, semipro, and minor league teams. At the end of World War I, teams continued to play under names other than Bloomer Girl, names such as the Philadelphia Bobbies, so named for their bobbed hair, and the All-Star Ranger Girls, who would produce future AAGPBL player Rose Gocioch. Now, another chance presented itself for women's teams to be noticed nationally.

With great excitement, Wrigley's broached his idea to the other owners of the major league teams. His brainchild met with little enthusiasm. None of the owners saw the prospect of a professional women's league developing into anything worthwhile. They also would not consent for their ballparks to be used when their team was on the road. The only one who would even agree to be represented as a trustee of the new organization was Branch Rickey.

Rickey would gain attention four years later by signing the first African American ballplayer, Jackie Robinson. What is not as commonly known is that Rickey almost single-handedly introduced the farm team system in the major leagues and pushed for pooled scouting, long before anyone else seriously considered the idea. Obviously, Rickey matched Wrigley in his taste for the new and pioneering.

Yet, traditionally mavericks move society toward needed change, intended or not. That Wrigley thought about the impact his decision would have upon future generations in relation to women's rights is doubtful. Not that he did not think women could play sports, but as Wrigley was above all else a businessman, he looked more at profit and loss than at the possibility of any great social reform. Nonetheless, his plans had greater lasting impact than he or anyone else could possibly imagine.

To put his proposal into action, he first sent one of his scouts to meet with the owner/manager of one of the softball leagues in the Chicago area. Since the league had a less than sterling reputation, and the manager himself was a somewhat unsavory individual, Wrigley abandoned the idea of using local talent and started from scratch. He sent his scouts all around the country and into Canada, convincing girls from various softball teams to come to Chicago for tryouts. Although in the beginning only sixty-four girls would be chosen, hundreds answered the call.

In the meantime, Wrigley planned where he would base his new enterprise. Since the owners of the Major League teams would not agree to lease their parks, he turned away from the bigger cities and looked closer to home. He happened upon several mid-size cities with fairly large war-producing factories. Not only would the employees of these factories give him a fan base, he could tout the women's teams as entertainment for the workers coming off of their shifts. This would satisfy the patriotic sensibilities of the time.

Wrigley approached area businessmen in selected cities. Four responded. Racine, Wisconsin, Rockford, Illinois, South Bend, Indiana, and Kenosha, Wisconsin all expressed interest in a professional women's softball league. What he offered these cities was basically a franchise. Several businessmen in each city would put up a sum of money and Wrigley's organization would provide the equipment, the uniforms, and the publicity. They would also recruit and train the girls and would assign each girl to a certain team, thus ensuring an equal distribution of talent. Any profits would go to the individual teams, but the money would go back into the community to fund local projects. With these details settled, play was about to begin.

That first year went well, with attendance gradually building up to a good-sized number of fans. The league also underwent a name change from the All-American Girls Softball League to the All-American Girls Ball League. While the game started out resembling softball, some changes were made from the beginning, specifically base stealing. This made the game livelier, with an element of suspense not usual in softball. The ball measured twelve inches—three inches larger than that used in Major League Baseball but slightly smaller than some softballs. The length of the base paths and the distance from the pitching mound to the batter's box were shorter than in Major League Baseball but longer than those in softball. Like baseball, nine players composed a team, as opposed to softball's ten, and the game consisted of nine innings rather than softball's seven. Although not yet Major League Baseball, nonetheless the small changes in the beginning, including the name change, indicated a far different game would evolve in the future.

When Dottie joined the league in 1944, it had expanded to include two more teams, this time in the larger cities of Minneapolis, Minnesota and Milwaukee, Wisconsin. The names chosen for the new teams were the Millerettes and the Chicks, respectively. That these two teams were doomed from the start, no one guessed. Hopes ran high that the boom the league enjoyed in the first year would continue, and indeed it did, but not in the bigger cities. However, adding more teams meant that more girls would have a chance at the big time and that ultimately more women would experience the thrill of professional baseball.

The letter inviting Dottie to the tryouts in Chicago came to 1212 Rosewood Avenue in the spring of 1944. Dated April 20, it read in part,

> Dear Miss Wiltse,
> Mr. Bill Allington of Van Nuys has recommended you and gave me your address. As a talent scout, for the All-American Girls Professional League, we are offering you an opportunity to join our league.... For the players it is a business opportunity which gives them a chance to become nationally famous and acquire a bank account.... We feel this League can be developed into one of the very largest Professional Sports in the world for girl players ... we would appreciate it if you would let us hear from you by return airmail, with some idea what weekly salary you would expect.

The letter was signed by J.A. Hamilton of the Wrigley Building, Chicago, Illinois, and was accompanied by a questionnaire requesting personal and educational information as well as specifics of Dottie's softball career, such as a list of championship teams she had played for and the number of no-hit, one-hit and two-hit games she had pitched.

Dottie's parents shared her excitement over the good fortune that years of hard work had brought to her, although Dottie admitted that her mother cried because she was going so far away. Still, Ellie managed to organize a nice going-away party for Dottie shortly before she left on her trip. Some of the gifts intended to send Dottie on her way included a writing kit from her grandmother and Aunt Blanche; a suitcase with a blouse and slip tucked inside from her mom and dad; and sweaters, pajamas, and stockings from several close friends. *The Los Angeles Examiner* joined the chorus of well-wishers with an article on May 9, 1944, headlined "Dorothy Wiltse, 'Million Dollar Baby,' Joins Chicago Ball Club on Long Tour." After capping her accomplishments throughout her softball years, the piece ended with "All Inglewood and a host of friends throughout Southern California join in wishing 'Cinderella' ...the best of good luck and success." The next day, May 10, Dottie boarded a North Western train in Los Angeles for the three-day trek to Chicago.

Five other California girls traveled to the tryouts in Chicago with Dottie. These included Levonne "Pepper" Paire, Annabelle Lee, Alma "Gabby" Ziegler, Faye Dancer, and Thelma "Tiby" Eisen. One can imagine these young women, most in their twenties, bubbling with excitement as they began a new phase of their lives. When asked if she was frightened going so far from home for the first time, Dottie responded, "Heck no. It was a train full of sailors." Naturally, she ascertained this fact pretty quickly. Drawn as if by radar, Dottie quickly homed in on car 806, where several young representatives of the United States Navy were en route to their next assignment. Time passed quickly once Dottie made friends with sailors such as Ray, aka "Camp," Bill the "Chaplain," "Bulldog" Burt, and "Silent" Chris. Hanging around with the service men had other advantages as well. As she wrote to her mother, "Having a lot of fun on the train. Everyone knows us. Call us the base ball girls. Pepper and I made friends with the head waiter and we get to eat when the service men do, which is first."

Train travel in the 1940s was quite different than it is today, with a formality in keeping with the times. White-jacketed porters carried the passengers' luggage, while similarly clad stewards with silver trays served riders in their seats with just the ring of a bell. The sumptuously furnished lounge cars and the dining cars with white linen tablecloths, china, and glassware added a touch of sophistication to the journey. Diners in The Challenger, the North Western's food car, were treated to entrees such as potted beef or baked chicken pie, complete with vegetables, potatoes, beverage, and dessert, all for seventy-five cents. Amidst this heady atmosphere the girls relaxed and planned for a different kind of ride ahead.

When the train reached its destination on Saturday morning, May 13, 1944, the girls headed to the Stevens Hotel on Michigan Boulevard at Balbo Drive, classified as the world's largest hotel. Overlooking Lake Michigan, the imposing structure must have presented a magnificent sight to Dottie, coming as she did from the small community of Inglewood. The girls roomed together on the sixth floor of the hotel for what was to be a one-night stay. After a day spent sightseeing in Chicago and dining at Williams "700" on South Wabash Avenue, the girls gathered their belongings the next morning and traveled to Peru, Illinois, outside of Chicago, for ten days of tryouts. While they had undergone a pleasant interlude, now they would be put to the test.

However, that they were more than prepared to meet this challenge became apparent right from the start. As anyone who watched them play could readily attest, the girls from California knew their stuff. Most of the other players labeled the California girls as arrogant, which Dottie frankly admitted they were, but perhaps what came across as arrogance was simply an overwhelming assurance about what they did so well. The proof of this came when the tryouts ended. While about a third of the 120 girls who had tried out failed to make the cut and were sent back home, all six of the girls from California were chosen for the league. They were the first women to be recruited from their state, but their performance ensured they would not be the last.

Dottie recalled how grueling the tryouts were. As she wrote to her mother in a Western Union telegram dated May 16, "Still in Peru. Work out yesterday. We do mean work." The girls arrived at the ballpark around 9:00 A.M. to be ready for workouts at 10:00. After a break for lunch at 12:30, more drills were conducted in the afternoon, with practice ending around 5:30. The girls trained in Washington Park, a big recreational field in the center of town. Sliding instructions in specially constructed sand pits, blackboard chalk talks, hitting, pitching, and catching instructions, and infield and outfield play composed the day's activities. Often mini-games were carried out on one diamond while the exercises were carried out on another.

As Dottie phrased it, "The setup in Washington Park was tops." Indeed, as noted in Peru's local newspaper, *The Daily Tribune*, Peru was selected because of its excellent sports facilities. That criterion was added to the fact that Wrigley Field in Chicago was considered too small for the turnout of 120 girls in 1944, although Wrigley, the scene of the 1943 tryouts, would again be used in later years. Chaperones and managers were on hand at all times, and in general a professional atmosphere prevailed. The girls were expected to try out for every position in order to determine their eligibility for a future team, but interestingly the powers that be kept Dottie strictly on the rubber. "Probably took one look at me and thought she can't do," Dottie reasoned. In addition to her poor running skills, her less than optimal hitting ability was a standard joke among her teammates.

After the training session ended for the day, the girls retired to the New Hotel Peru, which touted itself as a "friendly hotel," complete with its famous Royal Hawaiian Room. Dottie remembered it as a very old brick building, rectangular in shape, with awnings shading the front and side doors. From her room on the fifth floor, Dottie could look over clumps of trees and houses nestled together and see the Illinois River off in the distance. Downtown Peru's shopping district, with its main street typical of many such streets all across the United States during the 1940s, offered shops and other services to meet any of the girls' requirements.

Having a professional women's baseball league in town was a plus for many of the residents. The mayor of Peru, Albert H. Hasse, extended an official welcome at the beginning of the training session, telling the ballplayers, "Peru and Peruvians are happy to have you in their midst.... We hope that Peru residents show the girls that old Peru spirit and make them feel at home while they are with us." Sportswriters encouraged local residents to attend the exhibition doubleheaders staged by the girls on the weekend following their arrival and reported faithfully on the progress of the girls' training camp, detailing particulars such as their sessions on sliding and base stealing and commenting on the amount of talent on display. Max Carey, manager of the Milwaukee Chicks, was a featured speaker at the weekly luncheon meeting of the Peru Rotary Club.

Once the tryouts ended, four of the six California girls, Dottie, Faye Dancer, Pepper Paire, and Annabelle Lee were sent to the Minneapolis Millerettes, while Tiby Eisen and Alma Ziegler were platooned to the Milwaukee Chicks, both expansion teams for 1944. The fact that there were there at all, and that all would move on to stellar careers within the league, can be directly attributed to Bill Allington, Dottie's mentor from her softball days. As if to display that knack he had for sensing the promise in others, Allington had handpicked the girls from the hundreds he had managed throughout his girls' softball career. Some quirk of fate must have intervened to guarantee Bill Allington ended up where he did. Had he remained healthy and gone on to a major league career he may not have managed girls' softball in Southern California, in which case the All-American Girls Professional Baseball League would have been much poorer as a result.

Although Dottie never played on a team which he managed in the women's professional league, what Bill Allington taught her about pitching and competing remained with her throughout her career. In one of the letters he sent to Dottie when she first joined the league, he wrote,

> Say Dot. Here's just a thought. You have a wonderful chance now to have a manager who knows all the angles of pitching and I would like to have him show and teach you to throw a *change* of *pace*. Not a slow ball but to change up on your fast ball. If you master that pitch Dottie no fooling you will be able to pitch to your own children. I mean that long!!

Bill's suggestion was probably one of the reasons for Dottie's stellar reputation as well as her longevity as a strong pitcher. The change of pace Allington suggested would hopefully make Dottie's pitching arm last longer. Encouraging her to add more than one pitch to her repertoire meant she would be more effective keeping runners off the bases, since the batter would need to guess what type of ball was being hurled over the plate. Most pitchers today have an array of pitches, which allows some of them to remain effective in the game to the age of forty and beyond. Roger Clemens is one such pitcher.

At the time the girls started in 1944, Bill was not yet a manager in the All-American League. However, the fact that he showed up at the station in Los Angeles to see his six "girls" off gives a good indication of the pride he must have felt in his protégées. Because his confidence level matched theirs, he teased the girls about all the clothes they had packed, when he suspected all along that none of them would be returning to the West Coast any time soon. "Hell of a lot of luggage for two weeks," he commented. Due to Dottie's intervention and that of the other girls, Bill himself would soon be in the Midwest with them. An inkling of what was to come appears in the same letter in which Bill advised Dottie about her pitching,

> Your mother told me some nice news that you wrote about me being considered as one of the managers next year. Well Dottie you know what it's like being a professional player for two months, after ten years it kind of gets in your blood. I know all of you girls have played for me and I do appreciate it and only hope that if I do get a chance that I can come as close to living up to your recommendation of me as you girls have already succeeded in doing with the recommendation I gave you. From what I heard about the LA girls I guess you all made a lasting impression on your arrival and during the tryout period.

Bill also revealed his role as a father figure to Dottie and all the girls, as was evidenced earlier when he saw them off at the station. In another letter to Dottie, he says,

> I'm so glad you girls, "or should I say young ladies" are doing so well. Your mother said you have a 7 to 1 average now. That's swell. Just a little suggestion now. Dottie as the club goes on and keeps winning, you yourself will be anxious to pitch more and often and so will your manager keep calling on you out of turn. So here it is. Be doubly sure that you get plenty of sleep *every* nite and also doubly sure regular that your eating is correct. If you do that there is no

doubt in my mind that you will come home one of the happiest girls ever to put on a uniform. So will your Dad and Mother and I'm not leaving myself out of that either. So good luck Dottie and *stay in shape.*

That Dottie took his advice seriously is proven by her pitching performance that first year, with a 1.88 ERA and a .555 winning percentage. Dottie pitched 297 innings, with 205 strikeouts and 130 bases on balls. With statistics like those to start, some promising years lay ahead.

If it seems odd that some of Dottie's mentors were men, such as her father and her former manager, we need only to look at the time period. Men were the only ones from whom these women could learn. While women had excelled at other sports, such as running and swimming, no other women played professional baseball. Even those women who barnstormed around the country playing the game were never taken quite seriously, with many teams including men masquerading as women. The softball leagues were no better, some with names like the Num Num Pretzels Girls. Dottie's own mother never even liked the game of baseball at first, although she followed her daughter's career and was proud of her accomplishments. It took men who knew the game to recognize the skills these women possessed and to encourage them to hone those skills, despite their gender. The men who did this deserve credit for transcending society's barriers, thus fostering a love of the game in women who could play the game well.

The girls also depended upon each other to reach personal levels of success, a necessity in Dottie's first year of play since the Millerettes mainly stayed in the cellar throughout the season. One of the difficulties the girls faced was that the team was composed mostly of rookies, with the exception of Lillian Jackson, who had played for the Rockford Peaches in 1943. "None of us had been away from home before in our lives," Dottie explained. "It was all new to us to a certain extent. Plus, they hadn't balanced the team out."

Although other problems aside from the preponderance of rookies surfaced as the season wore on, another hindrance to the Millerettes' success was apparent almost from the beginning. Dottie, ever the competitor, remembered that the manager of the Millerettes, Claude "Bubber" Jonnard, did not push the team hard enough. Perhaps Jonnard, a former major leaguer who had pitched for the New York Giants, St. Louis Cardinals, and Chicago White Sox, never really took girls' baseball all that seriously. As a result of his un–Allington approach to the team, the California girls shared their own set of signals to spur on a win. Probably it was this display of spunk that kept the Millerettes going that year in spite of some tremendous obstacles along the way.

Yet it seemed an auspicious beginning for Minneapolis's new female ball club upon their arrival on Thursday, May 25, 1944, two days before their opening day game. The girls checked into the Sheridan Hotel at Marquette and Eleventh, prior to receiving their housing assignments five days later. Along with catcher Pepper Paire, Fay Dancer, and first basewoman Vivian Kellogg, Dottie was sent to the home of two elderly women at 2952 North Eighth Street. Neither of the women ever came to the ballpark, but they faithfully listened to the games on the radio. Dottie remembered that whenever she and the girls came home after a ballgame, cookies and milk waited for them on the kitchen table. "They were really sweet ladies," Dottie fondly recalled. Having a bit of home in a strange city must have helped the girls immensely as they adjusted to a world far removed from family and friends.

To officially welcome them to the city, the Minneapolis Aquatennial Society feted the Millerettes as featured guests at their planning luncheon, which took place at the Nicollett Hotel the day before their opening game. *Tribune* sports columnist Halsey Hall was master of ceremonies. The Minneapolis papers also heralded their coming with a newspaper article in the *Minneapolis Daily Times* calling upon community involvement to suggest a different name for the Millerettes, named after the minor league men's team, the Millers, so named to reflect the city's milling industry. Although the community was never as integrally involved with choosing a name as was the case in Fort Wayne, Indiana, the next year, several people did write in with suggestions. Names such as the Squaws and the Miller Maids were bandied about, with the Lakers, for the "City of Lakes," catching on as an alternative to the more commonly used Millerettes.

However, the concern over the name "Millerettes" possibly offending the minor league men's team served as a harbinger of trouble ahead, as did the tongue-in-cheek comments made by area sportswriters. Columnist Pat Purcell of the *Daily Times*, discussing the search for a nickname, suggested the Millerettes be called, among other things, the "Bubbers," after manager Bubber Jonnard, or "Wriglers," for Phillip J. Wrigley. Meanwhile, Halsey Hall of the *Minneapolis Tribune* commented, "Common courtesies and the sweet little niceties accorded ladies generally go by the board at Nicollett Park next weekend." Hall also questioned how long a sportswriter should wait after a game before entering the ladies' locker room, an interesting foreshadowing of the dilemma female sports reporters would face several decades later.

Once the team began play, however, the skeptical attitudes changed somewhat. Having disposed of the formality of presenting the mayor's wife with a giant bouquet of flowers after she threw out the first pitch, Dottie took the mound to show the hundreds of spectators gathered there what women's baseball was really about. Although the Millerettes lost the home opener 5–4 to the Rockford Peaches, their level of play took the community, especially the sportswriters, by surprise. Despite Halsey Hall's previous reservations, he knew quality play when he saw it, and he gave credit where it was due. Reporting on that first game, he wrote, "Chatter was the only feminine touch to the proceedings. In a welter of flaring skirts, headlong and feet-first slides ... bodily contact, good pitching and really brilliant outfielding, the Millerettes performed like genuine ball players ... Pitcher Wiltse would have won with better support."

Obviously, this benevolent attitude did not hold true for a writer from the United Press who wrote, "...there's a powder puff plot under way ... aimed at virtual extinction of the perspiring, swearing, tobacco-chewing baseball player." A photograph of Dottie accompanied these ill-informed comments. Ironically, she is poised for a perfect pitch, but the writer could see only the curves on the girl, not the arc of the ball. This emphasis on the feminine shifted as spectators realized the caliber of play and the competitive spirit the girls exhibited. Yet Wrigley made sure the feminine angle was never de-emphasized.

To this end, Wrigley stipulated the girls must attend charm school in order to portray the correct image to the public. He didn't want any "Curvaceous Cuties," harkening back to one of those dreaded softball team names, but Wrigley wanted the girls to project a certain image to minimize the often negative stereotype of female athletes. The typical female sportswoman of that time period, and for many years afterward, was pictured as coarse, masculine, and often uncouth. While Wrigley expected his girls to play well, he also demanded they conduct themselves as befitting their sex.

Wrigley transferred control of the league to his advertising executive, Arthur Myerhoff, after the 1944 season, but his charm school edict held sway when he was at the helm. In 1943, the school was run by the Helena Rubenstein Salon and in 1944 by the Ruth Tiffany

School, after which the concept of formal schooling was discontin-
ued. The charm school was part of the spring training camp in Peru
in 1944 and took place at the Hotel Peru where the girls stayed. At
their first class, the girls met with an unconventional method of com-
municating the material to be covered.

Rather than a series of lectures, the girls were presented with a
story dramatized in six parts by Frances McCune, the director of the
Tiffany School. The girls were handed pocket-size notebooks at the
first session that were "designed to forecast the personality development information which the Ruth Tiffany School will dispense,"
according to a news release prepared by Gertrude Hendriks, director of public relations for the League. In keeping with the times, the
first-edition books were designed in red, white, and blue, with a pen-
cil for note taking hanging from a patriotic red ribbon. Although the
book was meant in part as a program of the subject matter to be discussed, no actual subjects or speakers' names were listed. Instead,
phrases intended to provoke interesting conversations among the girls
illustrated each lesson. For example, "Come Into My Parlor," taught
the players how to walk, sit, and move with grace. Some other lessons included "Everyone Loves a Uniform," and "Oh What a Beautiful Morning," opposite to which was a blank page for the "Notes
of a Star to Be."

Dottie filled page after page with the pearls of wisdom she
received. She jotted down reminders on how to conduct a conversation, such as "Let yourself become interested in the person to whom
you are speaking—keep subject impersonal." She also meticulously
detailed how to properly don a coat. "Put right arm in first, then left.
Let fall over shoulders. Use one motion to arrange on. Don't wave
arm," she wrote. As for the correct way to walk like a lady, she had
been counseled, "Feet one directly in front of the other. Walk in
rhythm. No swinging of hips." Dottie also recalled walking with a
book on top of her head for good posture and balance and being
taught how to sit correctly, how to enunciate properly, in other words
without talking through her nose, and how to put on makeup and style
her hair. Dottie said there were some "dandy lookers" who came out
onto the field after fussing with their locks as they had been instructed.
All of this was intended to fulfill president Ken Sells's hopes that the
"All-American League girls will be recognized for the poised way
they walk down the street, the charm they radiate in conversation, and
the good-taste clothes they wear." Furthermore, as noted in Hendriks's press release, by "helping girl ballplayers to be by birthright

truly feminine, ball playing 'Tomboys' will have a chance to be lovely all-girl 'Marygirls.'"

When asked what she thought of the notion of charm school, Dottie said, "We laughed! Like mad crazy! We thought it was real funny." Dottie, Tiby Eisen, Faye Dancer, Annabelle Lee, and Pepper Paire even spoofed the theme of stardom when they each autographed one point of the star on the cover of Dottie's book. Yet looking back, Dottie admitted the importance of what she was taught, not only for her overall benefit but also for how she was viewed as a ballplayer. "I really think it was good," Dottie said, "because we were women playing baseball, not women trying to be men playing ball." That is an important distinction, recalling the issues women dealt with thirty years later when they entered the board rooms of high-powered corporations in large numbers. The women playing baseball in the All-American League never meant to imitate the masculine sex. They brought their own brand of talent and their own perspective to the sport, thus enriching baseball for all.

The femininity issue did not stop with charm school. The uniforms the girls wore also supported the wholesome impression the league was at pains to convey. They consisted of a one-piece dress with a short, flared skirt, from three to four inches above the knee, and satin boxer shorts underneath, designed after the field hockey and figure skating outfits of the time. Across the chest of the pink Millerettes uniform stretched a blue and grey Minneapolis emblem with a waterfall embroidered on it. The buttons on the dresses were maroon, as were the caps, emblazoned with a blue and grey M on the front, belts and wool tights, under which the girls wore white cotton stockings to protect against blood poisoning from the maroon dye in the case of being spiked. The girls improvised with rubber bands and shoestrings to keep the stockings from falling down.

Dottie's first reaction to the uniform was, "I ain't wearing that," just as one character later exclaimed in the movie *A League of Their Own*. In the beginning, she and the other girls thought that management would soon change the uniforms, but they never did. However, Dottie remembered that you "either put the uniform on or got the hell out." The length of the skirt was the main problem. Gradually, Dottie and the other girls shortened the skirt until management learned to look the other way. Although Dottie never felt the uniform was uncomfortable to play in because she pinned it to the side when she was pitching, it wasn't the same as the more practical softball outfit of short shorts. The main downfall of the uniforms was that they left the girls' legs unprotected when sliding into bases, leaving bruises and scrapes, called strawberries.

It is interesting to note that the artist who fashioned the uniforms also created the green pixies to advertise Wrigley's chewing gum. Whether the artist envisioned the women ballplayers cavorting sprite-like around the field is rather an amusing question to ponder, although interestingly sportswriters often used the term "cavort" in reporting on the women's games. What is more likely, however, is that the artist wished to convey a sweet, ethereal image to the public, a picture of appealing innocence. Instead, the grit and determination with which these women played baseball belied that view and forced the fans to concentrate wholly on the game.

The girls were also given a handbook, called *A Guide for All-American Girls—How to … Look Better, Feel Better, and Be More Popular.* The foreword to the guidebook states,

> The All-American girl is a symbol of health, glamor, perfection, vim, vigor, and a glowing personality…. The All-American Girl is fast becoming the perfect ideal for the younger generation because American youth is learning the distinction of being included on the All-American roster is indeed a privilege to be granted to only those who are especially chosen for looks, deportment and feminine charm, in addition to natural athletic ability.

It should be noted that athletic competence is listed almost as an aside. To reiterate that Wrigley was first and foremost a business-man, the novelty of women playing professional baseball lay in the fact that they clearly were women in every way who happened to be able to wield a bat, throw a ball, and run the bases. If Wrigley was not exactly looking ahead to a time of women's liberation when he created the league but instead was looking at opportunity in general, his insistence upon the feminine angle makes sense. Quite simply, the teams would attract more followers if they acted like ladies.

One fan of Dottie's who wrote to her shortly after the season began commented on this very trait. After commending Dottie on her pitching, he said,

> I believe compliments are also in order for the very lady-like manner in which you girls acted on the playing field. It was pleasantly sur-prising to say the least.

Even the Millerettes team song, sung to the tune of "Strike Up the Band," concentrated on this trait, although parts of it are obviously tongue-in-cheek. The first stanza begins, "We hail from Minneapolis, we're ladies one and all.... We hit with grace, we sit with grace, we spit with grace, and we eat with grace, and we eat with Joe. Look and admire, Minneapolis here we go."

It is apparent that an odd dichotomy acted here. These women were to be ideal women and at the same time exhibit true athletic skill. This balancing act must have been difficult, to say the least. To have to be sure makeup was properly applied before hurling a ball or cracking a bat required concentration on two areas when all of the focus should have been on one. It is hard to imagine male major league ballplayers checking to make sure every hair is in place before taking the field. These women adapted, though, and took the criterion in stride. Once they had themselves in order, they became immersed in what really mattered: the game.

After their home opener, the Millerettes played a doubleheader against the Peaches the next day. They split the series with a come-from-behind 7–6 win in the first game and a 0–2 loss in the second. On Monday, trailing Rockford two games to one, the Millerettes downed the Peaches in the last game of the series with a score of 7–6, justifying Jonnard's confidence that Dottie's curveball would even up the match between the two teams. However, a hint of troubled times ahead came with the many errors the Millerettes committed, with five of the six Peaches' runs resulting from those mismanaged Millerette balls.

Immediately after the game, the Millerettes left for a twin bill Memorial Day contest with Kenosha. They lost the opener at Lake Front Stadium 0–6 but captured the nightcap with a score of 16–14 after exploding with twelve hits in the fourth inning. A crowd of over 2000 stayed for the doubleheader, which lasted until nearly midnight. Having been rested for two days, Dottie was ready to take the mound against Kenosha on June 1, determined to fulfill the *Minneapolis Tribune's* prediction that she was the "Laker Hope" after the Millerettes' 10–2 loss to the Comets on the last day of May. True to form, Dottie held the Comets to five hits with her sharp-breaking curveball and amassed a total of ten strikeouts in the game, with the Millerettes winning with a score of 1–0. Although she wore number 2, Dottie was clearly number one.

In their next four-game series with the Rockford Peaches, the Millerettes won the first game 8–2, which left them in sole possession of second place. They lost the next by a total of three runs, 13–10, but split the doubleheader on Sunday at Rockford's Fifteenth

Avenue Stadium to even the series. Dottie's record was now 3–1, and she had struck out 29 batters over 36 innings. The start of a two-game matchup in South Bend on Monday, June 5, saw the Millerettes move to within one game of the league-leading Blue Sox with a win over South Bend of 7–5. The results of the second game would have to wait, however.

Across her schedule for Tuesday, June 6, in all capital letters, Dottie penned the words, "D-Day Invasion, No Game," to commemorate the Allied troops crossing the English Channel in the largest amphibious onslaught ever. As President Roosevelt reminded "Almighty God" that "our sons, pride of our Nation, this day have set upon a mighty endeavor," all Americans echoed this sentiment, each in their own way. A United Press illustration from the next day, June 7, showed a man in a baseball uniform, with his head bowed and his cap over his heart, standing on an engraved basepad which read "The Sports World," indicating that all sports figures stood behind the troops as they began the battle to recapture Western Europe from the stronghold of the Axis powers.

As the Millerettes moved on to Racine on June 7, they lost to the Belles behind the pitching of Audrey Haine, but the next day Dottie evened the score with a 4–0 shutout, allowing only four hits and striking out 11 Racine batters. Behind her mixture of curveball and a fast ball, only eight Belles reached the base lines and only one made it to third. Dottie was not nicked for a hit until Anna May Hutchinson smacked a double to left in the fifth inning. The Millerettes dropped into third place with a 7–0 loss to Racine on the following Monday, but they won the next game 1–0, with the single run coming in the ninth. In that game, Dottie allowed just three hits throughout nine innings of play.

By the time the Millerettes returned home to meet the Belles at Nicolett Park on June 16, Dottie had earned a 7–1 record and had pitched 36 scoreless innings. She was the only pitcher in the league with a sharp-breaking curveball, and sportswriters predicted she would establish herself as one of the best hurlers in the league. Even after the opening home game with Racine, a heartbreaking 3–2 loss in 15 innings, Dottie still distinguished herself by pitching a no-hit game for ten and two-thirds innings and giving up only six hits for the entire game.

Dottie's pitching played a key role in earning the respect the team commanded from many of their fans, even when their losses started mounting up like a pile of tottering coins. After the tough loss to

Racine, the same fan who wrote to Dottie to compliment her on her ladylike deportment on the field wrote again to offer this:

> May I take this opportunity of expressing my deepest appreciation to you for your splendid exhibition of pitching for the "Millerettes" in Saturday's game at Nicolett Park. I realize that our team was the loser, but nevertheless that does not in any way detract from the fine exhibition of ball-playing presented. Frankly, I was surprised at the talent which you girls have for the game. I can truthfully say that I enjoyed the game fully as much as [I would have] any men's professional team.

Several weeks later, after the Millerettes had left Minneapolis for good, a photographer writing to report on the status of some pictures Dottie had ordered broke off talk of business in the middle of the letter to comment,

> Incidently, keep up that swell pitching—8 and 2 with 69 strikeouts is pretty good—especially when the team has won only 14 or so. Yep, I still keep up with you 'gals' even though you've deserted our town ... good luck to you and your teammates.

The Millerettes needed all the support they could find. A downward spiral a week into a fourteen-day homestand brought them their fifth and sixth straight losses when Kenosha took both games of a doubleheader on June 23, with scores of 9–7 and 5–1, although Dottie gave up only six hits in the opener. One sports reporter suggested that perhaps the Millerettes should fire Millie the Mascot, the stuffed white Scottie who perched outside the Millerettes' dugout and who had seemingly started their run of bad luck. The team still had managed to produce a 14–15 record before the disastrous doubleheader, which is even more impressive when the number of wins is looked at in light of the number of errors the they committed. For example, in the game with Racine in which Dottie pitched over ten hitless innings, the Millerettes left 22 base runners stranded, a league record at the time. They knocked out fourteen hits, but their strategy was such that they were unable to get those hitters home. They forced so many games into extra innings that the press began referring to them as the Marathon Millerettes.

No matter how valiantly they fought, though, they couldn't quite keep up with the other teams in the League. By the time they finished their marathon homestand on July 1, they had lost 12 out of 17 games, including a humiliating loss of both games of a doubleheader against the first-place South Bend Blue Sox on June 25. The first game ended with a score of 1–3, while an early lead in the second game evaporated like raindrops on a summer day, leaving the Millerettes with a 3–9 defeat. However, in the third game of the series on June 26, billed in the *Tribune* as "Wiltse Wins Thriller Over Blue Sox," the fans applauded Dottie as she masterfully got herself out of trouble several times to win the game of 2–1. Nevertheless, before the month was out the two local softball stars, Lorraine Borg and Peggy Torrison, decided to return to their former amateur softball team, which fared better in the standings than the professional team they had joined.

As if to prove that fortune's well-oiled wheel often turns on a whim, following the win over South Bend the Millerettes promptly won the next game over Rockford to make it two in a row, but then began a terrible downward slide. July proved to be their undoing. Traveling to Milwaukee, they lost two games to the Chicks in Borchert Field on July 2, with the Chicks benefiting from 15 bases on balls and 12 stolen bases in the nightcap. The next day brought another Millerette loss, and the Fourth of July brought comparisons to dud firecrackers as the Millerettes lost a further two games to their sister expansion team. By July 5, they had earned the distinction of being the sole team in the cellar.

Nothing they tried seemed to work, even with the addition of infielders Catherine Blumetta and Betty Trezza and catcher Ruth "Tex" Lessing, who roomed with Dottie before they were forced on the road. The press took a jaded view of the team, claiming the opponents were winning on fewer hits than the Millerettes could belt out. Only the weather seemed to be on their side as heavy rain canceled the game scheduled with Racine for July 6, but the inclement conditions meant the beleaguered Millerettes were forced to play two doubleheaders on Friday and Saturday against Racine, with a doubleheader against Kenosha scheduled for that Sunday. Interestingly, although they were pounded yet again in the first doubleheader against Racine, 0–3 and 3–6, the press referred to Dottie as the Millerettes' "ace hurler" in game one as she held the Belles in check until the seventh inning when the Belles broke through with three runs. The Millerettes grabbed those two games back from the Belles on Saturday but lost both halves of the twin bill against the Comets on Sunday, 1–3 and 3–5 , again mainly due to errors.

However, when the Millerettes met the Milwaukee Chicks a few days later, Dottie again led her team to victory in fine fashion. After her team lost the opening game of a doubleheader, 0–1, Dottie pitched the Millerettes to a 12–4 win in game two. She allowed just four hits and fanned eleven batters, bringing her strikeout total to 106 and earning her the title of strikeout queen of the league. Even though the girls had difficulty coming together as a team, the individual performances of some of the players, such a pitchers Dottie Wiltse and Annabelle Lee, and league-leading hitters Helen Callaghan and Faye Dancer, showed the potential just waiting to be tapped.

This promise would ultimately have to be drawn out by another team. On July 17, the Millerettes left town for what was to be a four-week road trip. Unknown to them, this was the last they would see of the city that was their first home as a professional team. They began the second half of play on July 19 in Milwaukee. They played well, losing the first game to the Chicks by only one run, with Dottie's rash throw in the ninth allowing the winning run to score. Despite her wildness, Dottie still held the Chicks to just six hits over nine innings. While they lost the next game 1–2 on a squeeze play in the ninth, the Millerettes came back to win the third game of the series 9–1, with 23 hits, seven bases on balls, and 11 stolen bases. They then evened the series with a 5–4 win behind the pitching of Dottie Wiltse in the final game. These splendid exhibitions, however, were insufficient to stem the damage already done. On July 23, the *Minneapolis Tribune* announced that although the team would keep the name, the Minneapolis Millerettes, their home base would no longer be in Minneapolis.

Several reasons exist for the failure of the Millerettes to make a go of it in Minneapolis. The fact that the girls failed to come together as a team did not help, of course, since no one likes to watch a team consistently lose, but that was only one part of the problem. Minneapolis was an experiment of sorts to see how teams would fare in larger cities. Judging by the poor attendance figures at Nicolett Park, the answer was obvious. Girls' baseball vied with so many other forms of entertainment that it could not compete. In addition, the size of the ballpark, which the Millerettes shared with the minor league Millers, did not suit the game the women played. The shorter distances between bases and from the pitcher's mound to the batter's box tended to get dwarfed in a park meant for minor league teams aspiring to the men's majors. That much physical distance also created an emotional distance between the players and spectators. Most fans were unable to build an affinity with the players, while in the mid-size cities the smaller parks cultivated a homey feel between fans and players, so the fans could call the players their own.

Another problem in Minneapolis was its location. For example, when the girls traveled from Minneapolis to Milwaukee on the Hiawatha, they faced a three-hour train ride, with another 45 minutes tacked on to reach Racine. To get to Rockford took four hours, mainly by taking a bus to Lake Geneva and then transferring to the Rockford bus. In the story in the *Tribune* that announced Minneapolis's release of the Millerettes, Ken Sells, president of the circuit, cited problems with other teams. He said, "This action was taken after four independent clubs in the league—Racine, Kenosha, Rockford, and South Bend—objected to making the trip to Minneapolis because of the heavy traveling expenses with such small crowds attending the games."

However, the main reason the Millerettes never took hold in Minneapolis was the minor league Millers. The Millers were the Triple A club of what were then the New York Giants, and passing through its portals were such names as Ted Williams, Willie Mays, Jimmie Foxx, Hoyt Wilhelm, and Rube Waddel. Clearly, even had the Millerettes enjoyed a pennant-winning season, compared to the star-studded Millers they would still have looked like a shirttail cousin, and a rather ragged one at that. For this reason businesses in the area never really backed the Millerettes, although Nicolett Park hosted several promotional events, such as Leap Year Tilts, where ladies could entertain the man of their choice for just two dollars, and free admission for women on certain days throughout the season. Quite simply, though, with the Millers in town the idea of girls' baseball never really stood a chance.

Now homeless, the Millerettes were designated a road team. Called the "Orphans," they roamed from city to city, playing in the hometowns of the other teams, staying in hotels, and living a vagabond existence. The girls were never even told they would not be returning to Minneapolis, and Dottie remembered they had to replace the clothes they left behind as they moved from town to town. While in some ways it was a hard existence, the girls were young and still managed to have fun. Dottie related the story of Faye Dancer staying out past midnight and being forced to sneak back into the hotel where her team was housed. Dottie and a few of the other girls tied bed sheets together and hoisted her up through a back window. Luckily the girls were in good shape from their baseball exertions, or Dancer may have landed a bed in a hospital instead of one in a hotel.

The next morning, knowing that Comets manager Marty McManus was aware of their escapade and afraid they were going to get kicked out of the league, they came downstairs "looking like they were going to the best ball in town," as Dottie put it. They had on high-heeled shoes and the dresses the girls were required to wear in public, with makeup carefully applied and hair artfully arranged. Whether this was supposed to charm McManus, a career .289 hitter with the Browns, Tigers, Red Sox, and Braves, or simply show him they knew how to follow at least some of the rules, what they did worked. "When we started down, he just grinned at us," Dottie said. "He knew damn well what we did, but he never said anything."

Dottie recalled how mad Alma Ziegler was that Fay, a notorious prankster, was not straightening up. She had good reason to be. The league demanded the girls follow certain rules off the field as well as on, and not going anywhere without the approval of the team's chaperone was one of them. Failure to adhere to these regulations resulted in a five-dollar fine for the first offense, ten dollars for the second infraction, and automatic suspension from the league for the third. "It didn't take much for them to get rid of you," Dottie said. "There was always someone waiting to take your place." Dottie witnessed this first-hand the following year. In August, 1945, Betty Luna and Nalda Bird were sent home to California for insubordination at the same time that tryouts for outstanding players were taking place all over the United States and Canada.

As the Millerettes traveled from town to town, they also managed to pick up several wins along the way. They handed Kenosha a 7–1 loss on August 11, a game in which the Comets managed only three hits off Dottie's fantastic curveball, and followed that by two wins against Rockford on August 14 and 16 and a three-game sweep against Racine on August 18 and 19. Annabelle Lee even pitched the league's first perfect game on July 29. By the time the Millerettes played their last game in September, though, they still occupied the cellar with a 45–72 record and a .385 winning percentage, ending the season by splitting a doubleheader with the Chicks just after Labor Day weekend.

Still, even after suffering some heartbreaking losses, and not knowing which city would sponsor them next year, Dottie and the other girls were more than ready to return for another season of play. They had good reason for wanting to continue. Despite the team's abysmal record, Dottie's 20-win season argued well for the time ahead, as did Helen Callaghan's .287 batting average, the second highest in the league. The girls were paid well, most making more money than their fathers. Dottie's weekly salary was 75 dollars gross, with an additional two dollars and 75 cents per diem per day. Dottie could afford to buy clothes such as the sports jacket she purchased with a week's pay, because in her mind, "Hell, we were rich." More importantly, they had tasted a slice of professional pie. No longer were they "amateurs." They played ball for a living, something no women before had ever done. If, as Dottie noted, they did not think of things this way but were just girls having fun, that's all right, too. Either way, these women got to play the game of baseball.

The Orphans Find a Home: The Fort Wayne Daisies, 1945

Teeming crowds thronged the streets of Chicago when Dottie arrived to begin training for her second season of play on May 8, 1945. News had leaked out that Admiral Karl Donitz, who had succeeded Hitler after the latter's suicide on April 28, had pledged that the German military would lay down their arms that day at 11:01 P.M., officially ending the war in the European theater. As Dottie emerged from Union Station, she joined the thousands of people joyously celebrating Germany's surrender in a war that had seen more than three years of United States involvement and that would claim over 400,000 American lives by the time it ended several months later. Confronted with the heady masses flush with patriotic fever and with headlines screaming "Chicago's Joy Boundless," Dottie sent a telegram home to her parents that fittingly summed up the general mood, "Arrived Ch [Chicago] V E Day Everything is Perfect Love Dottie."

It was an auspicious start to the league's third year of operation and Dottie's sophomore season in professional ball. During the winter months, she had returned to work for Payne Furnace and Supply, where they had kept her job waiting for her. "I know I wasn't very valuable, so they could do that," Dottie chuckled. In early February, she received a letter from Max Carey, former manager of the Milwaukee Chicks, who had taken over as president of the league after the resignation of Ken Sells. Carey wrote in the hope that Dottie's contract for the upcoming season was satisfactory and to emphasize his plans to make the league even bigger and better. He ended his memo with a reminder that the girls were to purchase their own shoes that year, a concession to economics that would become more marked in the league's later years, and with the suggestion that the girls start preparing for the season at least thirty days before the start of spring training on May 9.

With that thought in mind, Dottie and several fellow Leaguers, including Nalda Bird and Betty Luna, took advantage of the year-round balmy climate in Southern California to ready themselves for the year ahead. The beaches there provided a perfect setting for the girls to practice sliding, to perform leg-strengthening exercises, and to work on their tans in the process. Also during the off season, Dottie's parents entertained Rockford's manager, Bill Allington, league president Max Carey, Alma Ziegler and a few others at a dinner party at their home on Rosewood Avenue. All of these activities centered around the sport of baseball primed Dottie for what turned out to be a phenomenal year ahead.

Spring training in 1945 began with a week of workouts in Chicago's Waveland Park, affectionately dubbed "The Mud Hole" by Dottie and her teammates since cold and wet weather plagued the players for a good part of their time in Chicago. Mostly the days were filled with the typical round of instructions in the basics of batting, running, and the fine art of stealing from 10:30 in the morning until 2:30 in the afternoon, intermingled with actual games. When the girls were unable to take the field, they were dispersed to various gymnasiums in downtown Chicago to keep in shape with indoor games and general calisthenics. Once they began actual play, Bill Wambsganss, manager of the newly formed Fort Wayne Club to which Dottie had been assigned, was highly impressed with the group of seventeen girls under his charge, especially in light of the soggy field. He particularly commented on the girls' stamina and their hitting and fielding ability, this from the man who completed the only unassisted triple play in World Series history in 1920 for the Cleveland Indians. Additionally, Wamby observed that the girls seemed to show more zest for the game than the men. Waveland Park had three diamonds, which allowed for the three simultaneous exhibition games played on May 12 among the six teams, with Dottie and the Fort Wayne team winning a tight battle against Rockford, 1–0, in their part of the competition.

The girls also reported to a general session meeting as part of spring training, the purpose of which was to stress the fundamentals of fielding. Ninety-six girls assembled to hear Max Carey and the six managers of the teams speak. Another important part of spring training was the allocation meeting, which took place that year at Chicago's Allerton Hotel where the girls were housed for the duration of the training camp. At this meeting Max Carey and the six club presidents met to select rosters for each team, using the rating charts contributed by scouts and managers to establish the ability of each player. This ensured a fair distribution of talent and fostered a fair sense of competition, the girls having signed a contract with the league rather than with an individual team as was common in men's baseball. Originally, the league planned to put all the girls in a main pool at the end of each season to recycle the talent. However, this turned out to be a money loser, as the fans became attached to certain players and paid to see these girls brandish their own particular skills.

The league compromised by keeping a nucleus of ten former players for each team and putting the rest back in the pool, with fresh talent coming from the new recruits. In addition to the rookies and the players who had been invited back, the seven men could chose from those girls who had made the cut in the local tryouts held in each league city, conducted just prior to the selection process. Since no farm system existed in the women's league, those rejected during spring training were often called upon as replacements for injured players during the season, giving the athletes another chance at professional ball. Spring training, therefore, provided league officials with a chance not only to monitor the progress of the new recruits as well as the returning players but to see which team would suit them best, or rather which team could use their particular talents.

Once the players were assigned to their teams, they set out for a five-day tour of army camps and veterans' hospitals in the Sixth Area Corps for a series of fifteen exhibition games. The league planned this phase of the preseason as a means of contributing to the war effort by offering some much needed entertainment both to war-weary combatants and lonely novices alike. Dividing the teams up into groups of two, the league paired Dottie's new team, The Fort Wayne Girls Club, with their sister expansion team from 1944, the former Milwaukee Chicks who had moved from Milwaukee to Grand Rapids in 1945. On May 17, the two teams traveled to Selfridge Field in Detroit, home of World War I ace Eddie Rickenbacker of the 17th Pursuit Squadron and home of the first all-black 332nd Fighter Squadron, more familiarly known as the Tuskegee Airmen. They also performed at Romulus Field while in Detroit, and then it was on to Michigan for a two-day stop at Percy Jones Hospital in Battle Creek and Fort Custer in Augusta.

At Fort Custer, Dottie, with help from Annabelle Lee, blanked the Chicks 3–0 in a game of flawless pitching, a payback for the 0–4 shellacking the Daisies took from the Chicks the night before. In between games, the girls visited with patients in the American Legion hospital at Fort Custer and with those servicemen at Percy Jones who were confined to their beds and unable to attend the games. The skills the women had acquired during charm school stood them in good stead as they moved naturally among amputees and other battle-scarred veterans, exchanging small talk as if they were chatting with friends from home. What a welcome respite they must have been for the soldiers, a perfect combination of competence and grace.

The tours turned out to be so popular that plans were made for more games to be played at military bases at the end of July. Yet it was not only watching the sport of baseball that meant so much to the men, or even the added bonus of having lithesome ladies shagging fly balls rather than the traditional spectacle of rugged manhood. For those serving their country in the armed forces, baseball moved beyond the concept of a mere game to serve instead as an enduring symbol of an ideal well worth fighting for, a reminder of the home they had left behind. A poem being circulated at the time by the Veterans of Foreign Wars to servicemen recuperating in hospitals aptly echoed this sentiment. Written by R. Hand, it reads,

> Beyond the railroad tracks in my hometown
> A sandlot lies, and smiling, we recall
> Such thrilling scenes that time can never down
> Enveiled within the magic call, Play ball.
> Built on such scenes we glimpse a sight sublime,
> America's great house that shall not fall,
> Laid firm against the tearing tides of time,
> Laid safe while boys and men play clean baseball.

Although the poem refers to men playing baseball, the All-Americans Girls Professional Baseball League proved that women not only shored up the home front by working in the factories and the fields, they also played their part in a national pastime that served both as a needed diversion and as an anchor in an increasingly volatile world. That the women in the league admirably fulfilled one of the league's stated objectives, "that members of the Armed Forces at their leisure and defense workers may have additional recreation," is in no doubt. The type of work they did was different from that which engaged the majority of women during the war years, yet its value was just as great and perhaps even greater. In the same way that *Home and Garden Magazine* cautioned victory gardeners not to ignore the morale-boosting effect of flowers in favor of the more practical vegetable garden, women's baseball, too, provided a needed sustenance to a nation weary of war and looking ahead to an uncertain peace.

Perhaps this fact was at last beginning to sink in, at least as far as the press was concerned. Unlike their counterparts in Minneapolis, the newspapers in Fort Wayne waxed much more optimistic about the prospects of the newest sports addition to their town. Perhaps it helped that the first business manager of the Daisies, Frank A. Biemer, was a former sports editor of the *Fort Wayne Journal-Gazette*. Either way, the press not only faithfully recorded the games but dispensed other information relating to the team, such as the possibilities for both a playing field and a team name and the announcement of the tryouts for local talent at Packard Park. So great was the enthusiasm for the newest sports venture in town that *The Gazette* did not even wait until a name had been selected before printing an advertisement on May 22 for the home opener, simply announcing "Fort Wayne vs. Grand Rapids." Unlike the fans in Minneapolis, the people of Fort Wayne were not only prepared for the coming of the team that would be known as the Daisies, they were actively involved in the team's fortunes right from the start.

A good example of this is the response of area enterprises to the request for team financing. One of the league's stipulations was that rather than one or two major backers, several local businesses contribute a sum of money to make up the total cost of the team franchise, thus ensuring widespread community support. As an added incentive, any profits from the team would go back into the community, although in 1944 the league received three cents on each admission for the first 90,00 fans per franchise to defray operating costs. On April 5, 1945, the *Fort Wayne Journal-Gazette* reported that no less than 45 organizations in the city had subscribed to the fund to back the league and would meet that night to elect a board of directors. *The Gazette* tellingly used the term "awarded" to inform its readers that Fort Wayne would definitely be a member of the All-American Girls Professional Baseball League and to alert them to the team's opening date.

This sense of pride was expanded upon further in one of the first Daisy programs to be produced. An excerpt form a short piece titled "The All-American Girl" stated that "Baseball as played by the All-American Girl is not only clean and wholesome entertainment for young and old alike, but it has lifted baseball out of the category of being a man's game. While driving through our great City, you will note that the vacant lots and playgrounds are mighty busy with groups of grade and high school girls enjoying the fun and excitement and the thrills of baseball." No reference to "powder puff ball" spilled from the pens of sportswriters here.

In another show of enthusiasm for girls' baseball, *The Gazette* announced a contest for fans to choose the name for the newest team in town. To capture their readers' attention, a headline in the Gazette, printed in all capital letters, shouted, "Wanted: Name For Team In Girls Pro Ball Loop." The article suggested the name carry "the feminine touch" and offered a book of season tickets as a first-place prize, with varying numbers of tickets for runners-up. Three days later the paper reported that fans were taking a lively interest in the contest, although originality was not at its peak. By May 22, after several more articles prodding the fans for submissions, it was announced that a name had been selected for the club, now to be known as the Fort Wayne Daisies. To reach their decision, the judges had pored over thousands of entries and over 100 different finalists before selecting the name submitted by Jeanmarie Hackman. While the paper thought it appropriate that a woman was the winner for naming a women's team, they also awarded Raymond Hawver two tickets for the opening game for his submission of the name Rose Buds.

This fan base was crucial to the team's success and was a good reason why the Daisies stayed in Fort Wayne from 1945 until the demise of the league nine years later. While the league functioned as an umbrella to the organization, providing such services as training of players, furnishing uniforms and equipment, and printing of tickets, each city, as a representative branch of the organization, was responsible for game promotion, local advertising, and ticket sales to make sure its team was financially viable. This differed from the first year of the league when Wrigley and his staff operated under the direction of a board of trustees, only requiring the teams' backers to match Wrigley's initial $22,500 subsidy fee. The franchise concept actually took hold in 1944 when local sponsors took on more responsibility for team affairs, but 1945 was the first year these sponsors had an official voice in league affairs. While this was a good thing, it also meant that the backers were held more accountable for the overall success of their teams. If no one showed up at the gates, for example, or attendance was sporadic, the onus fell on the city. Fort Wayne, however, with its rich sports history, knew quite well how to keep a team in town.

At the time the Daisies came to Fort Wayne, the city harbored several sports teams, including the impressive Zollner Pistons fast-pitch men's softball team. Called the Yankees of softball, they won numerous national and world championships and left town after a fifteen-year tenure with a .869 winning percentage. In addition, a men's semipro baseball team, the G E Club, played in Fort Wayne from the late 1930s to 1957 and also won national and world titles. Prior to that, Major League teams often stopped to play against men's baseball teams in Fort Wayne, including the Yankees and Babe Ruth meeting with the Lincoln Life Team in the 1920s. The Babe even christened League Park, in downtown Fort Wayne where the county jail now stands, by blasting a homer into the far reaches of the hometown park.

Aside from these sports, two other noteworthy teams held sway in Fort Wayne. One was the Komets, an ice hockey team that while never affiliated with a National Hockey League, had "working agreements" with various teams and saw several of its players advance to the NHL. The Komets are still in existence today and are the second oldest minor league hockey franchise in the country, second only to Pennsylvania's Hershey Bears. The other major league sport represented in Fort Wayne at that time, the Zollner Pistons Basketball team, was the winner of three world titles in the 1940s. The team relocated in the late '40s and is known today as the Detroit Pistons.

Fort Wayne was also a factory town, and during the war years that meant that factories were working at full capacity, trying to do their part to help the country win the war. Often league cities were chosen because of their proximity to a number of industrial plants, since women's baseball provided recreation for defense workers coming off their shifts. International Harvester, turning out trucks and military vehicles, Magnavox, producers of the electronic firing gear for automatic weapons and submarine detection equipment, and General Electric, which made superchargers for bombers, were just some of the companies centered in the city, which was also home to the 900-acre Baer Air Field. Contributing as they did to the war effort, the Daisies fit neatly into the fabric of the town. Often, plant managers invited the players into the factories at lunchtime where the many employees reveled in the talent right on their very doorstep.

Dottie's own introduction to the citizens of Fort Wayne came with a piece in *The Gazette* titled "Niece of Former Giant to Play Here." Although not quite accurate, as Hooks was a distant cousin, not an uncle, clearly the heady introduction indicated that all good things were expected of Dottie. "It is said Dorothy has developed some of the pitching tricks that made her uncle a star in the Majors," the article extolled. An accompanying photograph showed a determined-looking Dottie with her arm outstretched, as if just releasing one of her famous fastballs. Just how much a star Dottie was in her own right she made clear in the first year of what would be a five-year reign with the Daisies, almost her entire baseball career. Dottie continually reinforced this initial impression throughout her remaining years in Fort Wayne, making her the much loved darling of her newly adopted home.

The Daisies played their first home game against the Grand Rapids Chicks on May 23. After much discussion, a committee decided on North Side Athletic Field at North Side High School as the site of home games. The diamond was to be laid out on the southwest corner of the football field, with a seating capacity of 4000 and extra light poles installed, since most of the games were played at night. Although the new field promised to be more than adequate, a disadvantage to the site was that the Daisies would have to share the

field with high school athletes when school was in session. Also, when league officials found out that visiting teams would be using the same shower room as the Daisies, they ordered that visiting teams go back to the hotel and shower, since sharing the space meant breaching the rule forbidding fraternization among members of rival teams.

Once these glitches were ironed out, the Daisies proved their worth to their new fans by capturing the opening game, 4–1. Manager Bill Wambsganss chose Dottie as the starting pitcher, and the *Gazette* referred to her as "the heroine of the winning

Dottie is all smiles after she chalks up another victory for the Fort Wayne Daisies, 1945. (Courtesy of the Northern Indiana Center for History)

inaugural." Dottie struck out thirteen Chicks and allowed only three hits in the entire game. Sportswriter Robert Reed went on to say that "there was some good infielding on both sides, but the Daisies' hurler, Wiltse, was almost the whole show as she mowed the Chicks down." Dottie continued her fine performance in the last game of the four-game series, beating the Chicks again by a score of 4–1. She allowed just two scratch hits, one a bunt scooped up by the center fielder, Twila Shively, and the other a bounder that eluded third basewoman Marg Callaghan. Dottie would have recorded a shutout if she had not thrown high to second when she tried to complete a double play. Still, she fanned nine batters and worked her way out of trouble several times with two runners on base, helping Fort Wayne win the series three games to one.

Moving on to Rockford to play the Peaches on May 29, she won yet again with a score of 4–1. This time she held the Peaches to three hits. She struck out four batters and walked none. The Daisies scored two runs in the first on Pepper Paire's safe hit after a walk, a wild pitch, and a sacrifice, and they took advantage of two walks, a sacrifice, a wild pitch, and an error to add two more in the seventh. From Rockford it was on to South Bend, where the Daisies lost two games of a doubleheader, the second of which broke Dottie's three-game winning streak. Dottie's rival on the pitching mound for game two was none other than her fellow Californian, Nalda Bird. The Blue Sox left-hander scored her second win for her team by striking out twelve Daisy batters. The Daisies put on a good show in both games, though, losing each by only one run.

The schedule was a grueling one. With between 110 and 126 games per season, the girls usually played six nights a week with a doubleheader on Sundays. Time off during their four-month tour as professional ballplayers totaled no more than four or five days. Nor was there much free time during the day. "We had to be at the ball-park for practice by eight-thirty, nine o'clock, and we'd work out until noon," Dottie remembered. "Then we went back to where we were staying and did what girls normally did, washed our hair, wrote letters, whatever we could get done before we had to be back at the ball-park." Then, too, getting from city to city was not always easy. During the war years, the girls relied upon city transit and train travel. After the war ended, the girls traveled by bus, sometimes pushing the vehicle themselves when the bus broke down. Many times they were on the road all night, catching a few hours' sleep in the morning in order to be fresh for that night's game.

When the girls were on the road they were accompanied by the team's chaperone, who also oversaw their activities at home. Wrigley inaugurated the idea of the chaperone from the beginning of the league to ensure the girls projected the image he wished them to convey. The idea of a chaperone was not a new one, a variation of the concept having been in vogue during Dottie's softball years in California. Ruby Sober, secretary for the Mark C. Bloome softball team and later the general manager for Beverly Stadium, the former Fiedler Field, also monitored the girls' behavior on the field and made sure they had everything they needed, similar to a house mother on a college campus. Fort Wayne's chaperone in 1945 was Helen Rauner, who had served as assistant supervisor of women at the International Harvester Company.

While the chaperone performed several roles, such as arranging hotel reservations and meals for road trips, approving the girls' living quarters in the town in which their team was based, and taking care of cuts and bruises, she was also cast as keeper of the morals. A big part of her responsibility was making sure the girls maintained decorum both off and on the field. Hired by league headquarters in Chicago, the chaperone's job was to make sure that the girls complied with the rules and regulations set down by league management.

One of these rules stipulated that feminine attire was to be worn at all times when the girls were not playing ball. This meant that if the girls wore slacks on the bus en route to another town, they had to change into skirts if for any reason they left the bus. All social engagements were to be approved by the chaperone, and she had the authority to set curfews. Smoking and drinking in public were not permitted, nor was socializing with members of opposing teams. This last was difficult to enforce, as many of the girls made friends on one team only to be switched to another. However, the chaperone knew that her job depended upon her insistence that in general the girls conduct themselves properly at all times.

Since she was older and supposedly more experienced, making sure the girls adhered to the rules was not terribly hard to do. Another factor to consider, though, was the attitude of the girls themselves. They loved what they did and were careful not to jeopardize their hard-won situation. "Baseball was our life," Dottie stressed. "We didn't have what kids have today. We didn't have video games or computers. Without baseball, I don't what I would have done, and most of us felt the same way." Probably the girls found the rules fairly easy to follow anyway, since they were not used to challenging authority or the norms of that time. Although these women had flaunted some of society's rules by playing professional ball, the morals instilled in them remained strong.

Wrigley's idea of a chaperone was a good one for two reasons. First, knowing their daughters would be well looked after satisfied the parents of the girls. Many of the players were only in their teens when they joined the league, and a good number of the girls were far from home for the first time. If the families of the players thought that their daughters would be traveling to other towns accompanied only by a male manager, perhaps many of them would not have allowed their daughters to join the league in the first place. The chaperone acted as a moral buffer and gave legitimacy to the job the girls had undertaken.

Secondly, maintaining exemplary behavior off the field made sense in terms of pubic acceptance. These women were doing something no women had done before and so had to hold to higher standards than their male counterparts in order to be taken seriously. It was one thing for Babe Ruth to depict himself as a hard-drinking carouser; it added to his image as a tough major league ballplayer and an all-around hearty guy. The Babe's notorious feats at the plate while nursing a hangover are still part of baseball lore today. However, for the women in the professional league, such unwanted attention would doom their efforts from the start, taking away from their abilities on the field. The more they forced the spectators to concentrate on what mattered most, the game, the less important the issue of gender became.

After their initial road trip, the Daisies came back home for an eight-game homestand on June 5, with Dottie slated for the opener against the Kenosha Comets. Dottie by now had an early lead among the hurlers, having won three games with only one defeat. In those winning games she allowed only nine hits and three runs, and she struck out 25 batters in 27 innings of play. Now, helped mainly by teammate Vivian Kellogg, Dottie and the Daisies shut out the Comets by a score of 8–0, moving the Daisies closer to first place after the league-leading Peaches were beaten by the Grand Rapids Chicks. Dottie had a slight problem with control, walking seven, but still managing to strike out ten batters and allowing just one hit when the Comets' left fielder beat out a bunt down the first base line in the second inning. Kellogg started her productive night by bringing in a run in the first inning. She followed that by a grand slam in the fifth, bringing home Helen Callaghan, Fay Dancer and Dottie, who had reached base on a passed ball. Dottie contributed to one more run in the sixth with a walk, after which Helen Callaghan sacrificed and Betty Trezza brought her home.

The Comets' payback came the next week when a tight pitcher's duel between Dottie and Helen Nicol Fox saw the Daisies lose in a 0–1 game. Each hurler only gave up two hits, and they also came close on strikeouts, with Wiltse fanning eight and Fox nine. Dottie threw more bases on balls than Fox, walking six batters to Fox's one, but the walks were not the cause of Dottie's trouble. With two strikes and no balls Kenosha's right fielder, Audrey Wagner, knocked a homer deep into left field to score the only run of the game. Fort Wayne lost the opportunity to even things up in the eighth when Vivian Kellogg singled, stole second, and reached third on an error but was doubled up when she started for home and tried to get back to third. However, the Daisies did not lose any ground in the league since the Grand Rapids Chicks, tied with them for their newly acquired lead, lost to the Rockford Peaches, 3–1, in a game that lasted thirteen innings in Grand Rapids.

When the Daisies next met their closest rivals on the Chicks' home field, they lost their battle for first place when the Chicks defeated them in the first two games of a four-game stand. Dottie pitched three-hit ball in the third game, though, and handed the Daisies a 2–1 win. A tense moment came when Dottie's fellow softball teammate, Alma Ziegler, led off the Kenosha fourth inning with a single and then stole second. After a walk and a strikeout, Dottie hit Betty Jane Whiting with a pitch, loading the bases. Pepper Paire then misplayed a grounder, and Ziegler scored Grand Rapids' only run. The Daisies got that run back in the sixth inning and won the game in the seventh when Dottie's sacrifice sent Ruth Lessing to second, enabling her to score when Helen Callaghan hit a single and Betty Trezza was thrown out on a fielder's choice.

A five-game homestand against the Chicks beginning June 20 saw the Daisies three games behind Grand Rapids, Fort Wayne having lost the last game of the series in Grand Rapids by a dismal score of 0–6. Once back on their home field, they hoped for better luck. Sure enough, the Daisies captured the first game 8–3 behind the pitching of Audrey Haine, although Haine needed help from Dottie in the eighth when she loaded the bases and the Chicks brought in two runs. Dottie struck out the side and came in to finish off the Chicks in the ninth, bringing the Daisies within two games of Grand Rapids. Hoping to increase their lead, manager Bill Wambsganss decided to stick to his original decision and use Dottie in the second game of the series even though she had performed a relief stint the previous night.

The decision proved to be a wise one as Dottie made it two straight wins for the Daisies in front of 1200 eager fans. For the first five innings she mowed down the Chicks in order, until in the sixth, pitcher Connie Wisniewski beat out a hit to short and made it safely to first. The eighth inning brought Dottie some trouble when Grand Rapids scored two runs on three hits, but she settled down and held the Chicks to just those two runs, ending the game with a final score of 5–2 and leaving the Daisies just one game back from the Chicks. Dottie had allowed just five hits, walked none, and struck out nine, making her the league's leading twirler with an 8–2 record.

After a tough 3–12 loss to Racine in the first half of a double-header on June 24, which the Daisies recouped in the second game behind Annabelle Lee, Dottie pitched a two-hitter against Rockford at North Side Field for a score of 9–1 in the first game of a double-header on June 27. She retired 18 consecutive batters before Dorothy Kamenchek got the first hit off her in the seventh. Kamenchek got her again in the ninth when she banged a triple and scored when Vivian Kellogg bobbled a ball at first. The Daisies backed up Dottie's power pitching with a big breakout in the fourth with seven runs on six hits. As the *Gazette* noted, "This cluster was enough to ice the game with Wiltse pitching in top form." However, the Peaches came back in the second game behind the excellent pitching of Irene Apple-gren and some great defense, again playing errorless ball and beating the Daisies with a score of 4–1. Applegren baffled the Daisies until the seventh, seemingly a bad-luck inning for pitchers, when Marg Callaghan hit a double and Faye Dancer smacked a triple to right field, scoring on Audrey Haine's line drive.

Dottie's crowning achievement, however, came on June 29, when she pitched a no-hit game and came just short of perfection. Facing the Peaches in the last game of their four-game homestand, Dottie stranded the Rockford lassies at home plate until the ill-fated seventh inning when Helen Filarski, Rockford's third basewoman, reached first base via Dottie's only base on balls. As if the gods intervened as Filarski dared to challenge the invincible Wiltse, just moments later Filarski was caught trying to steal second and was summarily retired from the inning. Only 27 batters faced the Fort Wayne darling, and she fanned ten hitters, including the Peaches' pinch hitter, Dottie Fer-guson, to end the game in the ninth. In the eighth, Faye Dancer saved the game for Dottie with a dazzling catch in center when Rockford's Margaret Wigiser's hard-hit drive soared over the head of second basewoman Betty Trezza. Making a desperate lunge, Dancer came up triumphant, the ball stuck in her glove. Shades of Paul O'Neil doggedly chasing a high drive to right during David Wells's bid for a perfect game in 1999 comes to mind here, a beautiful example of baseball's perennial promise of saving grace. Dancer also caught one of the only other two hits of the game, both to the outfield, with Helen Callaghan snaring the other. Dancer was the batting heroine of the game, too, connecting for a double and a single which led to both Daisy runs.

All of Dottie's fine display of athleticism earned her a goodly number of fans, some in unlikely places. A simple business transaction often opened the way for members of the community to meet one of Fort Wayne's biggest stars. One letter from The Equitable Life Assurance Society began, "Dear Miss Wiltse, This is probably a peculiar way for a 'Daisies' fan to make your acquaintance." The insurance agent then went on to lament his bad luck in missing out on seeing Dottie when she called in at a colleague's office to collect her mail. Only then did he get to the point of the missive which was to refer Dottie to an article about life insurance in an enclosed pamphlet. He even offered several references should Dottie care to meet with him to discuss how the information applied to her as a professional ballplayer. Ending the letter not with a reiteration of his services but with his best wishes to Dottie for a successful season, he signed himself "a dyed in the wool fan."

Similarly, Dottie's request to Fort Wayne's newspaper, *The News-Sentinel,* for extra tear sheets of the feature the newspaper had recently carried of her led to accolades of praise from the paper's circulation manager. While the first paragraph of the letter he sent would have been sufficient to take care of the business at hand, the second paragraph dealt with a matter the writer felt was of equal importance. "May I say at this time," the letter continued, "that which you undoubtedly have come to know—that the very fine display of good sportsmanship, talent and genuine entertainment, coupled with the excellent deportment of you and all the members of the Fort Wayne Girls' Ball Club have and undoubtedly will continue to add glory and honor to yourselves and to the community." The letter concluded with more good wishes for Dottie's success. Clearly, in Fort Wayne, Indiana, the Orphans had found a home.

Dottie's near-flawless pitching performances continually nurtured

Dottie puts on her game face as she attempts to add to her strikeout total as a member of the Fort Wayne Daisies in 1945. (Courtesy of the Northern Indiana Center for History)

this sense of community commitment, so crucial to the team's success as a viable sports entity. By the time the Daisies met Racine at home at the close of June, Dottie was third in the league for pitching with a .727 winning percentage. Nor was Dottie finished with her spectacular coups on the mound. After being rained out for the opening game of the Racine series, the Daisies used Audrey Haine and Annabelle Lee for a doubleheader on July 1, resting Dottie for a game on July 2. To quote the *Journal-Gazette* on July 3, "Dottie Wiltse, leading hurler of the Daisies, almost pulled a Johnny Vander Meer with a second successive no-hit game as she beat the Racine Belles last night, 8–0," referring to Vander Meer's two consecutive no-hit games in 1938, on June 11 and June 15, and Dottie's previous no-hit game on June 29.

Ironically, the *Los Angeles Examiner* also had compared Dottie to Vander Meer prior to the start of her 1942 softball season, referring to her three no-hit, no-run games during the 1941 season. As columnist Morton Moss noted, although Dottie did not exactly imitate Vander Meer, she came pretty close. The same held true in the All-American League. Although Dottie was stopped in her bid for a consecutive no-hitter in the sixth inning on a slow roller to first by pitcher Jane Jacobs that Dottie could not get to fast enough, she later pitched a second no-hitter against South Bend on July 15. This meant that between June 29 and July 15, Dottie pitched two no-hit games and missed out on a third no-hitter by just one run. In the game on July 2, only three batters reached first base in nine innings of play while the Daisies belted out thirteen base hits, with the Daisy runs coming in the second, sixth, and eighth innings before a Ladies' Night crowd of 1500.

The Fourth of July never seemed to bring the team much luck, judging by their performance in Minneapolis the year before. The Rockford Peaches handed the Fort Wayne Daisies a double defeat on Independence Day, with scores of 1–2 and 0–1, before an all-time league attendance record crowd of 5,351 in Rockford. The defeat left the Daisies in third place in the league standings, with the Peaches the current leaders. However, Dottie lit the fireworks a day later when she saved her team from defeat and beat the Peaches by a score of 8–7. With Fort Wayne ahead in the ninth inning, after a roller-coaster game with both teams taking the lead, falling behind, and ending up in a tie, Rockford threatened to win the game in the bottom half of the inning when Snooky Harrell opened with a single off Fort Wayne's Audrey Haine. After Harrell was thrown out by catcher Lessing,

Dottie came in and promptly issued a walk to Helen Filarski. A Rockford single brought Filarski to third, aided by a bad throw by Pepper Paire. The throw proved costly as Filarski brought Rockford to within one run of the Daisies, but Paire made up for her error by throwing out Dottie's old batterymate from her softball days, Kay Rohrer, to end the threat.

After the series with Rockford, the Daisies lost the prime source of coverage for their games. Fort Wayne newspapers went on strike from July 7 to August 20, 1945. Promotion depended upon radio broadcasts, cards in the windows of area businesses, and announcements at games. Interestingly, despite the limited advertising, during those six weeks when the presses were stopped the Daisies continually averaged 1300 spectators per game. The Zollner Pistons, who vied with the Daisies for a fan base, averaged just 500, in spite of the fact that the Pistons were on one of the greatest win streaks in local athletic history. In addition, the Daisies charged 74 cents for an adult admission, while the men's softball games were free. Had novelty been the lure for women's baseball, attendance would have slackened after the first few weeks. Perhaps the passion the girls brought to the game, born of the joy of a privilege never before conceived, added that extra something that kept the fans coming back for more.

That and the fact that the Daisies were playing good ball. When the papers in Fort Wayne resumed production, the *News-Sentinel* reported, "Led by the Callaghan sisters, Helen and Margaret, Dottie Wiltse, Audrey Haine, Viv Kellogg, Pepper Paire and other standouts of the team, the Daisies have remained at a point where they still have a chance at the regular-season crown and seem sure to be one of the playoff contenders when the season ends Labor Day." As further proof that Fort Wayne held the Daisies close to its heart, the *Sentinel* listed the girls' baseball entry first when recapping the sports scene from the beginning to the end of the strike, followed by the Pistons and ending with blurbs of local golfers.

Dottie gave the papers something else to write about. The night before the presses began to roll once again on August 20, Dottie pitched and won both games of a doubleheader at North Side Field against the first-place Rockford Peaches, 5–1 and 1–0. A crowd of 3,000 people overflowed into the outfield to watch Dottie's masterful pitching performance, victory numbers 23 and 24, respectively. She had now earned the honor of second place in the pitching race with a 24–9 record, behind Connie Wisniewski of Grand Rapids, who stood at 28–9. The *Journal-Gazette* noted that "the slender right-hander had the Rockford hitters eating out of her hand" for sixteen innings, referring to the seven innings played in one game of a doubleheader rather than the traditional nine. Dottie struck out ten batters in the first game and got herself out of trouble twice, after loading the bases in the fifth and allowing a base hit and a passed ball in the ninth. In the second game she struck out just three batters, but the Peaches still could not connect with her pitches. Three infield rollers that the runners beat out composed the total Rockford effort in the nightcap.

It was Dottie who asked to go in for the second game after she completed the first. Manager Bill Wambsganss granted her request, assuring her he would use her every other night as the Daisies made their bid for the playoffs as long as her arm was fit. Dottie's appeal to Wambsganss foreshadowed one she would make to a different manager during a doubleheader three years later, almost to the day. Then, however, she would ask to be taken out of the second game because of something that had nothing to do with her arm. In this case, Wamby's decision to let Dottie pitch as often as possible proved a good one, as Dottie went on to win another doubleheader just eight days after her first one, pitching two other games in between. In just eight days, therefore, she pitched six complete games with a 5–1 mark and worked her way through an incredible 52 innings.

One of those two single-game wins came against Kenosha on August 24. Holding the Comets to three hits as payback for the defeat she had suffered against them only days before, Dottie allowed just two runners to get past second base, neither time as a result of a hit. She walked two and fanned six for a 3–0 decision. The Daisies trounced the Comets in the final game of the series, 11–2, behind the pitching of Audrey Haine. Then it was on to Grand Rapids to give Dottie a chance to trim the Chicks and move the Daisies ahead of the team they had been battling for second place in the league standings. It was here Dottie recorded her second double victory on August 27.

Pitching before a crowd of 3500, Dottie amassed seventeen strikeouts in the two games and granted the Chicks just one run, that in the first inning of the second game. The *News-Sentinel* quipped that "for the second time this season Dottie Wiltse pulled an 'iron man' stunt" and went on to credit her for the Daisies' newly won second-place position, four games behind the Rockford Peaches. Dottie's teammates helped in the first game by knocking fourteen hits off three different hurlers and scoring in every inning to take the first game, 14–0. In the second game, Faye Dancer slammed a homer into the left field stands, the first to do so in the Grand Rapids park in 52 games played there, and Penny O'Brien drove in the other two runs on two hits for a Daisy win of 3–1.

As memorable as that mighty pitching streak of Dottie's was in terms of her growth as an athlete, she looks back fondly on that time for an entirely different reason. A certain date remains forever fixed in her mind, namely August 19, 1945, the day of that first double win in Fort Wayne. Among the thousands of spectators watching her from the stands, a young navy man home on leave showed more than a sporting interest in Dottie's fine exhibition. Vowing he would meet her after the game, he called upon his friend Jimmy Haskins to help him in his quest. Haskins, a midget, had befriended Dottie after one of the many games he attended at North Side Field. Often he brought Dottie gifts of butter and other rationed food items from the club he belonged to, located near the flat Dottie shared with several other girls close to the ballpark. That night, in honor of her double victory, Haskins brought a case of beer to Dottie's apartment, with the added bonus of the handsome sailor, Harvey Collins.

When Harvey arrived at Dottie's flat lugging the welcome beverage, Dottie and her roommates, among them Tex Lessing, Vivian Kellogg, Pepper Paire, and Faye Dancer, thought it would be funny if they talked in pig latin, a popular pastime in vogue at the time. Basically, pig latin was moving consonants and vowels around to form a unique word. Most words in pig latin end in ay. For example, if a word starts with a consonant and a vowel, the last letter of the word is moved to the beginning and "ay" is added. Happy then becomes "yhappay." Similarly, if a word starts with two consonants, the two consonants are moved to the end of the line and again "ay" is tacked on to complete the word. Child then becomes "ildchay." The girls spent most of the night yapping away in this idiomatic fashion, never suspecting that savvy Harvey Collins knew exactly what they were saying. "He was smart enough not to let us know," Dottie chuckled. "And he sat there and listened to us all evening long and then he told us and answered us back in pig latin, and oh! we about all fell on the floor with some of the things we had said, you know."

Once Harvey left, Dottie went downstairs to call her parents with the news of winning both ends of the doubleheader. A few minutes later Harvey walked back in the door. He asked Dottie what she was doing the next day and if she knew how to play golf. "I laughed and told him no, but then he asked if I would be willing to try," Dottie remembered. "I told him I would, but all the while I was thinking of my father and I driving by a golf course in Inglewood and my dad saying, 'Look at those damn fools out there. Hitting the ball and then walking a mile to find it.'" Harvey and Dottie's first date would have to wait, however, as Dottie was off on a three-day road trip to Kenosha. "I completely forgot about him once we left town, to be truthful," Dottie admitted all these years later. Harvey never forgot, though. He called Dottie as soon as she returned to Fort Wayne to meet the Kenosha Comets at North Side Field. Taking her onto the golf course the next day, Harvey introduced Dottie to a sport she would also master once she hung up her cleats and left the diamond forever.

That Harvey's initial attraction to Dottie stemmed from watching her at her athletic peak, a situation that would intimidate many men, says much about him as a person and gives a good indication of the strong union that Dottie and Harvey would build together over the course of more than fifty years. Naturally, Dottie's 5' 6" 125-pound frame, coupled with her pretty, wholesome face, probably did not hurt, either. In addition, something else factored into the mix: simple curiosity. In one of those cases where coincidence seems to be stretched impossibly far, Dottie reminded Harvey of a another female ballplayer he had heard about through one of his buddies in the service, Bob Inman. Stationed on Johnston Island in the middle of the Pacific Ocean with Harvey, Inman had a newspaper photograph of a female ballplayer pasted on the inside of his locker. Inman was from California and so was the girl whose picture he displayed. Now here Harvey was meeting another woman ballplayer, and one from the very same state. Harvey later found out from flipping through Dottie's scrapbook that Inman's girl was none other than Barbara White, Dottie's best friend and fellow softball player. "That was the only picture the newspaper ever took of her," Dottie said with a laugh, referring to Inman's locker decor, "and it showed her leaping up to catch the ball and missing it by a mile."

Although Dottie never officially received permission from her chaperone to date Harvey, which, going by the book, she should have done, they still managed to see each other quite often in between games. By now the season was winding down and the Daisies were in full contention for the playoffs at the end of August. Although the Blue Sox beat them twice on August 30, the Daisies did not lose any ground to the first-place Peaches, Rockford having been beaten by Racine, 3–4. Another doubleheader against the Blue Sox the next night in South Bend, played to make up for a rained-out twin bill two nights before, saw the Daisies take the first game from the Sox to pick up a half-game on the first-place Peaches and extend their second-place margin over Grand Rapids to a game and a half. Dottie was the winning pitcher in that game, giving up only two hits and recording seven strikeouts during seven innings. The second game was tied one-all before rain again canceled the contest, but in a makeup game the next night in Fort Wayne Dottie came to the mound in the eighth inning to help Annabelle Lee post another Daisy victory.

The Daisies ended the regular season homestand on September 3 with a bang. A loss to the Belles the day before had left the Daisies needing an even break in their final two games of the season in order not to lose their coveted second-place finish. Instead, like the Yankees did that day against the Athletics in Philadelphia, they won both games of the doubleheader against Racine and clinched the second-place spot for the playoffs. Dottie was in great form in the first game, coming close to pitching her third no-hitter of the season until Racine's Sophie Kurys knocked a ball between Marg Callaghan at third and Pepper Paire at short in the ninth. Although Paire made a valiant bare-handed stab, she was unable to throw the ball to first ahead of the runner. Another hit almost robbed Wiltse of a shutout, but she settled down and came through, 5–0, with Lee following her example in the nightcap with seven innings of shutout ball for a winning score of 2–0. The Daisies had needed only one game to assure themselves of a place in the playoffs, but the extra win served as a good impetus as they moved toward postseason play.

The Daisies met with the Racine Belles on September 5 for the first game of the playoffs in Fort Wayne. Since the Daisies had finished second in the league standings, they were pitted against the fourth-place team, with the league-leading Peaches taking on the third-place Grand Rapids Chicks. The Daisies used Dwenger Park for the playoff series, the same park where they had played their final home games. Plans were under way to move the Daisies there the next year so they would not have to share their playing field with the high school teams. In the meantime, the necessary alterations had been made for the women's playoff series, with home plate moved the required distance. All games would start at 8:30. The league set ticket prices at $1.00 for adults and 25 cents for children. The tickets would be available at downtown stores to save people the hassle of standing in line. Out of the ticket price, the players would receive 40 cents, the clubs 35 cents, the league eight, and the federal government 17. With attendance totaling approximately 69,000 for the Daisies' home games, as reported by club president, Henry Herbst, the playoffs could conceivably draw quite a crowd and put some extra money in the girls' pockets.

According to the *Journal-Gazette,* league officials gave the Daisies an edge over their opponents. Their fielding mark of .945 was the best in the league, and Dottie was said to give Fort Wayne a pitching edge. Indeed, the *News-Sentinel* said, "Dottie Wiltse will carry most of the Fort Wayne hopes for the playoff championship." She fulfilled the *Sentinel's* expectations admirably in the first game, winning the opener 6–1. Over the box scores for the game, the *News-Sentinel* proclaimed, "Dottie Does It!" in bold print, and the *Journal-Gazette* seconded that thought with the words, "It was Dottie Wiltse all the way…" As she had done in the game with secured their bid for the playoffs, Dottie once again pitched two-hit ball, both hits following an error by shortstop Pepper Paire, and lost a chance for a no-hitter with two out in the seventh. Dottie's teammates backed her up with runs, making all six without the aid of an extra-base hit. The Daisies brought in three runs in the fourth inning and one in the fifth, while the final two runs in the eighth inning came on two passed balls, a wild pitch, and an error. Dottie added ten strikeouts to her season's total and chalked up another win for the season.

The Daisies took the next game, 8–2, behind Annabelle Lee and moved on to Racine for game three in the best-of-five series. With only two outs standing between them and a chance for the playoff finale, the Daisies saw Racine tie the score 4–4 on Janet Jacobs's homer in the ninth. The Daisies then dropped the game in the eleventh inning, 4–5, prolonging the series against Racine. Now it was up to Dottie in game four. She rallied the team beautifully, winning with a score of 10–3 and moving the Daisies up to the next round of competition. As a result of her outstanding work on the mound, manager Bill Wambsganss slated his ace to start in the conclusive battle against the Rockford Peaches, who had won their set against the Grand Rapids Chicks on Monday, September 10, in Rockford. The playoffs featured two three-of-five sets, with the winners of each tangling in a seven-game contest.

Rockford dimmed the Daisies' hopes somewhat by winning the first game, 2–1. Although Dottie pitched a good game, giving up four hits, striking out ten, and walking none, the Daisies were no match for Rockford's right-hander, Olive Little, who either struck out the opposing batters or popped them up. Dottie had not lost hope, though, as evidenced by the telegram she sent home to her parents after the game, "Lost two to one-Wiltse and Little still a long way to go-we will win yet," she wrote. The weather did not help matters, either, with rain forcing a ten-minute delay in the fifth inning and a strong wind creating dust storms over the diamond throughout the game. The weather was no excuse for the Daisies losing the next two games in Rockford, though, forcing them into a do-or-die situation at Dwenger Park on September 13. Actually it was not the pitching that caused them the most trouble, with Annabelle Lee hurling a 2–3 contest and Audrey Haine coming up with a 1–3 loss, but the failure of the Daisies to hit in the clutch. As usual, it was up to Dottie to keep her team in contention in game four.

This time the weather really did hamper them, with rain halting the first half of the third inning on Thursday night. Maybe the weather was actually on their side, though, as Dottie had gotten herself into trouble by loading the bases with two hits and a walk when the scoreless game was called. She came back to the mound the next night and showed the Peaches she had learned her lesson by shutting out the visitors 2–0. "Wiltse and Little still fighting," she informed her parents, again by telegram. More than 2300 fans braved the damp and cold evening to watch Dottie deliver seven strikeouts, two walks, and four hits. Dottie's tensest moment came in the sixth inning when Rockford's Dorothy Kamenshek singled with one out and reached second on a wild pitch. Jo Lenard then walked, and she and Kamenshek pulled a double steal. Two fly balls caught by Helen Callaghan ended the threat, and the inning was finished. The Daisies scored almost immediately in the first frame on hits by Pepper Paire, Penny O'Brien, and Faye Dancer, adding another run in the fourth on a double by Dancer and Vivian Kellogg's hit into left field, which scored Dancer.

Unfortunately, the Rockford Peaches proved to be more than a match for the Daisies. In game five, Rockford took the series, 3–2, and were crowned the championship team of 1945. The Peaches scored once in the third inning and twice in the sixth. While the Daisies came back with one run in the last half of the sixth and another in the eighth, they could get no farther, despite a brave rally in the bottom of the ninth with the tying run on third. Still, the Daisies had little to regret. Not only did the team prove they were contenders by winning a berth in the final playoffs, they had fared extremely well in their new city. Local officials estimated that the club income, including the money raised to start the club, would be several thousand dollars over

operating expenses. The *News-Sentinel* reported that "the club directors are looking forward to 1946 and are asking fans for opinions and
suggestions." A new ballpark was even being contemplated for the
Daisies' permanent home. Moreover, each Daisy player received $215
for her playoff share, a goodly sum for young ladies in 1945.

As for Dottie's personal achievements, she had placed second in
the league with 29 victories and ten losses for a .744 winning percentage. She led the league with 293 strikeouts in 345 innings, leaving her with the title of strikeout queen of the loop. The only other
pitcher anywhere near that number was Helen Fox of Kenosha with
220, the next highest number belonging to Rockford's Olive Little
with 142. Dottie's 0.83 ERA was only bettered by Connie Wisniewski's 0.81, just two hundredths of a point. Moreover, Dottie was
one of seven pitchers in the league who had pitched no-hit, no-run
games in nine innings and the only pitcher to do so twice in one year.
To cap off these heady achievements, Dottie was falling in love. As
she headed home to California at the close the 1945 season, Dottie
tucked away the thought of baseball in one corner of her mind and
concentrated on something else entirely.

Give Me Your Answer, Do: The Daisies, 1946

As Dottie packed up her belongings to return to California at the close of the 1945 season, she hatched up a good plan to make the trip home a little more interesting. Rather than drive across country alone, Dottie invited her teammate and close friend, Helen Callaghan, and none other than Harvey Collins to climb into her Model A Ford and join her on the trek back to Inglewood. The car was one Dottie had with her in Fort Wayne, the girls being allowed to have their own transportation, but only to use in the city in which they were based. For away games, the league stipulated that the girls must travel with their team, at first by train and later by bus once the war ended and gas rationing was no longer in effect. Dottie owned a car in Minneapolis, too, which she had purchased from a player on another team. That car served not only as a means of transportation but as a mobile advertisement as well. Dottie and her teammates tooled around town with the words "Powerhouse Wiltse, 1944" emblazoned on the side panels, with "Minnesota Special" written underneath. Perhaps they attracted a few new fans that way, drawn as people must have been by this intriguing proclamation.

In 1944, however, Dottie was in no condition to get behind the wheel of a car at the end of the season. In one of the last games the Millerettes played that year, Dottie had jumped into the dugout in a display of good humored exuberance and promptly broke her tailbone. Ignoring the pain, she went back out to the mound, but Bill Allington, now managing the opposing team, the Rockford Peaches, knew something was wrong and convinced Dottie's manager to take her out of the game. Dottie ended up in the hospital for a few days before she headed home, but she still faced a grueling train ride ahead. To make her more comfortable, Alma Ziegler, Pepper Paire, and Faye

Dancer bought a rubber cushion for Dottie to sit on during the long journey back.

Not that most of the other California girls were in any better shape than Dottie. When they finally detrained in Los Angeles, the ballplayers looked as if they had participated in several military battles rather than a slew of baseball games. Pepper Paire had a broken collarbone, Fay Dancer was on crutches, and Dottie walked with mincing steps, like a crab walk, because if she moved any faster she got a cramp all the way up her leg. Alma Ziegler, the only one who was relatively whole, carried all the luggage. "I wish we had sense enough to take a picture getting off that train, with our parents standing there and the looks on their faces. Everybody's got a crutch or something. We looked like we were home from the war," Dottie said. Dottie's mother must have been particularly alarmed, having suspected some such catastrophe would befall Dottie from the moment she joined the league.

Dottie's parents had something else to upset their peace of mind at the end of their daughter's second season of play. When Dottie called her parents to announce she would be bringing Harvey home with her, it "went over like a lead balloon," according to Dottie. The anxiety on her parents' part centered on the fact that Dottie was engaged to be married to someone else and had been for some time. The engagement was even mentioned in a short piece in the *Los Angeles Examiner* in June, 1944 shortly after Dottie arrived in Minneapolis. "Dorothy Wiltse, daughter of Mr. and Mrs. D.E. Wiltse, 1212 Rosewood Avenue, is winning acclaims with her spectacular pitching," the article began. After touching upon Dottie's pitching record, and that she had been "royally feted" by Mayor Kline of Minneapolis and his wife, the article ended with the news that Dottie's "...engagement was announced before her departure from Inglewood several weeks ago to William 'Gail' Jackson of the Navy, now stationed in the Aleutians."

Yet Dottie knew her own mind, and she must have sensed almost from the first time she met him that her destiny was with Harvey and not with the boy she had left behind. While Dottie does not remember it striking her that way from the beginning, she admitted that it hit her parents immediately. When Harvey, Helen, and Dottie finally arrived at Dottie's home on Rosewood Avenue after a week long drive, including a stop in South Dakota to meet up with some friends of Dottie's at a dance, one of Dan's first comments to his daughter was, "There's a goddamn sailor in the house." Then he took Harvey out to the garage, just the two of them, for a little heart-to-heart talk. "My dad was a real gruff guy, so I was dying in the house," Dottie recalled. "I was wondering what the hell my father was saying to Harvey. I never knew exactly who said what, but knowing Harvey he stood right in front of my dad and took everything he said and said it back." It is not difficult to imagine these two men confronting each other for the first time, both loving the same woman in different ways, but one needing to release the person he had helped form, the other needing to prove he could hold her well.

Whatever doubts Dan and Ellie had, though, Harvey quickly put to rest. Everybody liked Harvey, according to Dottie, and fortunately her parents were no exception, since it would not be much longer before Dottie and Harvey officially announced their engagement. In the meantime, Harvey needed to get back to base. Although his leave had officially expired by the time he reached California, he called his superior officer to report that his car had broken down and that he would be a few days late. Luckily for Harvey an armistice had been signed in both Europe and the Pacific, thus ending the war, so instead of getting into trouble he was granted a further 30 days' leave. "He was awfully good at getting leaves," Dottie said, shaking her head in wonder. "I don't know how he did it, but he always managed to get one. He had so much time off it wasn't funny." Perhaps Harvey's tactics stood him in good stead this time. Harvey and Dottie had only known each other for about a month when they arrived in California. That extra time they were granted may have been all it took to convince both of them that togetherness suited them better than being apart.

Dottie and Harvey's wedding took place on Sunday, March 10, 1946, in the front parlor of 1212 Rosewood Avenue, the forbidden room where Dottie and Barbara used to sit and gossip when Dottie's mother was not home. In announcing the marriage, *The Fort Wayne Journal-Gazette* referred to the bride as the "ace pitcher of the Fort Wayne Daisies baseball team," an unusual title to bestow upon a bride in the 1940s, or even today for that matter. About 25 close friends of the couple attended the double-ring ceremony, set against a background of white stocks and peach blossoms and conducted by the Reverend John Gray Ross of the First Methodist Church of Inglewood. Dottie's matron of honor was her best friend, Barbara White, who had chosen Dottie as her maid of honor the year before. Barbara had not married Bob Inman, the man who kept her picture in his locker on Johnston Island, but Jim Hoffman, who had been a year

ahead of Dottie in Inglewood High School. By the time Dottie got
married, Barbara was eight and a half months pregnant. "We were
kind of silly the day we went shopping for my bridesmaid's dress,"
Barbara recalled. "I don't know what the sales clerks thought, because
we let them think it was my wedding, not Dottie's." The girls finally
decided on a silver-blue dress for Barbara with black accessories and
a corsage of pink camellias.

The *Journal-Gazette* also reported that Dottie wore a dusty blue
suit with a pink blouse and navy accessories and sported a white
orchid. Dottie opted for a more informal type of wedding as Barbara
had done, also. "It didn't have anything to do with the war," Dottie
noted. "It was just that neither of us wanted a traditional type of wedding." Dottie's mother greeted the guests in a blue afternoon dress
and a corsage of yellow roses. Although Dottie was given away in
marriage by her father, the newspaper made no mention of Dan's
attire. Presumably, the fact that he was there was information enough.
Dottie's maternal grandmother, Mrs. R.A. Runswick, assisted Dottie's mother in welcoming the guests, while her Aunt Blanche, Ellie's
half-sister who worked with Dottie at Payne Furnace Company, provided the music, playing such songs as "Because," "I Love You Truly,"
and "Always." Barbara Hoffman remembered what a pleasurable time
everyone had. "We all just had a nice wedding there in Dottie's house,"
she reminisced. "They had a piano and we sang and just enjoyed ourselves."

None of Harvey's family was able to attend the wedding service, but his childhood friend, Carl "Bud" Offerle, hitchhiked all the
way to California to share his buddy's big day. Since Harvey did not
know if Bud would be able to make it, Dottie's childhood friend,
Steve Barrett, stood up for Harvey instead. Dottie and Steve had
stayed close from the time their parents took them to baseball games
together, their friendship cemented together even more firmly after
Steve's hardships during the war. The only tense moment of the day
came when Harvey stole the wedding cake out of the kitchen before
the beginning of the ceremony. "By the time the wedding was ready
to start my mother was a nervous wreck, because Harvey had taken
the cake outside and was horsing around running up and down the
street with it. My mother just about died, I swear," Dottie remembered.

Another of Harvey's practical jokes came into play as Dottie and
Harvey made their way back to the Midwest. Dottie and Harvey's "honeymoon" had taken place after the wedding festivities, with Harvey

and Bud going out to play golf, the two having started out as caddies together in Fort Wayne, and Dottie staying home to pack. The newly married couple had to leave Inglewood the next day because Harvey, a storekeeper third class, was due back in Lakehurst, New Jersey on March 26 for further navy duty. He had reenlisted after 43 months' service in the Pacific when his brother told him the war was going to last another five or six years. His brother, however, did not reenlist. "Harvey's brother never lived that one down, either," Dottie said. "Harvey would always tell him, 'If it wasn't for you, I would have been out a long time ago.'"

Dottie and Harvey boarded the train on

Dottie poses with her very own sailor, Harvey Collins, shortly before their wedding in 1946. (Courtesy of Dottie Wiltse Collins)

March 11 and headed for Fort Wayne, where they would make their home. When the train made one of its periodic stops along the way, Harvey told Dottie he needed to get off to buy some cigarettes, indicating he would be back in a minute. "Well," Dottie said, "I sat there by that window and I never saw him come out of that store again. The train took off, and I was petrified. Come to find out, he was hiding on the train. I could have killed him," she laughed. Once they reached Fort Wayne, Dottie and Harvey had less than two weeks together before Harvey left for his next tour of duty. Yet even though Dottie was abruptly single once more, she had plenty to keep her busy.

In late March she volunteered to work out indoors with The Bob

Inn girls' softball team. The Bob Inn was a local spot in town, popular with sports fans. Managed by Harold Grenier, the Bob Inn girls' softball team had been state champions in 1944 and 1945. A picture in the *News-Sentinel*, titled "It Must Be Spring" showed a smiling Dottie leaning towards the players as she demonstrated the correct way to grip a ball. Watching her intently were Kate Vonderau, Dottie's new catcher and a former Bob Inn player, and Fran Janssen and June Peppas, two Bob Inn players who would later join the All-Americans. Both would be instrumental in working alongside Dottie to keep the legacy of the league alive.

Shortly afterwards, Dottie left for spring training in Pascagoula, Mississippi. Now that wartime travel restrictions had been lifted, the league chose Pascagoula because the warm climate there allowed the girls to get a head start on the season. This was especially important since plans for a four-club winter league in Florida for two months had fallen through, mainly because of housing shortages due to the number of men's teams there. Once the girls arrived in Mississippi, they would be put through an intensive training session until May 5, after which they would barnstorm their way back north. Fort Wayne was to be paired with one of the new cities in the league, the Peoria Redwings, with scheduled stops in Pensacola, Florida, and Dallas, San Antonio, Houston, and Beaumont, all in Texas.

While regulars and rookies would report to camp on April 25, Dottie got there in advance of the other ballplayers so she could fulfill her new role as ace reporter for the *Fort Wayne Journal-Gazette*. The paper had contracted Dottie to write a series of articles on spring training in the All-American Girls League. Interestingly, she wrote under the name "Wiltse" rather than her married name of "Collins," whether to identify herself more easily or in a spurt of autonomy it is difficult to say. Either way, Dottie showed herself to be just as adept with a pen as she was with a ball. In the first article she dispatched to the newsroom, with "Daisies' Ace Pitcher" written under her byline, Dottie wrote, "Arriving here in advance of the vanguard of the All-American Girls Baseball League players, who are due to trek into spring training in the next few days, I was ushered to the spacious community building which is to be our headquarters." She compared the building to a "baseball equipment exhibition" and informed her readers that over 1600 pieces of baseball-related items were housed there, including 264 uniforms, 142 caps, 196 sliding pads, 224 belts, and 114 bats. To stretch the analogy even farther, she added to that the amount of gear each girl would bring to the camp, creating a picture of an overwhelming array of baseball paraphernalia. The piece ended with the observation that the amount of baseball equipment just about equaled the population of Pascagoula.

That number was about to rise, as newspaper men, photographers, club directors and their wives, plus some fans, were coming to town to "take in the girls' games," as Dottie reported in the *Gazette*. This interest in girls' baseball expressed by sports devotees, combined with the extensive preparation for spring training and the longer preseason practice sessions, demonstrated an even deeper commitment to women's professional ball and brought the girls' league closer to men's major league ball. Another similarity between the two was that the All-American pitchers reported to camp one week earlier than the rest of the team, along with any new girls. In her second report on spring training, headlined "New Girls Begin Arriving In Mississippi," Dottie pointed out one considerable difference between the women's and men's camps, though. Complimenting league president Max Carey and his staff on the fine job they did with the preliminary training camp arrangements, Dottie went on to remark that men's Majors League Baseball takes 50 or 60 players to spring training while president Carey had over 200 girls with whom to contend. She noted that all the details had been worked out to perfection, including the initial travel arrangements.

Since most of the girls came by train, the league arranged for five different railroads to provide transportation for the girls, with agents in each district providing complete train itineraries and informing the girls where to pick up their tickets. Due to economic constraints, a constant consideration for league officials, the league would pay for Pullman sleeping cars and meals for only those girls who needed to spend two or more nights en route. All others received coach accommodations. Some of the players from California and New York chose to fly to Pascagoula, on their own dime, of course, and some of the girls came by car, although the league advised against it. As Dottie informed her readers in the same article in which she praised president Carey, "Two of the new girls arrived today by automobile, but they apparently had not read the league's instructions about 'gas buggies.' Now they will have to put it in storage, as they will not be allowed to drive to the towns where they play exhibition games....So someone will have to pilot their car to the town to which they are assigned and there they can use it for pleasure driving, so I am told."

Once the girls arrived at the camp, they proceeded to the recreation center and the desk of league secretary Marie Keenan. The secretary then assigned them to their sleeping quarters, gave them an order for a uniform, and handed them printed instructions relating to the training schedule. A bulletin board in the recreation center listed each day's routine, which the girls were to check each evening. All this had been spelled out for the girls in a memo sent by Keenan several months prior to the start of camp. What they probably had not fully anticipated was the amount of work involved to prepare for the rigorous schedule of the regular season. Aside from the daily workouts, prior to which the girls were graded and assigned a squad, the girls attended a lecture each evening on league rules, conduct, and charm. Although formal schooling for conduct and charm had been abandoned after the 1944 season, the league continued to stress the importance of femininity through more informal means during subsequent spring training camps. All this left little time for recreation. However, as Dottie remarked in another story for the *Gazette*, "one of the nice things about Pascagoula is that there is not very much to do, outside of taking in a movie, but why talk about that when there is work to be done, and believe you me, they have plenty of that mapped out. I think the most popular spot in this town will be my little cot."

Dottie and the Daisies left Mississippi in early May for Pensacola, Florida, to play their first exhibition games on May 6 and 7. Appropriately, a U.S. Naval Air Training Center was based there; Dottie made sure to purchase a souvenir postcard highlighting that fact. The games were sponsored by the *Pensacola News-Journal Company* and were to be played at Legion Field, with proceeds going towards the construction of an electric scoreboard at the Pensacola High School athletic field. All of the exhibition games were locally sponsored and benefited area causes. It was the first time for girls' pro ball in that city, and *The Pensacola News'* Wesley Chalk reported enthusiastically on the upcoming games, urging fans in an article on April 24, more than a week before the girls' arrival, to make plans now to attend what promised to be very entertaining games. He went on to say, "The game is fascinating and fans will be surprised to see the talent on the two clubs. The gals play the same type of baseball as played by the men. Curve balls, sliding, running...everything that goes to make the Doubleday version is a part of the feminine touch."

Those in the stands got more than they bargained for just by watching Dottie alone. Pitching in the first game of the twin bill in Pensacola before 2300 fans, Dottie blanked the Redwings 5–0 in the first game, striking out ten batters, allowing only one hit, no runs, and never once finding herself in a spot of trouble. This was the first box score of the Daisies' 1946 season, and it was the first time that Dottie Wiltse appeared under the name of Collins. Although Peoria took the next two games, one a second contest in Pensacola and the other the first of two games played in Pascagoula, Dottie evened up the series in the second game in Mississippi, on May 9. While not as impressive as in her Florida debut, she worked herself out of a jam in the sixth inning when a single, a double, and a passed ball put the tying runs on base, winning the game 7–0.

Moving on to the Lone Star State, the Daisies made it four victories when they won a doubleheader in Houston. Dottie was responsible for the first win, with a score of 4–2 in twelve innings of play. It was a tough loss for former Daisy Annabelle Lee, who pitched shutout ball for her new team until an error and four straight hits allowed the Daisies to tie the game in the ninth. Next, Dottie dazzled the San Antonio fans by hurling her third straight victory on May 12, and putting them two games in front of Peoria in the exhibition series, five games to two. Although the damp weather saw the pitchers having trouble with control, Dottie kept the Redwings to five hits on six runs for an 11–6 win.

In Beaumont, the teams' last stop, the Daisies captured the last two games of the tour on May 16 and 17, winning against the Redwings, 12–4 and 3–2 respectively. Dottie pitched the first three innings of play in the second game but then was forced to retire with an arm sore from her twelve-inning marathon performance two nights before. At the completion of the series, the Daisies had the edge over the Redwings, seven games to three.

Ending their tour in Beaumont seemed a fitting close to the Daisies' preseason and a precursor to what lay ahead. The publicity surrounding the teams' arrival there reinforced the league's steadily growing stature, not just in the Midwest but throughout the United States. An advertisement to sell tickets for the two games played in Beaumont showed a woman baseball player swinging a bat, with one leg upraised as if ready to hit the ball into the distance. To the left of the picture, encased in a black bordered oval, the words "Bang-Up Baseball!" appeared in bold print, with "Swell Entertainment" written in the same style underneath. Just above the announcement of the names of the teams and the location, date, and time of play, the flyer enticed the citizens of Beaumont to attend the games by prompting them to "Thrill to the Top Girl Professionals of the All-American Girls Baseball League as they compete in Mile-a-Minute ball" and describing the upcoming diversion as "The Nation's Finest Girl Players in an Exhibition Game the Whole Family Will Enjoy." The tantalizing words "Glamour," "Thrills," and "Excitement" danced around the outside of the announcement in all capital letters.

Coupling this with the praise they met as they began their tour in Pensacola, and the generally positive reception they received in all the towns in which they played, the Daisies returned to Fort Wayne eager to begin another season of play. Part of their excitement came from the new talent gracing the team, with players such as catcher Katie Vonderau, former Bob Inn girl from Fort Wayne, and pitcher Alice "Moose" DeCambra. With the end of the war and related war work and services, more girls were able to devote themselves to baseball. As Dottie reported to the faithful fans in Fort Wayne from camp in Mississippi, "...I thought I could take it easy and watch the rookies go through their stunts. But after ... trying to keep pace with the new "crop" of girls, I found out different. The new girls in the league are a classy lot, and believe me every veteran is going to have to hustle to hold her position." The 1946 season beckoned as a banner year for all.

In Fort Wayne, however, all was not so smooth at first. The Daisies almost lost the city they had come to call home. The main difficulty centered around the lack of a playing field for the team. While the Daisies would have liked a park of their own, restrictions on building materials prevented them from doing so, although preliminary plans were under way to build a new park the next year if the ban was lifted. The Daisies, therefore, needed North Side Field for one more season of play, but a remonstrance submitted to the school board against the use of the field was put up by the residents in the vicinity of the high school. North Side eventually gave the okay for the games to be played there, but they stipulated that games could not be played on the field until June 7 and that the Daisies must conclude their schedule there by September 3 to avoid conflict with the school athletic programs. In addition, the school board also requested that the starting time for games begin at an earlier hour and asked that the club curtail its noise level, as the park was in a residential neighborhood. That last appeal implied that the school board thought they could monitor conduct at a sporting event in the same way they could in a classroom. How to quiet a crowd at a sporting event must have given club officials a great deal to ponder.

Until they could use North Side Field, the Daisies were granted the use of Dwenger Park for the first nine home games of the season.

They shared the park with two men's baseball teams, the General Electric League and the Federation League, and periodically with the Zollner Pistons men's softball team, pending completion of Zollner stadium sometime that summer. The field was less than desirable, located as it was between a dog pond and a sewage treatment plant and not far from a railroad. However, two new dugouts were added to the facilities to ready the field for women's ball, as well as an electric scoreboard. Prior to these final details being sorted out, however, the fans in Fort Wayne showed how much they loved their Daisies. A number of dedicated Daisy followers started a petition to keep their favorite team in town and paid to have copies of the petition printed in the

Dottie relaxes before the crowds arrive to watch her pitch at North Side Field in Fort Wayne, Indiana, in 1946. The car is the one that Dottie drove across country with Harvey and Helen Callaghan the year before. (Courtesy of the Northern Indiana Center for History)

Fort Wayne Journal-Gazette. A four-by-four printed slip asked "Do You Want To Keep The Daisies in Fort Wayne?" Those who did were told to fill in their name and address on the lines below and to return the form to Vim Sporting Goods Company, in care of the Daisies' leading pitcher, Dottie Wiltse.

The fans not only bestowed quite an honor upon Dottie by choosing her to collect the petitions, they also wisely used the team's biggest draw. Using Dottie as a lure ensured a steady stream of replies. One petition was signed separately by a husband and wife to garner more votes, with the words "Lots of luck Dottie" printed on the bottom of the form, right above the admonition "Keep the Daisies in Fort Wayne." Dottie also received several letters assuring her of the writers' support. One such letter began, "Dear Dottie, Certainly shall do all we possibly can to keep you girls here." Another read, "Miss Wiltse, Sure lots of fans want to see Kellogg ... Dancer, Callaghan ... Man [Manager] Wams [Wambsganss] here this summer as our home team." All in all over 2,000 signatures were received. The relationship that Fort Wayne shared with its Daisies, and more specifically with Dottie, would remain strong and continue to grow long after the girls ceased to play ball.

Opening day was set for May 22, with 56 games slated to be played at home. Seven players from the 1945 team were included on the 1946 roster, with each team allowed to keep ten players from the previous year for a total player limit of 18. Returning to the club in addition to Dottie were Vivian Kellogg at first base; Irene Ruhnke at second; Marg Callaghan at third; Helen Callaghan and Faye Dancer in the outfield. Audrey Haine joined Dottie on the mound. The two main losses from last season were pitcher Annabelle Lee and catcher Ruth Lessing, although Kate Vonderau would prove herself an able replacement for Lessing. With the entry of two new teams into the league this year—the Peoria Redwings, who had partnered with the Daisies during spring training, and the Muskegon Lassies—veteran stars had to be redistributed to make the newest additions viable contenders. Annabelle Lee was one such player, reassigned to the Wings.

The Daisies arrived back in Fort Wayne on Sunday, May 19, chugging in at 3:15 P.M. on the Pennsylvania Railroad. The ten rookies had made hotel reservations until they were assigned housing with families in the area, while those girls who already had a place to live went directly to their homes. Dottie and Harvey had purchased a white bungalow on the other side of town from the ballpark, and since Harvey was away in service, Dottie rented rooms to Marg and Helen Callaghan. The house had two bedrooms, one bath, a living room, a dining room, and a kitchen. "A couple who were real good fans told us about this place for sale across the street from their house," Dottie remembered. Dottie described the house as small, while Marg Callaghan recalled it as a "pretty fair-sized house," which says much about the power of perspective, but the fact remains that Dottie and Harvey's new home served as perfect living quarters for the girls. The three of them did well together, although Marg and Dottie often referred to Helen as "Queenie" since she tended to disappear whenever there was any housework to be done.

Before the Daisies began play, club officials mapped out several activities for them. First, club personnel and sports writers officially greeted the players at the club's business office located in the Vim Sporting Goods Store on South Calhoun Street. As reported by the *Gazette*, the girls would also have to go through a "snap-shot ordeal" as a number of fans were eager to take their pictures. Next, the players took time out for a few radio interviews and a luncheon hosted by the Lions Club at the Chamber of Commerce. However, aside from these commitments, the girls were prevented from accepting any of the many invitations that came to them from private homes and civic clubs since so much activity would have interfered with their daily workouts. Yet even though they could not honor all of the social engagements presented to them, the warm welcome they received once they returned to Fort Wayne undoubtedly boosted their morale immensely before their opening series with the South Bend Blue Sox.

The main concern as the Daisies began the 1946 season, according to the *News-Sentinel*, was the pitching. In an article previewing the season, the *Sentinel* asserted that "Dottie Wiltse, one of the best in the girls' game, can be counted on to win her share again. But the three rookie moundsmen sent here [Meryle Fitzgerald of South Dakota, Syracuse native Georgia Campbell, and Sis Arnold of Fort Wayne] are unknown quantities." Additionally, the article also expressed concern with the number two pitcher, Audrey Haine, who last year was number three. Comparing the Daisy pitching staff to the other teams who had at least two reliable hurlers, the article concluded that the Daisy staff fared poorest unless Haine and the rookies came through. "Wiltse can't carry the entire mound load!" they quipped. Manager Bill Wambsganss was not as worried, although he had experienced enough baseball to take nothing for granted. He told the *News-Sentinel* that he felt the '46 team was better balanced than the '45 team. "We'll have to see how some of the rookies react to competition and whether the veterans can pick up where they left off last year before deciding just how well we will do and what clubs are the ones to beat," he told the *Sentinel*, even predicting his club could give the powerhouse Peaches and the strong Grand Rapids Chicks a good run for the title.

The first game against South Bend on May 22 failed to meet his predictions. That game also enabled the Blue Sox to break the Fort Wayne hex after the Sox had failed to win one game in that city during the 1945 season. As for Dottie, even number one twirlers can have shaky starts. The game was close, 6–5, but Dottie had problems with control, issuing eight bases on balls, throwing two wild pitches, and being tagged for thirteen hits in twelve innings of play. Local dimout regulations still prevailed due to the shortage of coal, so the twilight game started at 6:15. However, when the game was still tied at the end of ten innings the superintendent of the city utilities ordered the lights to be turned on so the players could find their way around the field. Not that this condition helped the Daisies much. Some defensive bloopers and their failure to tie the score in the twelfth when Kellogg was caught stealing spelled doom for the Daisies on opening night. It was up to Audrey Haine the next night.

The fans, however, would have to wait one more night for victory, and it would not be Audrey Haine in the spotlight. On Friday, May 24, Dottie redeemed herself, bouncing back from Wednesday's fiasco to defeat the Blue Sox, 7–3. This time, instead of putting her in as a starter, manager Wamby used her in a relief role when rookie starter Mary Moraty folded in the middle of the second inning. "Collins turned in a praiseworthy performance," according to the *News-Sentinel*, "and earned a well-deserved victory" when she worked her way out of trouble in both the seventh inning, when she issued three walks to the first three batters, and in the eighth, with two hits and an error. Dottie's teammates backed her up by overcoming a 2–0 deficit with seven runs in the sixth inning of play. RBIs by Faye Dancer and Helen Callaghan, two each, and a couple of fine double plays, both involving Marg Callaghan, helped the Daisies to their first win of the season.

The Daisies also captured the series finale the next night, 4–2, to even up the match with two games apiece. Although she had pitched twelve innings on Wednesday night and eight in her relief role on Friday, manager Wambsganss had sent Dottie back to the mound on Saturday because he felt only Dottie could be counted on to balance the books with the Blue Sox. Dottie did not let him down, although she again exhibited some wildness in the seventh inning when she walked two batters, after which Viola "Tommy" Thompson reached first on a sacrifice and Sox shortstop Senaida Wirth sent home the tying run with a single. However, the Daisies put the winning runs over in the eighth with two perfectly executed squeeze plays. Vivian Kellogg hit a ball to left, and Faye Dancer sacrificed her to second. Ruhnke then moved Kellogg to third and stole second. Rookie Kate Vonderau then laid down a beautiful bunt and Kellogg reached home. From there, Irene Kotowicz brought Ruhnke over the plate with another bunt to clinch the game for the Daisies. At the completion of Saturday's game Dottie had worked a total of 29 innings, more than three full games in just four days.

Dottie contributed to a win in Muskegon, Michigan, with both pitching and hitting on May 27. She struck out ten Lassies and gave up six bases on balls, one of which forced in a run to tie the game in the sixth after two singles and an error filled the bags. However, Dottie won that run back in the tenth inning. After striking out the side in the ninth, she hit a single in the next frame, moving catcher Vondereau to third and allowing her to come home on Helen Callaghan's safe hit to the outfield. The final score stood at 2–1 and the series was even at one game apiece. Although Dottie lost to the Lassies two nights later, she pitched no-hit ball until the sixth when Charlene "Shorty" Pryer smacked a single off a Collins pitch. The Daises held the lead 2–0 until the seventh inning when Muskegon scored, later winning the game in the eighth on a double, a hit batsman, a sacrifice and a single. Collins struck out six, walked five, and completed a double play with first basewoman Vivian Kellogg.

When the Daisies next met with Muskegon on their home turf in the beginning of June, their pitching staff was to be strengthened by the addition of Elise Harney, who came over from Kenosha in a three-team deal that sent Audrey Haine to Grand Rapids. Harney had pitched in 43 games in 1945, with 14 wins and 22 loses, giving her an ERA of 2.60, according to the *News-Sentinel.* Harney had been in school when the season started and had not yet pitched for the Comets before being traded to Fort Wayne, but Wambsganss considered using her on June 4 for a game in the Muskegon series if she arrived early enough as expected. In the meantime, he slated Dottie as the starter for the first game of a doubleheader on June 2. Dottie lost that game 4–6, but Faye Dancer, called in from the outfield to take the mound, made up for the loss in the second game. Dancer put on a dazzling display, allowing the Lassies only one hit, by the leadoff hitter, Sara Reeser, thus immediately spoiling any chance for a no-hit game. After that, though, only four runners reached first base on one walk and three errors, and the Daisies won 6–1.

The Daisies made it two in a row the next night, beating the Lassies behind the pitching of Alice DeCambra. DeCambra, like Dancer, came in from the outfield to relieve rookie Mary Moraty, who again found herself in trouble early in the game. Moraty's career as a baseball player was short-lived. She never moved beyond the 1946 season. Since the other newcomer, Elsie Harney, had not yet arrived on June 4, Dottie pitched the final game of the Muskegon series and the finale at Dwenger Park. North Side Field was available for their next homestand against the Redwings. Collins pitched a two-hitter, her "best ball of the still-young season," to quote the June 5 edition of the *News-Sentinel*. She held the Lassies hitless until the eighth, when both runs scored in the 5–2 game, but she came back to pitch another hitless inning in the ninth. The Daisies gave Dottie great support, "with Kotowicz and Helen Callaghan authors of the best defensive gestures," to quote again from the *Sentinel*.

Yet the *Sentinel* could not know that the best was yet to come. After coming to the rescue of Faye Dancer in the eighth inning of the second game of a series with the Redwings on June 6 and turning back the Redwings 6–3, Dottie set the league strikeout record when she whiffed sixteen Redwing batters in Peoria, Illinois, on June 7, 1946. The former record was 15 strikeouts made by Olive Little of Rockford. Ironically, the victims of Little's 1945 performance were the Fort Wayne Daisies. Dottie's strikeout number was ten better than the previous year, when she averaged six strikeouts per game. Besides fanning the sixteen batters, Dottie allowed only three hits and just one clean one, a double by Kay Blumetta in the ninth, leading the Daisies to a 13–0 shutout. Second baseman Irene Ruhnke batted in five runs, bringing her to within one of tying the record in the RBI department.

In commenting upon her amazing feat, the *Journal-Gazette* noted, "Like her uncle George [Hooks] Wiltse she throws an out-breaking curve ball that has opposing batters fanning the breeze." Dottie's batterymate, Kate Vonderau, vividly remembered trying to catch her curveball. "I would give her a target behind the plate in one spot," Kate said, "and by the time I had caught the ball I was about two feet to the right of where I had started. It was kind of funny to see people swing at the ball and they'd swing and swing, and it just wasn't where they thought it was going to be. It was way off the end of their bats. It probably wasn't funny to the people who were trying to hit the ball, but it was kind of amusing to us."

After winning two in a row in Peoria, the Daisies returned home to North Side Field, all the pregame preparations having been completed at the park, according to business manager Frank Biemer. The Daisies would host the Redwings, who were making their initial bow of the 1946 season in Fort Wayne, for a doubleheader and two single games before leaving on a four-game, four-night match in South Bend. Business manager Biemer also announced that Viola Schmidt, a Fort Wayne native now pitching for Rockford, would join the local squad on Sunday, prior to the doubleheader. It was hoped that with both Schmidt and Harney on the pitching staff, along with Dottie, Fort Wayne would become a more imposing presence in the league. Schmidt, however, never really got of the mound, so to speak, since she saw very little playing time. By 1946, a limited sidearm pitch was allowed from an underhand delivery, and the league lengthened the distance between the base paths to 70 feet and the distance from the pitcher's mound to the batter's box to 43 feet. Also, the ball was now 11 inches, down from the original 12, which meant that batting averages went up in general as the smaller ball benefited the hitters. All of these changes brought the game closer to major league baseball, but they also meant that many of the girls, brought up within the boundaries of softball, would be unable to adjust to the slowly evolving game.

Dottie was the opposing pitcher for the Redwings' first game in Fort Wayne on June 9, and when the Redwings faced the formidable moundswoman they probably wished they had never come to town in the first place. In the opening game at North Side Field, over 3000 fans spilled onto the outfield to watch Dottie post a 10–1 win for the Daisies and hold the Wings hitless until the final inning. Former Daisy Annabelle Lee got back at the Daisies in the second game with a 5–2 win over her opponent, Elsie Harney. Harney, making her debut in Fort Wayne and pitching her second game, did well, but her teammates committed numerous errors and also failed in the clutch when at bat.

That doubleheader at North Side on June 9 also contributed to a new league record. With four doubleheaders played that Sunday in the All-American Girls Baseball League, attendance soared over the 100,000 mark with the season just two and a half weeks old. Over 12,000 were on hand to watch the action in Racine, Muskegon, South Bend, and Fort Wayne on that memorable early summer day. The individual league attendance mark for one season was 117,000, established in 1945 by Allington's championship Rockford Peaches. What had started out as a whim of Wrigley's to keep baseball alive during the war years had grown to proportions beyond the parameters of perhaps even his imagination. The 1946 Fort Wayne Daisies yearbook described the spirit of the All-American Girls' Baseball League as an effort "to contribute to the ideals of sportsmanship the application of unselfish cooperation with one another in the building of an outstanding national game, unhampered and unretarded by selfish motives." Judging from the positive response the teams received from their communities, the girls admirably fulfilled that tenet of the league's philosophy and another one as well: "To forever keep in mind the paramount thought behind every action, 'The Game Is the Thing.'"

On June 13, the Daisies tied the Peaches for second place in the league standings by winning against the South Bend Blue Sox. Dottie again relieved Faye Dancer in the eighth inning, fanning the first batter she faced to retire the side and easily closing out the game in the ninth. The Daisies then lost both games of a doubleheader against the Sox the next night, with Dottie the victim of an 8–1 Sox win in the first game. She yielded six runs in the first inning alone, and the double defeat dropped the Daisies into fourth place in the standings. Dottie then made up for that loss by pitching a shutout against Racine in the second game of a doubleheader at North Side Field on June 16, yielding just two hits and throwing eleven strikeouts.

Dottie's performance was even more impressive when Grand Rapids came to town on June 19 for a four-game series against the Daisies, and Dottie handed "Iron Woman" Connie Wisniewski her first defeat of the season after Wisniewski had won ten in a row. That 1–0 shutout thus fulfilled the Gazette's predictions of the previous day that "if anyone in the league can stop Connie it is Dottie." Wisniewski had edged Dottie out for the batting title in 1945, but Dottie showed her she still had her stuff. According to the News-Sentinel, Dottie "had her hook breaking the proverbial country mile Wednesday and the Chicks, when they weren't taking strikes, were whiffling in vain." Dottie mowed down 15 Chicks with strikeouts, one back from her league record, and she allowed only four hits. An article by Roger Nelson in the Gazette crowed that the league-leading Chicks were singing "Daisy, Daisy, give me your answer do," as they questioned what it was about Dottie's pitches that kept them swinging at air.

Dottie pitched her third straight shutout three nights later, blanking the Chicks 4–0 and giving the Daisies an even break in the series. Dottie coasted to the win after Marg Callaghan's home run gave the Daisies an early four-run lead in the second. Following the Michigan nine back to Grand Rapids the next night, Collins posted her second straight win over Wisniewski and won her third straight verdict over the Chicks in the second game of a doubleheader. Referred to as the "Grand Rapids nemesis," Dottie tantalized the Chicks several times during the game, but she pulled through in the end, winning 5–4. Dottie also grabbed the batting honors that night. She hit a double with the bases loaded in the ninth and later scored the winning run.

The Daisies ended the month of June by trouncing the Comets in three out of four games. Dottie was on the mound in the first game, fanning twelve and pitching no-hit ball until the seventh inning with two outs. After the Daisies lost the second game of the series, Dottie came back with a spectacular 8–2 win in the finale of a double-header on June 29. Aside from walking the first batter in the game, Dottie was close to perfection when she retired nineteen batters in succession. Only Audrey Wagner's long drive over Helen Callaghan's head in left field spoiled Dottie's bid for a no-hitter. Dottie also came within two of the strikeout record of 16 she had posted earlier in the month. Including the twelve strikeouts she had posted on June 26, she had struck out a total of 26 batters in eighteen innings of play. The series with Kenosha also hoisted the Daisies above the .500 mark and assured their fourth-place spot in the standings over the Rockford Peaches, who had been rained out of play.

Despite some lack of control throughout the season, such as the game in Rockford where she walked seven, made two wild pitches, and hit a batter, Dottie also played some fine ball. A picture of Dottie in the *Journal-Gazette* tossing a ball with her "game face" on verified this. The caption underneath read, "Dottie Wiltse Collins is below the sensational pace she set last year ... but is still the Daisies' top hurler. Streaks of wildness have robbed her of some her effectiveness but she has inserted some brilliant performances along the way." For example, although she lost to Peoria on July 26, she twirled four-hit ball, striking out five and walking only two. Similarly, in a loss to Muskegon on July 16, Dottie allowed only two hits and struck out six. Back in Fort Wayne a week later, however, Dottie trounced the Lassies on another two-hit game, this time with a shutout of 10–0 which broke a five-game losing streak for the Daisies. Two nights later, on July 24, Dottie again pitched a two-hit game against Muskegon, winning with a score of 5–2 and contributing to the Daisy run total by scoring the first run for the Daisies in the third. That game saw Daisy manager Bill Wamby pull a Billy Martin when he was banished from the game after a spat with home plate umpire, Don Fryback. The argument ensued when Helen Callaghan was thrown out at the plate after her sister, Marg, hit to the pitcher.

Dottie's achievements were not only noted within the confines of the All-American Girls Baseball League. Other clubs were eager for her talent, and they persistently courted her with tempting offers. Right after the 1944 season, Dottie received a letter from Eddie McGuire, the publicity director for the National Girls Softball League. After describing the makeup of the league and inviting her to be a part of it, he explained the schedule for the season, the rules of the game, and the uniform, for some reason focusing on the undergarments worn by the women softball players. A year later, on December 18, 1945, John E. Johnson, the owner of the Chicago Chicks, one of the teams in the league, sent a letter to Dottie inviting her to join the Chicks for the 1946 season and asked her to respond with her salary requirements. Like Eddie McGuire before him, Johnson tried to lure Dottie with the amount of money she could make. Since the softball games were played at night, full-time employment could be managed during the day, thus ensuring close to a double income for several months of the year. The All-American Girls League, on the other hand, made sure the girls received adequate earnings and provided meal allowances and housing expenses when the girls were on the road, but they did not allow other employment during the season, preferring the players devote themselves fully to the game. Another early attempt to lure Dottie away from baseball came in the form of a telegram from Marty McManus, a former manager in the league and now manager for the Bloomer Girls softball team. McManus urged Dottie to wire him collect, reiterating the greater possibilities for pay in the softball league and the easier schedule since all games were played in Chicago and no travel was involved. He even ended by offering to secure her daytime employment.

In addition to the softball league trying to lure the All-Americans away, another threat came from south of the border. Rumors circulated that Señor Jorge Pasquel, of the Mexican Baseball League, planned an outright onslaught on the AAGPBL talent, tempting the girls with cold hard cash. As reported in the *Fort Wayne News-Sentinel*, league official Frank Avery wrote to Pasquel, "While we are able to protect ourselves with our own players, we believe that for the sake of Mexican-American relations, we can show you why it would be wise for you to stop, look, and listen." Avery went on to say that Pasquel would find "most of our girls are loyal to the All-American organization" and that "neither the American people or the Mexican people will stand for a raid." Avery ended with a veiled warning to Pasquel that the girls had signed contracts with league management and that it would be management with whom he would ultimately deal. Avery also suggested the possibility of Mexican girls' baseball teams playing the American girls in a world series, a vision of international sports competition which came to fruition in 1999 when Japan met the United States in Fort Lauderdale for the American Women's Baseball League's South Florida Diamond Classics.

While Pasquel failed to make inroads in the girls' league, he fared much better with men's major league ball. On Tuesday, May 28, the *News-Sentinel* reported that three players from the St. Louis Cardinals had departed for Mexico. Pitchers Fred Martin and Max Lanier joined infielder Lou Klein in the Pasquel brothers' Mexican Baseball League. A photograph above the article showed Martin and Lanier laughing and talking as they loaded the trunk of Martin's car for the drive to their high-salaried positions. Club officials worried that the "Pasquels' persuasive pesos might lure other members of the squad..." However, Cardinals' owner Sam Braedon vowed he would not try to stop other Redbirds from flying the coop. "What's the use," Braedon said, "you can't force a man to work for you if he does not want to." Obviously, although the officials in the girls' league showed some concern, they counted on the integrity of the women they had recruited to honor the conditions under which they played.

As the season came to a close, Dottie continued alternating some fine pitching performances with her share of losses. She pitched one-hit ball until the seventh inning in a 6–4 loss to Peoria on August 1, after which she was relieved by Faye Dancer in the eighth. That night at North Side Field was Nylon Night, with several pairs of the coveted hose given out to some lucky ladies. Shortly thereafter, Dottie was within three putouts of a no-hit game when the Daisies met the Belles in Fort Wayne on August 8. She missed the no-hitter but pulled a Daisy win with a one-hit game and a shutout, beating the Belles 3–0. By the end of August, the Daisies had closed the gap to four and a half games in back of the fourth-place Rockford Peaches after a great pitching duel between Dottie Collins and Rockford's Carolyn Morris led to a 1–0 Daisy win.

After that, though, things tumbled downhill. The Daisies lost three games to the Peaches on August 24 and 25, including both games of a doubleheader, which clinched the Peaches' fourth-place spot and virtually eliminated the Daisies from a playoff berth. They then lost one more game to Kenosha before Dottie downed Rockford, 3–2, on August 31. In that game, Dottie granted the Peaches only three hits, none after the second inning, and struck out five. The Daisies ended the season by getting an even spilt with Rockford in a doubleheader season finale and ending up fifth in the league standings.

Dottie exited the 1946 season with a 22–20 record, a winning percentage of .524, and an ERA of 2.32. She also struck out 294 batters and issued 187 walks during the 44 games in which she pitched.

Although the papers were correct that Dottie's control was not as effective as in 1945, with the number of hit batsmen jumping from 20 in 1945 to 31 in 1946, she had definitely buckled down from her first year of play when she hit a total of 44 batters. A career, however, is never measured by one year alone, nor can it be assessed completely until seen from a distance. Several more years of expert play awaited Dottie Collins before the final summing up could be ordered.

A Pregnant Pause:
The Daisies, 1947–1948

A subtle shift in focus occurred in Dottie's fourth season of play, one that foreshadowed her eventual decision to leave the game. Having been married now for just over a year, and settling in for the first time as a couple since Harvey's permanent return from service, Dottie opted to stay home with her husband rather than leave for spring training. Dottie's situation was unique in some ways since most of the other women in the league did not face this choice between personal responsibilities and commitment to the game they loved. Citing some statistics about the female ballplayers in their April 18, 1946, edition, the *Journal-Gazette* revealed that twelve of the women in the league were married and three of the them had families, a low number considering that the eight teams in the league that year comprised over 100 women. Dottie, therefore, juggled responsibilities different from those of many of her fellow leaguers.

Then, too, participating in spring training entailed more of a commitment in 1947 than in previous years. In November, 1946, league president Max Carey reported that Havana, Cuba, had outbid several other cities to host the girls for spring training. Obviously proud of the location, he told the *Journal-Gazette*, "At last we've got a real major league training set-up, which we should have had a long time ago. These girls are major league caliber, and they're going to be training like major leaguers." Sponsored by the Havana Stadium Corporation, training would consist of a four-day exhibition tour of Cuba, followed by an official training program. Over 170 members of the league, including 155 players, eight managers, eight chaperones, sportswriters, umpires, and league officials left Miami, Florida, in eight Pan American Airways Clippers on April 21, 1946, for the shores of Cuba, the first time in baseball history that an entire league had been taken out of the country. The *Fort Wayne News-Sentinel* called it "a highlight in the history of the All-American Girls' Baseball League."

The Cubans welcomed the girls wholeheartedly. In the end they drew more fans than the Brooklyn Dodgers, who also had spring training there. The Daisies fared well, despite a heartbreaking loss to Muskegon on Friday, May 2, which would have enabled them to play in the finals the next night. However, the Daisies were not the same caliber of team minus Dottie Collins, and no one knew that better than the new skipper of the team, George Johnson. On April 19, he wrote the following appeal to Dottie, "Dear Dorothy, I would appreciate much, if you could possibly join us on the training trip, after we leave Havana, Cuba and come back to the mainland to start north. In other words, as soon as the series is completed in Cuba, I shall notify you what cities our club plays and hotels ... I know all the girls and myself will appreciate your joining us on the way home." He followed up his letter with a telegram to Dottie on May 5, which read in part "Entire team awaiting your arrival. Need pitching help now."

Dottie was like the tip of a compass, the focal point around which the entire team revolved. League president Max Carey knew this, too, and he tried to goad Dottie into making the trip to Havana in the first place, using an interesting bit of bribery in the process. In mid–January, Carey wrote to Dottie to ask her to reconsider her decision not to join the league in Cuba. After reminding her of what she would gain from an educational standpoint in terms of experience, and informing her that she would forgo her spring training salary if she did not make the trip, Carey then told Dottie that the Daisies "have been reorganized and they are looking forward to having a good club this year, and if you do not come to camp that certainly would throw a monkey wrench into our general setup." He concluded by offering to do what he could to help her change her mind and expressed the hope that she would travel to Havana with the league. Coming from a person in a position of such authority, these were pretty heady arguments indeed. That Dottie transcended the pressure and never wavered from her decision says much about her strength of character. Little did she know that this sense of centerness, finely honed during her years as a ballplayer, would later serve as her lifeline at a time when she needed it most.

Despite her decision not to go to Havana, Dottie did join the team in Fayetteville, North Carolina, in early May. Previously, the Daisies had staged several exhibition games in Knoxville, Tennessee, and

Gadsen, Alabama, with manager Johnson relying upon players converted from other positions to solve his pitching dilemma. Alice DeCambra, regular second baseman, hurled a great five-hitter to beat the Peoria Redwings on May 5, and veteran Irene Kotowicz and rookie Betty Tucker did their share, also. However, it was mound ace Dottie Collins everyone was waiting for, and as usual, Dottie did not let them down. Coming onto the field against the Redwings on May 12, Dottie fanned fourteen of the opposition and allowed just seven hits before a crowd of 2500 fans. The Daisies played errorless ball in that game and they so moved the crowd with their fine exhibition that, as reported by *the Journal-Gazette*, the next night's game was expected to test the capacity of the stands, which held about 3500 fans.

Dottie followed up that performance with a 10–3 triumph over the Wings in Selby, North Carolina, and a 12–1 two-hit victory in Columbus, Ohio. Although Dottie was a little wild in the exhibition game in Selby, with seven passed balls and four bases on balls, she still managed to give up only two hits before being relieved by Alice DeCambra in the fifth. The Daisies ended their 14-game series with Peoria with nine wins to the Redwings' five. The spring exhibition games proved to be more popular with each passing year. In 1947, the All-Americans visited 31 cities in Florida, North and South Carolina, Alabama, Georgia, Kentucky, Tennessee, Virginia, West Virginia, Ohio, and Michigan. Since the games not only provided an introduction to girls' baseball but benefited area communities as well, with the proceeds from the Columbus, Ohio, games going to charities sponsored by The Childhood League and the Junior Chamber of Commerce, the exhibition tour attracted more than its share of public appeal. Nearly every city visited in 1946 called the league office in Chicago to request engagements for 1947—a sure sign as to the popularity of the All-Americans' spring circuit.

Fort Wayne was well prepared for the Daisies by the time they returned home on May 18, having begun preparations for the 1947 season shortly after the previous one ended. Aside from the choice of George Johnson, a former umpire in the American Association for thirty years, as manager, the Daisies appointed Marian Stancevic of Port Jervis, New York, as the Daisies' new chaperone. "We are most fortunate," said Daisies president Hans Mueller, "in securing the services of Miss Stancevic. She is well qualified by her background of physical education training and teaching experience to assume the responsibilities of chaperoning the Fort Wayne Daisies. It has been and will continue to be the policy of our board to hire only those persons whose character ratings, moral standards and practical experience are above reproach." Since the chaperone's character reflected on the team as a whole, this emphasis on her impeccable value system ensured that the ballplayers would uphold the standards of the league by conducting themselves properly both off and on the field.

Once the matter of team stewards had been resolved, Daisy officials finally settled on a playing field for the sole use of the Daisies. The board chose Memorial Park, a former general recreation center on the east side of Fort Wayne between Washington Boulevard on the north and Jefferson on the south, with Glasgow Avenue running along its western edge. Dwenger Park, where the Daisies played in 1946, was located just to the north of Memorial Park, so if games were played simultaneously, the fans in Memorial Park could see the lights in Dwenger in the distance and vice versa. In early April, team management stressed that everything would be in readiness for the opening game on May 21 despite a spate of rainy weather that had recently blanketed the city. Plans were under way for considerable improvements in the playing site, as well as additional seating for the large number of anticipated fans. Once the renovations were completed, the grandstands ran all the way up a hill, around the park, and down to where a fence separated the park from the road. Steps led down to the playing field, above which was a food concession stand and the Daisy box office. Locker rooms with showers stood on the other side of the park from the field. "We really packed them in," Dottie remembered. "It didn't look like we could have packed them in very much, but we did. First the men came out, and they enjoyed it so much they got the wives to come out and bring the kids."

Perhaps this permanent site, more than anything else, expressed most clearly that the former orphans had truly found a home in Fort Wayne. Memorial Park would serve the Daisies from 1947 until the demise of the league in 1954. Today, a monument to the Daisies graces the edge of the park in the form of a large rose and gray boulder with a diamond carved into the left side and the insignia of the All-American Girls Professional Baseball League on the other. The proud inscription reads, "All-American Girls Professional Baseball League, Home of the Fort Wayne Daisies, 1945–1954."

Daisy officials and Dottie were also busy drumming up publicity for the team in the months before the season began. Prior to spring training, Dottie and Naomi Meier, who had moved from Rockford to Fort Wayne that year, represented the Daisies' ticket booth at the Sportsman Show in the Armory, which ran from Thursday, March 27, through Sunday, March 30. Various exhibits, including a cutout of a female ballplayer, adorned the edge of the table where visitors gathered to buy tickets for upcoming games and to hear information about the new season. Dottie and Naomi also took a night out to instruct a group of girls in softball at the Jefferson Recreation Center beginners' school in mid–April.

While the girls were working individually to promote the team, the Daisies' board of directors busily planned a number of ways to increase attendance for the year. One of the most productive of these was the establishment of headquarters for the Fort Wayne Daisies on the mezzanine floor of the Hotel Anthony. Centrally located in downtown Fort Wayne, The Anthony provided a place for fans to secure reserved, unreserved, and box tickets for Daisy games and to obtain information about the upcoming season. A direct telephone line was also installed so fans had the option of ordering tickets by phone and having them mailed. Another avenue to more ticket sales involved the appointment of a speakers' committee to address local clubs and societies about funding for local playgrounds should the Daisies show a profit beyond operational costs in 1947. It was a good ploy to get people out to see the games, since the more tickets sold, the more money would go into community improvements. A ticket order form in the *Journal-Gazette,* inserted almost two months before the first home game, further nudged fans and would-be fans into attending the games, promising as it did "48 thrill-packed nights, glamour, action, excitement, and baseball at its best."

Daisy management conjured up an even more innovative advertising angle shortly before the start of the season. On Saturday, May 17, at 2:00 P.M. several Daisy officials rented a plane and dropped 5,000 daisies on the citizens of Fort Wayne as they flew over the city. Although one wonders how the people felt about being bombarded by flowers falling from the sky, there was a purpose to the stunt, aside from bringing attention to the symbolism of the daisies. A total of 200 flowers among the 5000 were good for free tickets for the home opener on May 21, when the Fort Wayne Daisies were to meet the South Bend Blue Sox. An advertisement in the *News-Sentinel* on May 16 prepared the citizens of Fort Wayne for this floral display with a large announcement that read "Daisies Will Rain from the Skies," with the date and the time the flowers would be dropped listed underneath. The bottom of the page detailed ticket prices and information for impending games, along with the businesses where fans could purchase tickets. The only incongruity in the ad were the drawings of the rather limp-looking daisies around the border, hardly a fitting symbol for a team predicted to be a competitor in the league standings for 1947.

An added boost for the Daisies, and the league in general, came from an article in the April 1 issue of *Forbes Magazine*. According to the *Journal-Gazette*, the author of the piece, Norman Klein, noted that executives in Fort Wayne and seven other cities in the Midwest came upon girls' baseball as the solution to "restlessness, production difficulties, and disturbed morale." Klein commented that "the plan has resulted in notably heightened enthusiasm among plant workers and their families, new town pride and all-round friendliness, and a sharp cut in juvenile delinquency." Klein also liked the fact that the clubs were locally organized and gave back to the community in which they were based. More importantly, he emphasized that the girls were playing "real professional baseball which in no way resembles amateur softball."

The *Gazette* supported the author's contention that girls' baseball had a wide appeal in Fort Wayne, citing the wide array of fans who followed the Daisies, ranging from bosses and workers in industrial plants to clergymen and teachers and men and women of all ages. The *Gazette* also stated that "Coming to Fort Wayne two years ago, the Daisies have captured the fancy of sports-minded men and women in this city and throughout the area towns and cities ... the girls baseball club has brought and will continue to bring good, clean entertainment, furnished at moderate prices."

With such an auspicious beginning, the 1947 season got under way. Dottie was again slated as the starting pitcher for the home opener with South Bend on May 21. Heralded in the *News-Sentinel* as "the Daisies' lissome right-hander who won 22 and lost 20 in 1946," the accompanying photo of Dottie proclaimed that "she has been dazzling All-American Girls Baseball League batters for two years with her sweeping curve ball." To make sure she was at her peak, Dottie rested up for Wednesday's opener by skipping the short trip the team made to Grand Rapids for a game with the Chicks on Monday. However, the weather determined that she would have another day off, as heavy, all-night rain washed out the diamond at Memorial Park. The game was called before noon.

The extra break failed to help the team as a whole, though, as the Blue Sox downed the Daisies 1–3 on Thursday, May 22, before a crowd of 4000 disappointed fans. While Dottie allowed only six hits, recorded seven strikeouts, and walked three batters, her teammates had difficulty against the pitching of Phyllis (Sugar) Koehn, a sub-marine hurler, and could not score even when they managed to get on base. In addition, the Sox capitalized on the Daisies' inability to stop their opponents from stealing bases, particularly Bonnie Baker, who stole three and scored all of the Sox runs. As Marg Callaghan commented, "Dottie was one of the best pitchers in the league in the years that she played, but I think sometimes we could have given her more support."

Unfortunately, that support failed to come through in Dottie's next start against the Grand Rapids Chicks, although the game was a tight one. Again the Daisies were granted extra time off when rain intervened to cancel the final game of the series with South Bend on May 24, but once more this failed to help them when they traveled to Grand Rapids the following day. Dottie dropped her second in a row when the Chicks employed some good fielding to beat the Daisies, 2–3. Up against her old nemesis, Connie Wisniewski, Dottie's six-strikeout game failed to halt the Chicks' masterful bunting to get the runners home. Alma Ziegler singled in the first, was sacrificed to second by Doris Tetzlaff and then scored from second on a safe bunt from Twila Shively. The winning run in the sixth also came from a bunt, this time from the bat of former Daisy catcher Ruth "Tex" Lessing, who brought Jane Stoll home from third. Fort Wayne ral-lied in the ninth, but Teeny Petras's brilliant double play ended the Daisies' hopes and the game.

After losing the second game to the Chicks, with rain calling the third game on Tuesday, the Daisies occupied the cellar in the league standings, their only win a game against South Bend during the open-ing homestand. A series with the Muskegon Lassies, now steered by former Daisy manager Bill Wambsganss, represented their next chance to move out of their early-season slump. After the losing the first game at Memorial Park on May 28, the Daisies came back to win a doubleheader against the Lassies on Decoration Day, with scores of 4–0 and 14–4. Dottie Collins was the winning pitcher in both games. Called the "heroine" of Friday's doubleheader, along with catcher Ruby Heafner, who delivered five hits and drove in five runs, Dottie fanned twelve batters in the first game and issued only one walk for her first shutout of the season. The first and only hit off Collins came in the second inning when Mickey Maguire smashed a triple to left field. This time Dottie held the Lassies back with some terrific support, with single runs in the third and fourth innings and two more in the fifth. In the eighth inning of the second game, the

Daisies blew a 4–1 lead when Alice DeCambra, starting pitcher, loaded the bases on a hit and two walks and Doris Sams knocked out a hit that brought two runners home. Dottie then came in to relieve DeCambra and the rest was history. Even though a run came over the plate when Dottie first took the mound, evening up the score, she soon retired the side and the Daisies flew past the Lassies in the home half of the inning, collecting ten runs with four hits, five stolen bases, a pair of walks, and five Muskegon errors.

A loss to the Lassies on Saturday brought an end to the Muskegon series and sent the Daisies on the road to meet the league-leading South Bend Blue Sox. Now that the war had ended and the girls traveled by bus, the schedule could be grueling, considering that close to half of the 120 games played in a season were on the road. The girls made the best of the situation, though singing, reading, and sometimes playing poker, although only for pennies as Dottie assured her mother in a short note she wrote home. If the bus broke down, the girls often waited long periods for help in those days before rapid communication. Yet Dottie looks back upon these journeys as fun. "You could just stick your luggage on right there, and you didn't have to worry," she said, thinking back on some hectic train rides with luggage getting misplaced along the way. This constant traveling, though, was the reason that the majority of the games were played at night. "Sometimes we would get in at four or five o'clock in the morning, and all we wanted to do was go to bed. So we couldn't play an afternoon game," Dottie said.

It must have been difficult for Dottie to be away from her husband at times. Even when she was at home, nights were spent at the ballpark, and Dottie's mornings consisted of making the beds, cooking the breakfast, and doing the dishes before dashing off to practice, which lasted until well into the afternoon. Yet during the years when she combined a baseball career with marriage, she pledged herself completely to the game once the season was under way. Later, when she realized that she could not give herself wholly to the game or her family, she made a choice rather than do an injustice to either.

Dottie's catcher in 1947, Mary Rountree, specifically remembered that about her. "Everybody knew that Harvey was the light of her life," Mary said. "Harvey was the guy she loved. But when we were playing ball, her mind was on playing ball. What pitch to throw next, or how to get this or that going so we might have an edge. Everything was strictly baseball, until after the game was over and she would be going to meet Harvey." Dottie's former catcher, Kate Vonderau, agreed with this picture of intense concentration and gave that as the reason for Dottie's success on the mound. "When Dottie pitched, you almost always expected that you were going to win that game," she said. "Other pitchers that I caught for did not have the same kind of control. Dottie was a winner."

Dottie's stats from 1947 make that evident. That season Dottie recorded a 1.33 ERA, a league-leading 244 strikeouts, and a winning percentage of .588. She contributed to those impressive numbers in the second game of a doubleheader with the Sox on June 3 in South Bend. Pitching her second shutout in a row, Dottie blanked the Sox by a score of 3–0, with just three hits in nine innings. She also struck out eleven batters, which, coupled with her previous efforts, brought her string of strikeouts at this point in the season to 40 in just over 37 innings of play. Irene Kotowicz hurled two-hit ball in the seven-inning opener to move the Daisies up one notch from the cellar and topple the Blue Sox from their first place position. Moving on to Peoria, Illinois, a fourth straight victory on June 5 catapulted the Daisies into third place in the league standings. In that game, Irene Kotowicz was credited with the win, but Dottie relieved her in the seventh inning and pitched hitless ball until the end. Coming home to Memorial Park on Sunday, June 8, Dottie had chalked up 43 strikeouts in the 40 innings she pitched and had permitted only seven runs to score.

Dottie would meet an old friend when the team returned to Fort Wayne to meet the last-place Kenosha Comets. The Daisies' president, Hans Mueller, announced the signing of William "Daddy" Rohrer as the new manager of the team. Current manager George Johnson had been recalled by Max Carey because of the need for good umpire talent in the circuit, Johnson having formerly served as chief umpire of the league. Rohrer had his own baseball ties to the city. First drafted by the Chicago White Sox, he was then sold to the Dayton Vets in the former Central League, where he played a number of games against the Fort Wayne Chiefs. In addition, Rohrer had not only managed one of Dottie's softball teams in California and watched one of his biggest stars work her way up to the top, he had witnessed his daughter Kaye's similar upward climb.

Being familiar with baseball and many of the California girls in the league helped Rohrer adapt more easily. However, now the tables were turned somewhat and he depended on his girls, whereas before they relied on him. Shortly before Rohrer's first game as manager, a picture in the *Journal-Gazette* showed Rohrer squatting down between Dottie Collins and catcher Ruby Heafner. Daddy's cap was twisted to the side as he turned to catch some advice from a smiling Dottie, as Ruby Heafner leaned in and listened intently. Something must have worked, as Dottie and the Daisies beat the Comets in the seven-inning opener, 8–0. Dottie extended her streak of scoreless innings to 27 and upped her strikeout total in these innings to 29. She remained hitless until the seventh when Marge Villa hit a single to left.

The honeymoon was over in the nightcap, the debut of catcher Mary Rountree, when the Daisies lost that game 7–4 behind the pitching of a wild Irene Kotowicz. The next game of the series in Fort Wayne saw the struggling Comets rally for a 10–8 win, with the *Sentinel* suggesting the cellar-dwelling Comets had found a haven in Fort Wayne. The final game of the series against Kenosha on June 10 represented a heartbreaking loss for Dottie Collins, who had struck out nine batters in nine innings. The *Journal-Gazette* reported that the Daisies "pulled a 'Merkle' in the ninth inning that lost them a 13-inning ball game, 2–3, in almost unbelievable fashion after they had it literally won and tucked away in their bat bags." The "Merkle" referred to the New York Giants' first baseman, Fred Merkle, the precursor to the ill-fated Bill Buckner of the Boston Red Sox. In a 1908 game against the Cubs, with the score tied in the bottom of the ninth in a heated pennant race, Merkle failed to touch second base after the winning Giant run crossed home, returning instead to the clubhouse after becoming alarmed at the fans who had mobbed the field. Subsequently, the league president, Harry Pulliam, ruled the game a tie that would have to replayed at the end of the season.

In the Daisy version of the Merkle error, the Comets sent three pinch hitters to bat in the bottom of the ninth. It seemed that Dottie Collins had struck out all three to give the Daisies a 2–1 victory. The Daisies were even gathering up their equipment to return to the clubhouse and the crowds were snaking toward the exits when someone on the Kenosha bench realized that catcher Ruby Heafner had dropped the ball on the third strike called on batter Jean Cione. Since Cione made no move towards first, Heafner never threw the ball to the first sacker. However, Cione's teammates soon got her moving, and before the Daisies could react she had reached second. As so often happens, that one break was all the Comets needed to turn the tide their way. The next batter beat out a single to bring the tying run over the plate. In the thirteenth, a triple followed by a single did the trick for the Comets. They left Fort Wayne with three out of four wins, thus knocking the Daisies into fifth place in the standings.

Things were not much better once the Daisies reached Rockford the next night. They lost a doubleheader to the Peaches, the second game another great pitching duel in which Dottie suffered another tough loss in extra innings. After striking out twelve and giving up only one base on balls, compared to Millie Deegan's eight strikeouts and two walks, a misplay cost Dottie the game. Dorothy Kamenshek sent a high fly towards center, and both Faye Dancer and rookie right fielder Marie Kruckel charged after the ball. While Kruckel got her hands on the ball, she dropped it when she saw Dancer coming her way. Kamenshek reached first safely, proceeded to steal second and third, and finally scored on Dottie Ferguson's single to left, breaking open the scoreless game in the twelfth. In the final two games of the series, Rockford swept Fort Wayne with scores of 3–2 in both games.

Coming home to try and break their slump on June 15, the Daisies failed to do so in a doubleheader with the Racine Belles, but in the third game of the series they turned a fifteen-inning marathon to their advantage It was the third extra-inning game Dottie had pitched in seven days. As the *Journal-Gazette* noted, "the scales of justice finally got around to balancing in her favor." She pitched no-hit ball for eight innings and never let the Belles come close to a base hit until Sophie Kurys led off the ninth inning with a double and then stole third, a move that was hotly contested by the Daisies. The umpire ruled in favor of the Belles, and that one hit led to the run that evened the score and sent the game into overtime, although Dottie contained any further damage in the ninth. After Kurys's tying run, Dottie walked Pepper Paire and recorded two putouts with fly balls. She then walked Maddy English to load the bases and ended the inning by forcing Irene Hickson to ground out.

However, Dottie still had her work cut out for her, especially in the fourteenth and fifteenth innings, with the Belles collecting several hits off of her during those frames. In the fourteenth inning, Mavis Dabbs, the Daisies' right fielder, saved the game for Dottie by grabbing a Maddy English fly ball, which would have scored Ellie Dapkus who had tripled with only one out. Before Dapkus reached the plate, however, Dabbs fired to Ruby Heafner and got Dapkus out by a long shot. In the top of the fifteenth, Dottie hit the first two batters but then retired the side with two pop-ups and a strikeout. The Daisies rallied in the bottom of that inning and pulled off a win with a combination of plays. Two runners reached base when Marg Callaghan walked and Marge Pieper was intentionally passed after Faye Dancer flied out to center. Betty Whiting then sent a nice drive to left, but unfortunately for the Daisies, Edie Perlick made a great running catch. Next, Helene Machado, nicknamed "Chow" for collecting table scraps from the players to feed the street dogs in Havana, connected for a long shot after going hitless in six previous at-bats. That dinger sent Marg Callaghan over the plate from second base with the winning run. With that victory, the Daisies broke a string of nine straight defeats and were ready to roll.

The Daisies made it four in a row when they defeated the Rockford Peaches at Memorial Park on June 20, again in a hectic fifteen-inning marathon. In that game, Dottie lost control in the eighth with two out and was relieved by Alice DeCambra, who did a fine job of halting the Rockford runs for the remainder of the game. Unfortunately, a few days later the Daisies slid downhill with a third straight loss to the Racine Belles on June 23 after losing both halves of a doubleheader the night before. Dottie was partially responsible for the lone run the Belles scored to win that single game, which she forced in after hitting first basewoman Marge Danhauser with a pitch. She made up for that error on June 26 when she pitched a two-hitter against the Chicks at Memorial Park to give the Daisies a 1–0 win. A headline in the *News-Sentinel* announced "Daisies Snap Loss Skein; Nip Chicks," conjuring up an interesting picture of a bunch of chickens anxiously fleeing a field of frenzied flowers. However, the Daisies were not all that menacing, as they lost two to Kenosha, bringing the Comets up from the basement and putting themselves back into it. Dottie pitched the June 30 nightcap and suffered another one-run defeat, even though she struck out ten batters. Coming into Muskegon on July 4, she hurled a one-hitter against the Lassies and broke a seven-game losing streak for the Daisies.

Despite their roller-coaster ride through the first half of the season, most of it at the bottom of the loop, Daisy fans stood by their team, and the team stood by their fans. Dottie received many accolades from the citizens of Fort Wayne, including a letter that read, "You pitched a wonderful game. We had faith in you. Good luck." Some fans later sent Dottie one dozen roses because "her wonderful performance was appreciated." Even after the 1946 season ended and before the next one had begun, an admirer sent Dottie a Christmas card with his hopes that she would return to the Daisies in 1947. He ended his note with the sentiments, "We need you and we love you." Beyond the fact that she was a great ballplayer, the Daisy devotees appreciated Dottie because of who she was as a person as well.

"She was always being bombarded by people, and not just kids, wanting to talk to her before the game," recalled Judy Widen, whose father, Ernie Berg, became business manager of the Daisies in 1948. "She was always nice and willing to sign her name on the programs. It must have been distracting for her before a game," Widen reflected, "but she never put anybody off. She was always willing to smile and wave and chat with the fans. I remember her as the leader, the one the players looked up to and admired. She was so talented and had so much natural ability. She seemed so tall to me as a kid, with such long wonderful arms that were amazing to watch when she whipped that ball across the plate." Kate Vonderau, Dottie's catcher in 1946, concurred. "I was just a youngster when I first started playing in the league," she said. "Dottie had been in the league for years, and she was a star, but she made me feel comfortable, even though it was hard to catch her ball, it curved so much."

Other followers flocked to the team in general. Vivian Kellogg most vividly remembered the fans who came from the elderly men's home in town. The Women's Service Club would go to the home and bring the gentlemen to the ballpark. Two of the men always sat on the first base side, where Vivian held down the bag. "One night as we were leaving the park," Vivian said, "these two gentlemen came alongside me and I told them I was sorry we lost the game. And they said, 'Well, that's all right, Kelly. We just want to be here when you split those shorts.'"

A slightly more wholesome story involved two bachelor farmers in town. The Daisies were their whole life, and they attended every game. The players always noticed them in the stands because when they took off their hats to cheer their bald heads shone brightly against the dark tan of their faces and arms. These two men so loved their Daisies that they regularly invited the players over for Sunday dinner once the season ended and they did not have to be at the ballpark. As the girls tucked into chicken dinners with corn and lettuce and peach pie they experienced a true farm feast, with all the bounty of the land spread out before them. To honor their devotion to the team, the characters of the two farmers were portrayed in cameo parts in the movie *A League of Their Own*.

The Daisy organization kept busy throughout the season coming up with ways to boost this fan base. One idea they hit upon benefited not only the Daisies but some of the area's less privileged children as well. More than 800 youngsters across various economic strata would have the chance to see a Daisy game, courtesy of members of the Daisy Knothole Gang. To join the Knothole Gang, an organization or individual pledged to invite 100 children to see a Daisy game at Memorial Park at a special price for the block of tickets. Some of the sponsors included the Fort Wayne Lions Club, the Fort Wayne Navy Club, and the Mayflower Mills. In addition, special "group nights" were planned, whereby an organization would buy a block of tickets and resell them to members or employees for a designated game. The American Legion Post 47 planned to watch the matchup between the Daisies and the Peoria Redwings in early July, with a number of other groups, including the Mizpah Shrine, expressing interest.

Furthermore, the girls took themselves out into the community. Using their knowledge and experience, the girls agreed to assist the recreational staff of the City Park Board in Fort Wayne in forming a girls' softball league. Teams would be organized at all of the city's parks and playgrounds throughout the course of a week. Three members of the Daisies were to be present at each park every day during the first week in July, with the exception of the day they played in South Bend. Aside from helping to organize the girls' league, the Daisies would provide equipment such as gloves, bats, and balls, and would help out with coaching and umpiring once the league was organized, their schedule permitting. Dottie was to appear at Memorial Park with Marg Callaghan and Alice DeCambra on the first day of training, joining up with Ruby Heafner, Vivian Kellogg, and Faye Dancer, among others, later in the week.

The coaches also did their part to help the fledgling softball stars. Daddy Rohrer of Fort Wayne and Leo Murphy of the Racine Belles were on the bases for the championship tilt of the Girls' City Softball Tournament, which ran from July 31 to August 8. The final game was to be played at Memorial Park as a preliminary to the Daisies-Belles game. Fort Wayne Girls Ball Club president, Hans Mueller, said, "Fans should find the spectacle of baseball managers calling balls, strikes, and putouts an entertaining sight." He further stipulated, "Usually managers are the ones who beef about the umpires' decisions. This will be an opportunity for managers Rohrer and Murphy to put the shoe on the other foot." At the conclusion of the tournament, the Daisies and Mueller would cosponsor "the President's Trophy" to be presented to the winning team. The gold trophy would permanently remain in the park of the winner.

The rest of the 1947 season saw the Daisies battling the Kenosha Comets for the bottom rung of the ladder. The best they managed in the standings was sixth place for a short time in mid–August, although Rockford soon knocked them down a rung to the second-to-last spot. Still, Dottie hurled a three-hitter against the Blue Sox on July 9 for a Daisy win of 2–0 and a six-hitter against the Chicks a week later. In the game against the Chicks, though, Dottie's teammates could not seem to make it across the bag, and the Daisies lost 1–3. By this point in the season, the Daisies knew that any chance of grabbing a berth in the four-team postseason playoffs was fast disappearing. A tough loss to Muskegon on July 20, in which Dottie pitched three hit-ball but had no runs to back her up, just about polished off any hopes for the season. Aside from the lack of run support, two Daisy errors cost Dottie that game, including one of her own when she fumbled Sara Reeser's sacrifice after walking Charlene Pryer. A great pitching duel between Dottie Collins and South Bend's Jean Faut later that month ended in another loss for the Daisies, although Dottie went from the second to the eighth inning without allowing a hit. However, her teammates again failed to score while the Sox backed up Faut with one run in the ninth.

A four-hit shutout over Peoria, a two-hit 2–1 win over Rockford, and another two-hit 2–1 win over Racine in early August rounded out what Dottie intended to be her last year in the big leagues. On August 13, the *News-Sentinel* announced that Dottie Collins would not return for the 1948 season. The day before the news of her retirement appeared in the *Sentinel*, Dottie helped the Daisies capture a series finale with Rockford, 4–3, by yielding nine hits and adding seven strikeouts to her total. In one of the last games of the season she produced a terrific three-hit shutout against South Bend, fanning ten batters and retiring 17 hitters over one stretch. Finally, she closed the 1947 season on September 2 by pitching the Daisies to their 45th win of the season with a 7–4 victory over the Grand Rapids Chicks. She added ten to her strikeout total in that game and walked just four hitters. It had been a grand stretch of time in Fort Wayne. In her three seasons with the Daisies, Dottie recorded 821 strikeouts in 994 innings during 135 games; her highest ERA in those three years was 2.32, and she averaged a winning percentage of .618.

Immediately after the last game of the '47 season, Dottie and Harvey started for California, intending to see if they wanted to make their home there. First on her agenda, though, was baseball. Dottie had convinced her teammate, Marg Callaghan, to come to California with her and Harvey so Marg could play ball with her for a few weeks in the California-Arizona League. After that, Marg would return to her home in Vancouver and Dottie would enter a new phase of her life as a full-time wife and later mother, or so she thought. What she did not bargain for was that the siren call of baseball would soon lure her back to the field.

Shortly after she returned to Inglewood, she received a letter from Max Carey, dated October 23. Carey began the letter by expressing his regrets that one of the "number one girls in the league" will be severing her connections with the All-Americans. He then proceeded to come to the point when he wrote, "I don't see why you cannot continue your relations with us by representing us in Southern California as a commissioner. I know you will be looking at a lot of girls off and on and when you feel that you would like to recommend a girl for the league please do so and you can earn yourself $100 per girl." Carey was an astute businessman. Dangling that sum of money before Dottie was almost a sure way to keep her in the loop of the league. Moreover, he offered to keep her on the "Mail Bag" list, a chatty newsletter put out between seasons to keep the girls informed about what their fellow leaguers were doing. In this way, he subtly enticed her with what she was missing, since what he would be missing if Dottie did not return for the 1948 season was one of the biggest draws of the league. Attendance in Fort Wayne had been 77,000 for the 1947 season, nine thousand below the 86,000 needed to break even. Questions had been raised as to whether Fort Wayne would host a team in 1948. While those doubts had been put to rest, losing Dottie Collins would give the Daisies a definite disadvantage for the next season, despite the acquisition of shortstop Dottie Schroeder from the Kenosha Comets and Kay Blumetta from the Peoria Redwings. As the *News-Sentinel* noted, "Collins' ... absence would be a severe blow to the Daisy cause and her presence in the fold greatly enhances Fort Wayne pennant hopes."

Carey's tactics worked, and in the next letter he sent Dottie he thanked her for her interest in scouting for the league and promised to keep in touch with what was happening with the All-Americans. As Carey probably suspected, scouting alone was not enough for Dottie, because before long she started to reconsider joining the league. First, she attempted to make some compromises in order to achieve a balance between her home life and the career she had so diligently nurtured. Writing to Max Carey in the spring of 1947, Dottie asked if she would be allowed to pitch only at home and not travel with the team when they were on the road. Carey reported that the league Board of Directors had expressed some reservations about endorsing this arrangement. Ultimately, Carey put the choice in the lap of the new Daisy manager, Dick Bass, with Carey intimating that perhaps

Bass would let her pitch one game during a road trip and then send her home. Although Bass was unable to comply with her wishes, the *Journal-Gazette* informed its readers in late April that Dottie had tentatively decided to join the team. On May 13, during a rain delay in the Daisies home opener, Dottie officially signed with the Fort Wayne Daisies, the "day's only ray of sunshine," according to the *News-Sentinel*.

Several changes appeared in the 1948 season for the league in general and the Daisies in particular. The most considerable of these was the introduction of overhand pitching. Reporting on spring training in Opa-Locka, Florida, on April 9, the *Journal-Gazette* called the change "revolutionary" and further contended that "overhand pitching put the final and official 'baseball' stamp on the game which in five years had made the All-American Girls Baseball League internationally famous." While Grand Rapids manager Johnny Rawlings and league president Max Carey both predicted that eliminating pitching restrictions would open opportunities for girls with strong arms who were not proficient in other positions, overhand pitching actually forced many girls to leave the league.

Dottie pointed out that when the league first began it was not that different from the softball that the girls were used to playing. "Most of the girls left the league and went back to playing softball because they felt that this wasn't the thing for them ... we kept changing, see, as we went along," she said. "They were like me to a certain extent since they didn't have the ability to go to short or second or third." Yet those girls that quit the league also differed from Dottie. Dottie acclimated herself to the overhand style just as easily as she had to the side-arm delivery in 1946. The Daisies' program for 1948 gave a short blurb on Dottie that read, in part, "Dottie's ... using a wide side-arm delivery has resulted in one of the most effective deliveries seen in All-American Girls' League competition." Dottie's ability to adapt so easily to changing conditions gives a true measure of her innate athleticism. Another good indicator is that no one taught Dottie how to throw overhand. She taught herself.

Other changes in the game included extending the base lines two feet, to 72 feet, and moving the pitching mound five feet farther back from home plate, to 48 feet. The league had also decided to expand, adding teams in Springfield and Chicago, both in Illinois. As with Milwaukee and Minneapolis in 1944, the larger cities would prove inhospitable as host cities, the Sallies and the Colleens disbanding after one year and taking to the road as rookie touring teams. In spite of that, these changes indicated the league's commitment to growth. That the league would reach its peak in 1948 and thereafter begin a downward spiral no one could know, but at least every effort was made to keep women's baseball alive and well. The individual teams reflected this as well.

The first major change the Daisies made in 1948 was the appointment of a full-time business manager. The Daisies' board of directors knew that if they were to succeed after three seasons they would need a businesslike operation year-round, not just during the season. This was especially important since only Fort Wayne, of the eight league cities, failed to make a profit in 1947. To this end, they chose Ernie Berg, a former secretary to the City of Fort Wayne's Trucking Association, as business manager. Berg's duties included hiring groundskeepers, umpires, and other personnel, running the box office, getting the programs printed, and primarily public relations and advertising.

Ernie's daughter, Judy Widen, remembered her father cooking up all sorts of pregame events that drew people to the park, events such as fireworks on the Fourth of July, long ball hitting competitions, and special ladies' nights, when women could attend the games for free. Ernie also talked to civic clubs during the winter months, constantly drumming up patronage for the team. Periodically, he even took the place of a sportswriter and wrote the play-by-play stories himself if one of the reporters could not make the game. "After we closed up the park and locked the gates," Judy recalled, "we would race downtown to the offices of the *Journal-Gazette* and drop off the story. What a wonderful childhood I had growing up with the Daisies."

There were changes not only behind the scenes in the Daisy organization but in the more visible positions as well. The Daisies chose Dick Bass as manager for the 1948 season. Bass had played minor league baseball for several years and then began his major league baseball career on September 21, 1939, for the Washington Senators. He ended his big-league endeavor that same day after pitching one game against Cleveland, due to some mix-up in the deal that brought him up from the minors. In 1942, Bass was so badly injured in a defense plant explosion that for more than a month doctors wondered if he would live. Not only did he defy death, but he later came back to pitch fourteen straight wins in 1947 for the Kingsport, Tennessee, farm club of the Washington Senators in the Class D Appalachian League, prior to which he operated a school for pitchers and catchers for the Washington Senators.

In the winter of 1948, Bass had attended the minor league meeting in Miami, Florida. There he met up with Bert Niehoff, now the chief scout for the New York Yankees and formerly the manager of the South Bend Blue Sox from 1943–1944. Niehoff told Bass about the managerial opening in Fort Wayne, and because Bass respected Niehoff's judgment he went to the city to meet with Daisy officials. Soon he had signed a contract with the Fort Wayne entry in the All-American Girls Professional Baseball League. The team also hired Fort Wayne native Geraldine Reiber as chaperone. Reiber was a graduate of North Side High School, the home of the Daisies' first playing field, Harvey's alma mater, and the school that Dottie's children and grandchildren would attend.

In Dottie's first appearance of the 1948 season, she pitched four-hit ball to lead her team to a 5–2 triumph against the Springfield Sallies in Memorial Park on May 18. Moving on to Rockford, she hurled a six-hitter three days later against the powerful Peaches and handed her team a 5–2 Daisy win. Her teammates backed her up with an eight-hit attack for her second win in as many starts. After a few successful relief stints, Dottie suffered her first loss of the season in game one of the series against the Lassies in Muskegon on May 25, although she held the Lassies to just three hits and recorded seven strikeouts. Both teams were hitless until the seventh inning, with a brilliant pitching duel waged between Collins and Nancy Warren of the Lassies. In the last game of the Muskegon series, Dottie finally beat the Lassies, with the four-for-four performance of Mary Rountree contributing to a dynamic Daisy attack of twelve hits. The win gave the Daisies an even break in the match with Muskegon and edged them closer to the top of the standings.

A doubleheader win in South Bend, one of the victories behind Dottie's 2–0 shutout, brought the Daisies to within three and a half games of the league-leading Grand Rapids Chicks by the beginning of June. After taking an entire three-game series from the Peoria Redwings, with Dottie getting credit for the 8–5 win in the final battle on June 4, the Daisies went on to meet the number one Chicks at Memorial Park. In the crucial first game on June 9, Dottie spun a six-hitter with seven strikeouts to win the opener against the Chicks with a score of 7–2. A small brouhaha erupted in the ninth inning when one of the umpires refused to give Dottie Collins a new ball, and Dick Bass stormed out of the dugout in protest. In the end, the umpire stuck to his original decision, and some rabid fans ran onto the field to argue with him after the game. The umpire quickly scuttled to the safety of the press box until the commotion died down, probably vowing never to make that mistake again.

Dottie's fantastic hurling again helped the Daisies beat the Chicks 10–1 when they met a week later in Grand Rapids. The Daisies staged a fourteen-hit attack behind Dottie's four-hit pitching. That win cut the Chicks' lead to just two games over the Daisies and brought Dottie's record to 8–1. A defeat at the hands of the Belles on June 23 brought Dottie's loss total to two, but she racked up her ninth win against the Chicago Colleens shortly after that, winning 8–3 in overtime on Sunday, June 27. Unfortunately, the Daisies did not play the Colleens on a Friday night. If they had, they would have been part of history. For the first time in the annals of television, a sponsor was found to telecast girls baseball, the Patricia Stevens, Inc. modeling school. The league announced that WBKB in Chicago would broadcast the home games played by the Chicago Colleens at Shewbridge Field on 74th and Aberdeen Streets on Friday nights. The Friday before the Daisies arrived in Chicago, WBKB televised the third women's baseball game when the Colleens played the South Bend Blue Sox. If only that trend to televise the games had continued, perhaps a wider audience would have developed and the league would have enjoyed a longer lifespan, although various factors, not just audience appeal, led to the league's ultimate demise.

After the series in Chicago Dottie picked up two more wins, one against the Redwings and the other against the Lassies in a game with the largest paid attendance in Fort Wayne that year, with 3,316 fans packing the stands in Memorial Park. Dottie dropped a game to the Sallies on July 8, the loss caused by Dottie's wild pitch and an error by the otherwise phenomenal shortstop Dottie Schroeder, but Dottie still held the top pitcher's spot in the league with an 11–2 record and .846 winning percentage at the beginning of July. In trying for her 12th victory, she suffered two consecutive defeats to the Sallies and the Peaches, respectively, but received credit for saving another game against the Sallies on July 14, finally grabbing an even dozen. A lucky number 13 for Dottie came on July 21 against the Blue Sox when she blanked the Sox for five innings on four hits, which made for a 5–4 Daisy win. The Daisies then went on the road and lost seven straight, four to the Belles and three to the Blue Sox. In the final game against South Bend, Dottie pitched beautifully up until the seventh inning when three errors, four singles, a stolen base, and a triple combined for five Blue Sox runs against the Daisies' four. The loss plummeted the Daisies from second place down to fourth in the league race.

Commenting on the team's misfortunes, the *News-Sentinel* noted that Kay Blumetta and Dottie Collins had been bearing most of the pitching burden that season. Yet only Dottie, her manager, and her catcher knew that she was carrying more than the bulk of the pitching duties. On August 1, 1948, after losing the first game of a doubleheader to Peoria in a brilliant pitching duel with Dottie Mueller, Dottie Collins announced her retirement from the game, at least temporarily. She was almost five months pregnant at the time, a fact that interestingly neither the *Fort Wayne Journal-Gazette* or the *News-Sentinel* made mention of, simply stating that Dottie would not be back for the rest of the season. Dottie's doctor was more progressive than the press and told her she was in good enough shape to continue pitching up to a certain point. "I had started playing ball when I found out that I was pregnant," Dottie recalled. "I knew eventually I would have to quit, but I was doing all right. I had Dick Bass awfully scared, though," she continued. "He'd keep saying, 'Are you all right? Are you all right?' And I got so tired of hearing that. But after that game with the Redwings, Dick and I started up towards the clubhouse and he said, 'How do you feel? Okay?' And I said, 'Yeah, but I think I've had enough.' And I did. Somehow or other I knew."

Dick Bass was not the only one who was nervous about Dottie pitching while pregnant. Mary Rountree, the future Dr. Rountree, remembered Dottie telling her she was expecting a child and thinking, oh Lord, help me. I need a line drive. "And so I used to start calling for her to pitch on the outside of the plate," Rountree said, "thinking if I pitch to the outside, they'd hit it to the right side of the field. And if I keep the pitch inside, they'd hit it way to the left side of the field and I wouldn't get anything in the center. I tried to keep the center of the field wide open so that nothing got a line drive back to her. I was a wreck," Rountree finished.

Dottie, on the other hand, was as unfazed about her condition as if she had been pitching with a common cold. She pitched 175 innings in 24 games in 1948 and left with a 2.01 ERA, 101 strikeouts, and a .619 winning percentage. As for the future, she knew she had to sit out the rest of her term, but she expected she would be coming back. "I really didn't think anything," she said. "I didn't know. I just assumed I'd go back to baseball. I didn't know anything else." Soon that would change, and she would learn many things that would move her beyond the diamond onto another field of dreams, but baseball was not ready to take its final bow in Dottie's life just yet.

Ladies Don't Grow Up to Play Baseball: 1950–1983

The *Journal-Gazette* heralded the start of the Daisies' 1950 season with the news that one of Fort Wayne's favorite stars would be returning to the mound. "Dottie Collins Returns to Daisies Firing Line," a headline in the newspaper proclaimed on April 22. The article reported that Dottie had been working out indoors, and she felt certain that she could regain her old form. If so, the Gazette predicted "she would be a great asset to the pitching staff, which otherwise shaped up about the same as last year." Dottie had sat out the 1949 season to try on the new role of motherhood, but once again baseball drew her back into its fold and she decided to go back for one more shot at professional ball. Dottie could not know at the time how demanding it would be committing to a number of baseball games in addition to caring for a child, plus the fact that she would be away from home several times a week during the season. However, to the delight of Daisy fans, for one more year Dottie would give herself to baseball.

What must have been especially difficult for Dottie was leaving her family to report to spring training, held that year in Cape Girardeau, Missouri. Training would be followed by nineteen exhibition games before the team returned to Fort Wayne. Since Dottie had been away from the game for a while, Max Carey, now at the helm of the Daisies, pampered Dottie somewhat during the initial training at Capaha Park. However, he need not have bothered. Dottie soon proved that her arm was just as strong as ever, even after a year's absence from the game. Sharing the pitching duties with Kay Blumetta in Centralia, Illinois, on May 5, she helped down the Lassies,

5–3, and followed that performance with a 9–0 shutout over the Racine Belles in Middletown, Ohio, just a few days later. Dottie worked the first five innings of the shutout and scattered five hits, with Blumetta coming on in the sixth to finish off Racine with only one more hit in the game.

Dottie's fine showings convinced the Daisy board of directors that she was more than ready to assume her duties for the club. Based on this fact, the Daisies announced the release of pitcher Donna Cook several weeks prior to the start of the season. Cook was traded to the Grand Rapids Chicks in an effort to distribute player talent evenly. Besides Dottie Collins, Millie Deegan, Kay Blumetta, and Maxine Kline rounded out the Fort Wayne pitching staff. They were an impressive foursome. The Daisies ended the exhibition series with nine wins in thirteen starts, and the *Journal-Gazette* noted that "Dottie Collins, on paper at least, looks as if she will be a winner. If she can turn in twelve or fifteen victories it will help mightily." While Phil Olofson of the *News-Sentinel* was more cautious, stating, "her value is debatable until she proves herself in early-season activity," Dottie's mound performances in 1950 clearly demonstrated that she could fulfill the *Gazette's* expectations and more.

Dottie suffered a minor setback in the last game of the series that opened the season on May 18 in Muskegon. In her first start that year, Dottie walked the first four batters she faced and then gave up a single. Maxine Kline entered the game at that point and received credit for the victory, giving the Daisies two games out of three over Muskegon. Dottie fared better in the last game of the Daisies' opening homestand against the Grand Rapids Chicks on May 23, her first appearance on the Memorial Park hill since July, 1948. Although she again had difficulty in locating the plate at first, she finally settled down and allowed only four hits for the rest of the game. A slew of Daisy runs seemed to steady her pitching, resulting in a 9–2 Daisy win. Bob Reed of the *Journal-Gazette* speculated, "Collins seems to need only to gain her old confidence to become a consistent winner." She found it when the Daisies met the Chicks in Grand Rapids on May 29, with an impressive one-hitter against the opposing team. The Daisies won that game 5–0, with Dottie pitching near-perfect ball. The only hit came in the seventh inning when Doris Satterfield, the Chicks' outstanding left fielder, smacked a single to center. Dottie walked six batters and struck out four.

That Dottie was able to combine baseball with motherhood, she attributed to the support of her family, specifically her mother-in-law,

Hetty Collins. Harvey's mother was a unique woman in many ways, and she knew all about overcoming adversity. As a child in Lone Oak, Arkansas, Hetty had suffered a severe illness that led to deafness at the age of ten. She continued with school in spite of her handicap, but quit after the seventh grade, finding it too difficult to cope. Despite these obstacles, she went on to marry and raise three boys, Thomas, Edward, and Harvey Lee. "Everybody loved Grandma Collins. She was the old-fashioned type of grandmother," Dottie reminisced. Ironically, Dottie would turn out to be one of the most atypical of grandmothers, being more concerned that her grandsons knew how to throw a ball properly than worrying over such domestic details as Hetty focused on. Coming into Hetty's house to pick her daughter up after a game, Dottie would notice long stockings on her baby, an accessory that Patty did not have on when Dottie dropped her off. "Her legs are cold. They need to be covered," Hetty would scold her daughter-in-law. "I'd say, 'Yes, Mom. Yes, Mom,'" Dottie remembered. "She was the best mother-in-law in the world."

Often times, Dottie would look up from the mound and see her mother-in-law and Harvey sitting in the stands, Patty tucked in between them, and all three cheering her on. It was only right that Patty should be there, since she was ushered into the world in a true baseball manner. The January, 1949, issue of the All-American Girls' newsletter, the *Mail-Bag*, declared that "a bright new star is on the horizon for the league in 1966!" The newsletter then provided a description of the birth announcement, the cover of which was adorned with a pink ball with bats extended over it. On the inside, babies either swung at pop-up balls or cavorted in full uniforms and gloves. The wording on the back of the announcement cleverly extended the baseball metaphor. Framed in the center of the card, the notice read "The birth of Patricia Lee on Wednesday, December 22, 1948 at Methodist Hospital Ball Park. Batting Average 6 lbs 12½ oz. Now Playing with the Pink Sox. Developing catching smile and pitching style. Pennant-type diapers used in training. Short-stop at hospital will be followed by a Home Run to 439 E. Taber, Ft. Wayne."

Now the fans had something else to latch onto, besides Dottie's phenomenal pitching feats. Many Daisy supporters took a vicarious interest in the players' lives, avidly following such happenings as the courtship and marriage between Harvey Collins and Dottie Wiltse. Judy Widen remembered this quite clearly. "Dottie and Harvey were the Fort Wayne equivalent of a celebrity match," she said. "They were both so popular and so physically attractive. Everybody in town was

The world is coming up Daisies as both Dottie and her two-year-old daughter, Patty, show off their twin pink Fort Wayne uniforms in 1950. (Courtesy of Dottie Wiltse Collins)

excited about their marriage and felt part of their romance." Now they had the chance to watch the antics of a darling little "Daisy," which added a fresh dimension to the game. So taken were the Fort Wayne faithful with the newest addition to Dottie's family that one woman made a miniature pink Daisy uniform for Patty to wear to the park. Perhaps Dottie received some added incentive as she watched a reflection of herself wink back at her from the stands.

It certainly seemed that way when she held the Peoria Redwings to two hits and fanned nine batters at Memorial Park on June 5, her fourth victory, 9–1. Well on her way to her fifth triumph in Peoria four days later, Dottie was summarily deprived of that win in the ninth when a four-run Redwing rally erased the 5–2 margin Dottie had going into the final frame. Still, she led the Daisy hurling staff by early June with four wins and one loss, with Maxine Kline's 5–3 record coming second. A subsequent win against Racine and a 13–1 shellacking against the Comets, in which Dottie allowed only six hits, gave her wins number five and six and an .857 winning percentage. The game with the Comets on June 19 was the fifth straight victory for the Daisies and increased their hold on first place in the league, with both South Bend and Rockford a game and a half back.

That lead lasted only a short time before the Sox knocked the Daisies into second place after they downed the Daisies two games straight. Counting on his ace to even the score, Max Carey sent Dottie to the mound when the Blue Sox came to town on June 23. The score would remain skewed in favor of the Sox, however, as Dottie lost that game, 4–7, before a crowd of more than 2500. The main problem was that the Daisies failed to bring runners home, leaving ten runners stranded in the last five innings of the game. Dottie made up for that loss on June 27 with a 1–0 victory over ace pitcher Mirtha Marreo of the Lassies, battling her opponents before a crowd of 1064 faithful fans who braved unseasonably cold weather to watch the Daisies play. It was the first shutout at Memorial Park that season and Dottie's third. She edged close to her 1946 strikeout record of sixteen batters, fanning twelve Lassies over the course of the game. She allowed only four runners to get on base, and just two of the four reached second base, with no one advancing beyond that. Another mound duel with Marrero came the next week in Kalamazoo, the Lassies having moved there from Muskegon in 1950, but this time Marrero came out on top with a 5–2 win over the Daisies.

The Daisies played that game under threat of suspension, as Fort Wayne had been ordered by league officials to transfer first basewoman

Vivian Kellogg and left fielder Betty Luna to Kalamazoo and they refused to do so. Fort Wayne and South Bend had offered to give up one player each to help the struggling Lassies, but only if Rockford, the dominant force in the league the past two seasons, followed suit. When league president Fred Leo then demanded that Fort Wayne relinquish two players, Fort Wayne's president, Harold Van Orman, "hit the ceiling," according to Phil Olofson of the *News-Sentinel.* Part of Van Orman's anger stemmed from the fact that Fort Wayne had been the first team to volunteer one of its players to strengthen the Lassies. Also, the team was engaged in a tight battle for first place, a battle that could be lost with the departure of two of its stars. This is turn could spell disaster for the financial success of team. In the end, the dispute was resolved when Betty Luna went to Kalamazoo for Fort Wayne native Sally Meier.

In addition to informing its readers of the Daisies' dilemma, the *News-Sentinel* also included a short paragraph comparing the length of Daisy games in 1949 to those in 1950. On average, the games lasted from six to eight minutes longer, according to reporter Phil Olofson. He attributed this change to the livelier ball, which caused AAGPBL pitchers to lose control as they tried for the corners and often missed. Several times during the season Dottie was pulled from games due to such wildness, as in the July 5 battle with the Chicks when she was tagged for three runs in the first inning and was pulled after walking the first batter in the second. On the other hand, the *Journal-Gazette* claimed that the pace of girls' baseball had quickened due to several factors. The *Gazette* noted, "During the past three seasons the game of girls baseball has advanced in great strides and cannot be classed in the same category as softball." The piece continued with the observation that the ball the girls used was only slightly larger than a regular baseball and the pitcher's mound was only five feet closer than the sixty feet used in men's baseball. Therefore, the article concluded, "With the smaller ball in use, the game of girls' baseball has speeded up immensely, both on offense as well as defense."

Girls' baseball had evolved from the time of its inception, and it was becoming increasingly clear that women could play the same type of strategic, thrilling game as men. Unfortunately, just as women's baseball was finally coming into its own, the death knell was sounding for the league. Total paid attendance for the league hit an all-time high of over 910,000 in 1948, but that year also marked the failure of the league to retain its two newest franchises, bringing the number of teams back down to eight by 1950. In 1951, the league would dismiss the overall management organization, making each team responsible for players, management personnel, and its own publicity and scouting. This signaled another downward slide as teams struggled to cover costs previously undertaken by Arthur Meyerhoff's corporation. Moreover, societal changes were making their inroads on the league.

The 1940s saw women streaming out of their homes into jobs never before considered the province of women. Rather than "Go West, Young Man," the slogan of the 1940s seemed to be "Seek Fulfillment, Young Woman." Now, with the advent of the 1950s, the emphasis had shifted to the nuclear family, which was seen as the bulwark against the chaos of the Depression and the Second World War. Those who reached adulthood during and after World War II married in unprecedented record numbers. In 1950, 66 percent of the population was married, compared to 23 percent who were single, with the remaining eleven percent either widowed or divorced. Interestingly, the All-American Girls Professional Baseball League had managed to defy those statistics up to that point.

The *Fort Wayne Journal-Gazette* noted this fact on April 8, 1950, in an article titled, "Marriage, Motherhood Grab the Gals." Reporter Bob Reed wrote that up to this point the league "had been singularly free [from], or at least not too badly handicapped, by what would be expected to be the most natural inroads into playing personnel—marriage and motherhood." Now, however, he asserted that "the law of averages had caught up with the AAGPBL and the gals are dropping out right and left." Citing several players who would not be back that year due to pregnancy or marital bliss, including Dottie's close friend Helen Callaghan Candaele, who was expecting her second child, he capped his piece with a quote from league president Fred Leo. Leo philosophized that the league couldn't expect anything different after seven years of operation. He ended with the comment that he and league officials are "proud and happy that these kids go on to the fulfillment of a worthwhile life, reaping the benefits that we know our game provides."

While this sentiment intimates that baseball afforded the players invaluable fundamentals for future life endeavors, which indeed it did, clearly this view conflicted with that of society's. The climate of the 1950s demanded that women guard the home and keep the worries of the world at bay. Little room existed for any kind of diversity in women's roles. In this atmosphere, the women of the AAGPBL seemed an anomaly, perhaps even a threat against the existing order. A caption underneath a newspaper photograph of several Daisies at the piano enjoying a songfest, taken in May, 1950, informed readers that "away from the demanding rigors of baseball and excited crowds, the Daisies enjoy the normal existence of other girls," as if the game they loved somehow put them outside the established norm.

The choices Dottie Collins made in her life reflected these two different time periods. Yet the choices she made were of her own volition and depended on neither societal or family pressure. When Dottie finally made the ultimate commitment to full-time motherhood, the decisions was hers alone. "I felt it was time to do something else," Dottie said. "I just had had enough." Harvey never pushed her into quitting baseball, either. "He was very supportive of me playing," Dottie said. "He never asked why I was leaving the game. He just fell into place with what I wanted." Dottie's decisions always marked a forward progression. Rather than sacrificing one way of life for another, she found fulfillment in both. Even when she switched from softball to baseball, she looked upon the move as an upward one. "The softball was when I was a kid," she said, "and the baseball was when I was an adult." When the professional softball teams in Chicago tried to tempt her into their ranks, she refused, partly because she felt it signified a step backwards from her baseball career.

As strong as Dottie was in her convictions, though, she must have struggled with some niggling doubts regarding her fitness as a mother during the period when she juggled parenthood and a career, an age-old dilemma that countless women continue to face. Even today, Dottie steadfastly affirms that she never reneged on her duties as a parent when she was playing baseball. "The only time I traded her for the baseball was when she was a baby," Dottie explained, almost in justification for what she had done. She reiterated this standpoint further by stressing, "And then I never went to all the games. Never went to all the games."

That Dottie returned to baseball at all despite the other responsibilities in her life showed her dedication to the sport. Once she came back to the game, she determined to give it her best. "I always said I made a big comeback," Dottie laughed. "And quit the next year." While she was playing ball that last year of her career, though, no one suspected from her performances that the combination of two demanding careers was slowly wearing her down. She posted a 13–8 record and a 3.46 ERA in 26 games. Even when she suffered a sprained side in early July, she came back after two weeks rest, refusing to use that ready-made excuse to exit the game gracefully. In her first game back after being sidelined, she held the Comets to four hits in the seven-inning opener of a doubleheader. Betty Weaver Foss, the league's batting champion in 1950 and 1951, backed her up with a home run in the fourth inning that cleared the right field fence and landed in front of the scoreboard. Foss missed out on another spectacular homer in the next inning when Jean Buckley leaped up and made a one-handed catch. Foss's hitting prowess was renowned. During spring training, Dottie had told her manager, Max Carey, that she would do whatever he wanted her to do, but she wouldn't pitch to Betty Foss. "I wanted my mouth left intact," Dottie said.

With the win against Kenosha, the Daisies notched their tenth straight victory and their 14th in the last 16 games, bringing them to the top of the AAGPBL standings. Dottie won her eighth game against the Lassies in Memorial Park on July 28, limiting the Lassies to six hits for a 7–3 Daisy win. Dottie also contributed two beautiful hits for her team, one of them driving in a run. Since she was known for her less than sterling hitting potential, she "...surprised everyone with those two safe blows," to quote the *Journal-Gazette*. She again won against the Lassies in Kalamazoo on August 1, but the second-place Comets won two games from Peoria and moved to within one and a half games of first place. With pitcher Kay Blumetta sidelined with a sore arm, Daisy manager Max Carey relied on Dottie perhaps more than he should have, calling upon her to pitch in the next series against Peoria on only two days' rest. Dottie collapsed in four and two thirds innings, walking eight and leaving the Daisies even more precariously perched on the top rung of the ladder with a 2–9 loss. A double loss to Rockford on August 5 and 6 brought the Daisies' lead down to half a game, with their bitter rival, Rockford, now just behind them in second place.

The battle intensified. The Peaches had grabbed the lead by the time the two teams next met at Memorial Park, edging out the Daisies by one game. However, the Daisies regained the lead in the league standings behind the exceptional pitching of Dottie Collins with a 6–3 defeat of Rockford on August 11. Dottie held Bill Allington's powerful Peaches to eight hits, and her teammates contributed a trio of two-run innings for the win. This was Dottie's second triumph over the Peaches, who had beaten her once that year. Probably Dottie did not feel as much pressure against the Peaches as some of her teammates, since much of the antagonism between the two teams stemmed from the previous year when she did not play. In 1949, the Peaches completely dominated the Daisies, winning the league championship in the process. The next year brought a reversal of roles, with the

Daisies holding an 8–5 advantage over the Peaches by the beginning of August. In addition, the resentment over Rockford's attitude when the Lassies asked for player assistance earlier in the season added fuel to the rapidly burning fire and helped heat up a most exciting race. For the first time since 1945, the Daisies' win column was significantly higher than their loss column, and they were in a good position to grab it all. On an individual basis, this was also to be Dottie's last chance for a piece of that pennant pie.

Towards the end of August, the Daisies were in the midst of a three-team fight for the league lead, with Kenosha creeping up on the Daisies. After Fort Wayne lost to Racine on August 19 and to Kenosha on August 20, Kenosha moved to one game in back of the Daisies, who trailed Rockford by half a game In a game against Racine on August 23, Dottie was on her way to another shutout, with a 5–0 lead, when the floodgates opened and the runs came pouring in. Maddy English started the rally with a single; then June Peppas walked and Betty Trezza singled to load the bases. Edie Perlick brought in the first run, and Irene Hickson walked to bring in the second. Joanne Winter's single sent two more runners over the plate to bring the Belles within one run of a tie. Just when things seemed to be looking up for the Daisies with a fantastic catch by Sally Meir, Meir threw the ball away trying for a double play, and two runners advanced. A single by English tied the score, and an error by Tiby Eisen determined that Racine would be the winner. Millie Deegan, who had pitched the first game of the twin bill, came in to relieve Dottie after that, but the damage was done and Racine won by a score of 6–5.

A week after that fateful game with Racine, another ninth-inning collapse seemed imminent, but this time Dottie came through with the victory. Again she pitched superb ball, and again she went into the final frame with a potential shutout, with the Daisies leading the Comets 4–0. However, a double, a walk, and a single filled the bases, after which two runs scored. With the tying runs on second and third, Dottie ended the heart-stopping inning behind some great defensive fielding by Evie Wawryshyn, pushing the Comets three games back from the Daisies and four games from the lead. By August 28, a Rockford loss at Kalamazoo and a rainout in Fort Wayne launched the Daisies to the top of the loop by half a game. Their lead was short-lived as a defeat at the bats of the Belles on the last day of August put them one game back of the Peaches and gave Dottie her eighth defeat. She pitched an otherwise brilliant game, striking out twelve batters in a row from the third inning to the eighth. According to the *News-Sentinel*, "a herculean effort by the Daisies is necessary if they are to overtake the Peaches." In other words, the Daisies would have to win six of their remaining seven games to finish on top, although they were practically assured of a playoff spot. The Daisies managed to grab the league lead by half a game going into one of the final games of the season and bolstered that position by winning both games of a doubleheader against the Blue Sox at Memorial Park on September 2. Dottie hurled four-hit ball in the opener and sent a runner home with a wonderfully executed drag bunt. The next day, however, the Sox got even and knocked the Daisies out of first place with a 6–1 win, while the pesky Peaches blanked Peoria, 2–0.

The final standings deprived the Daisies of the pennant, with Rockford on top by two games, but they earned a spot in the playoffs, which would begin on September 5. The first-place team, Rockford, would play the third-place Kenosha Comets. The second-place Daisies would play the fourth-place Grand Rapids Chicks. The winners of each three-of-five series would go on to compete against each other in the final four-of-seven match. Since the Daisies and the Peaches had secured the top two spots in the standings, each would host the opening game of their respective series. Max Carey chose Dottie Collins as the starting pitcher for the first game of the playoffs. As usual, Carey knew whom he could count on in the clutch, even though Dottie had lost five out of seven of her last starts. Carey's judgement was correct. After the game, the *News-Sentinel* reported that "the willowy right-hander came up with one of her brightest pitching performances in Tuesday night's opener, throttling the Chicks with a six-hitter for a 4–0 victory." It was her second shutout against the Chicks that season.

The teams split the two games in Fort Wayne when the Daisies lost to the Chicks on Wednesday night, 4–3. They then moved on to Michigan, where the Daisies beat the Chicks in game three. In the fourth game, Collins again came through with the win, sending the Daisies into the final stretch against their old nemesis, the Rockford Peaches. Dottie held Grand Rapids to four hits, walked two, and struck out five to wallop the Chicks 14–3. The only runs from the opposing team came in the first inning, two of those the result of Dottie's wild throw to third on a pickup bid. Tiby Eisen's three hits, a double and two singles, dominated the eleven-hit Daisy attack, but the twelve walks by three Chicks pitchers, Marge Silvestri, Earlene "Beans" Risinger, and Mildred Earp, did not hurt either. After the game, the Daisies left for Rockford, the site of the first two games of the championship series. Both the Daisies and the Peaches won the first round by the same margin, three games to one.

In the second round, Rockford won the opener on Saturday night, September 9, 3–1. Maxine Kline was the loser, tagged for fifteen hits. The Daisies' only run came in the first inning on a double, a single, and an error. Sunday's game was called in the second inning due to rain, but the Peaches dried themselves off and won Monday's game 7–2. AAGPBL officials declared that the third, fourth, and fifth games would be played in Fort Wayne, partly because the Peaches' park would not be available later in the week and also to reduce the stress of travel, since the two cities were over a hundred miles apart.

The confines of Memorial Park were more friendly to the Daisies. They beat Rockford 7–3 behind the combined pitching of Dottie Collins and Millie Deegan. Dottie started out well, allowing one hit to thirteen batters in the first four innings. Her teammates came through for her with five runs, two on Vivian Kellogg's double down the first base line and two on Kate Vondereau's hit into right field. The *News-Sentinel* noted, "according to the accepted standards of baseball, Collins should have been relaxed and comforted by the 5–0 bulge," but "instead she collapsed like a tent in a hurricane." She walked three batters in a row in the fifth inning and served Lois Florreich a fantastic pitch that Florreich sent to left center to bring two runs across the plate. After Dottie Key became the fifth straight batter to get on base, which accounted for a third Rockford run, Carey pulled Collins and brought in Millie Deegan to retire the side. Deegan held the Rockford attack at three for the next two innings, and the Daisies scored two more runs in those innings to increase their lead by four. In the eighth inning, with the Peaches at bat and two outs on the scoreboard, Lady Luck smiled on the Daisies when the game was called because of rain. Whether or not Rockford could have come from behind was a moot point for the Daisies.

The Daisies also won the fourth game of the series, 5–3, to even up the match, but the Peaches handed the Daisies a heartbreaking loss in game five. It all started in the eighth inning when a spectacular catch by Rockford's Jackie Kelley and an unsuccessful steal by Dottie Schroeder deprived the Daisies of the run that would have made an extra inning unnecessary. That extra inning proved to be the Daisies' undoing. In the tenth inning, with one batter out, Dottie Collins hit Dottie Key with a pitch. Key moved to second on Dottie Kamenshek's sacrifice, and Snookie Doyle was walked intentionally.

Now, with runners on first and second, Jackie Kelley smacked a ball right to the pitcher's mound. Dottie Collins was unable to stop the ball but deflected it off between short and third. Unfortunately, Dottie Schroeder, the Daisy shortstop, had moved towards second and couldn't catch up with the ball in time to get Key out at the plate in what seemed to be the battle of the Dotties. Another bad break came when Jackie Kelley, now on first, tricked Collins into throwing to second base in anticipation of Kelley's steal. That allowed Snookie Doyle to come home, and also proved to be the winning run. A rally in the bottom of the tenth, in which the Daisies brought one run across, was halted by a Rockford double play when Dottie Schroeder attempted to bring Betty Foss home from third with a squeeze play. Instead, the bunt resulted in a pop-up to Nicky Fox, who then doubled Foss off third to end the game. Up until the fateful tenth Dottie had pitched well, holding the Peaches to seven hits and walking four, but the Peaches ended up on top, 4–3.

With the Peaches leading the series, three games to two, the teams returned to Rockford for the final two games of the playoffs, should both be necessary. This time, Rockford's home field proved more amenable to the Daisies as they blanked the Peaches 8–0. Maxine Kline was the winner, with Betty Foss's bases-loaded home run in the third inning giving Fort Wayne a much needed extra edge. Now, with the series tied at three games apiece, Dottie's swan song was about to begin. As she took the mound for the Daisies in the crucial seventh game of the series, after Millie Deegan's wildness put her out of the game in the third, Dottie Collins wound up for her final two innings of professional ball. She held the Peaches to a pair of hits in those two innings, but the Daisies as a whole just could not pull themselves together. They knocked out eleven hits but left ten runners stranded on the bases, compared to the Peaches' eleven hits and four stranded runners, resulting in a 11–0 Rockford win. It was Rockford's third consecutive championship and the second year in a row that they beat the Daisies for the league title.

It was a tough way for Fort Wayne to end the season, but what was more lamentable was that Dottie left the game without ever touching the brass ring, a disappointment to say the least. In the end, though, that was not what really mattered. Like other baseball greats who never achieved the ultimate prize, such as Ted Williams, Ernie Banks, and the man behind Donnie baseball, Don Mattingly, Dottie's reward stemmed from the games well played, the talent well used, and the deep appreciation for the chance to play ball. What a spectacular ride Dottie enjoyed for six seasons of play. She had pitched in over 1600 innings in 223 games. She struck out 1205 batters and walked 673. The number of games she won totaled 117 compared to 76 losses for a winning percentage of .606. Her lifetime ERA in the All-American Girls Professional Baseball League was an impressive 1.83.

Probably, Dottie picked the right time to leave the game, as the league folded after the 1954 season. While a variety of factors led to the league's collapse, such as the advent of television, the end of gas rationing, which meant people could take advantage of diverse forms of entertainment, and the abolishment of the overall management structure, one major factor was the lack of an adequate farm system. The league found new recruits through the tryouts each city held in the spring and also picked up some talent as the teams barnstormed their way back to the Midwest from spring training camp. Certain teams also had their own miniature farm team. During the 1951 season in Fort Wayne, for example, the Future Daisy League was organized to give teenage girls the opportunity to play girls' baseball. They played in a supervised league and followed the same rules laid down by the All-American Girls' League. The idea for this league came about through the efforts of the Daisy Fan Club, whose aim was to foster a closer relationship between the fans and the Daisy organization and to bolster enthusiasm for the team.

However, none of these efforts were enough without a more comprehensive system. "They couldn't get enough new girls coming in," Dottie said. "The ballplayers got older and started retiring and no one took their place. That was what really caused the league to fold, in my opinion." Another problem, according to Dottie, was the lack of discipline in the later years of the league. "It got to the point where you couldn't control the girls any more," she said. "Where with us, if they told us to sit, we sat." Dottie also cited the special set of circumstances that produced the league. "It was wartime," she said. "We needed baseball and the country needed us." It seems regrettable, therefore, that not only did the league itself cease to exist for almost thirty years but the memory of it did as well.

In those intervening years between the league's demise and its rise from obscurity, Dottie settled down to raise her family. Her son, Daniel, named in honor of Dottie's father, was born in 1954, so now she had two young lives to nurture and mold. In a cruel twist of fate, Dan Wiltse passed away of a sudden heart attack shortly after the birth of his namesake. He was only in his fifties. Dottie remembered the telephone call from her mother in the middle of the day, relaying the unexpected news and summoning her back to California. She also recalled how frantic she was trying to catch the first plane going out west. "Harvey couldn't get off work immediately, so he put me on a plane with two kids," Dottie said, clearly envisioning the scene even after many years. "And that airplane took off and I forgot the diapers, I forgot the milk, I forgot everything." What she never forgot, though, were the special moments she and her father shared, the most memorable of which involved baseball.

"I think the biggest thrill of my dad's life was when he came back here to Fort Wayne, that had to be around 1950, I guess, the last time he was here, and we took him to a Yankee game," Dottie said. Since no baseball teams existed on the West Coast until after Dan's death, he chose the New York Yankees as his "home" team, the team on which his idol and fellow Californian Joe DiMaggio played. He followed the Yankees first on radio and later, to the delight of Dottie and Harvey when they came to visit, on television. "The screen was about as big as a matchbox cover, but we thought it was great," Dottie said. Yet Dan never saw a major league game in person until that summer he visited his daughter in Indiana. His exhilaration as he watched his favorite team from the stands is understandable. After years of honing his own skills on the field and then helping his daughter develop hers, he finally had the opportunity to experience firsthand that electrically charged atmosphere that can only come from sitting just a few feet away from the field, where the consummate athletes perform for the delight of the fans.

Luckily, Dan enjoyed himself thoroughly at the game, since he was less than taken with the environs of the Midwest. He and Dottie's mother had come to Fort Wayne several times to watch Dottie's games when she played in the All-American Girls League, but they usually never stayed that long before returning to California. That summer they extended their stay, probably to have more time with their only grandchild, who was now almost two years old. Dan occupied himself by laying out a sidewalk for Dottie so it would be easier for her to bring the garbage out to the back alley and puttering around in the yard, Harvey "not knowing what a hammer was," according to his better half. At one point Dan told his daughter, "You people work all summer long to get a nice lawn and flowers and the whole works, and then the snow comes and it's all gone. If I lived in this god-forsaken country I wouldn't have any lawn or anything. I'd cement the whole goddamn thing."

Dottie stayed close to baseball in the 1950s, following the Yankees as often as possible, usually when the Yankees were playing in Cleveland or Detroit. During one trip to Detroit, Dottie and Harvey stayed in the same hotel as the players. The Yankees were on a losing streak, and some of the New York press had come to Detroit to report on the hapless team. Dottie remembered sitting in the hotel bar with Harvey and listening to the reporters interview the Yankee manager, Casey Stengel. "It was the most interesting night I spent in a bar because they were all over Casey Stengel," Dottie remarked. "It was a real education to sit there and listen to him answer their questions." Dottie also got to meet Mickey Mantle, her favorite Yankee, using some family connections she had never called on before.

Dottie's uncle on her mother's side was the one who grew up in San Francisco and became friends with the legendary Billy Martin, later buying a tavern with him. Martin played for the Yankees from 1950–1957, so he was with the team on that road trip to Detroit. The second night the Yankees were in town, Dottie got her courage up and called his room. "Martin answered the phone," Dottie remembered, "and I told him who I was, and he thought that was great. He said, 'We'll meet you downstairs in the lobby.'" Dottie and Harvey found Martin and Mickey Mantle in front of the magazine rack, and they quickly struck up a conversation. Both of the ballplayers were especially interested in the fact that Dottie had played with the All-American Girls League, which Dottie found to be true of many other major leaguers she encountered over the years as well. She also recalled another part of their discussion, this one involving Billy Martin's particular passion. "Billy Martin was a nut on cowboys and Indians," she said. "That was the one thing he lived for. He wanted to be a cowboy with guns and shoot everybody, he said. It was really funny. Mantle was real quiet. Didn't have much to say. But it was interesting to meet them," she finished.

Aside from following her Yankees and experiencing the joys of motherhood, Dottie found something else to occupy her time and to keep her athletic abilities well oiled as well. The birth of this new-found interest took place in a family tavern where Dottie and Harvey usually spent Saturday nights. Mostly they had a few beers and played pool and shuffleboard, meeting up with a few other couples, including Gert and Charles (Mac) McAtee. Mac and Harvey had been good friends all through high school and had returned from service in World War II at about the same time. Now married and with families, they retained their friendship through a mutual interest, the game of golf. At one of these weekly get-togethers in 1956,

Gert and Dottie decided they were tired of listening to their husbands' incessant talk of their glowing golfing feats, so the very next day they headed to Foster Park and took to the links. One of Dottie's first shots hit a tree and landed behind her, but she was a natural athlete and soon caught on to the game. "Dottie was good at golf from the beginning," Gert remembered, "once she learned to get a golf grip on the club and not grip it like a baseball."

That did not take long. After a couple of years of practice, Harvey and Mac convinced the girls to join the Ladies of the Elks Golf Group, both of them playing in the men's league through the Elks. Harvey had always loved the game of golf and often caddied when he was young. Sometimes he even hitchhiked to the Fort Wayne Country Club and camped out overnight to get the best jobs when play started in the morning. Now an active participant at the Elks Club, Harvey encouraged his wife to realize her own potential on the greens, in the same way he had stood behind her during her baseball years. "Harvey liked an independent woman," Dottie said. "He was a very confident man." Because Harvey was so comfortable with himself, he could let his wife be her own person and so both could grow in their own unique ways. Soon, Dottie was chalking up golf championships just as quickly as she had accumulated wins on the mound.

Dottie emerged onto the competitive golf scene in Fort Wayne in 1958, going up against other golfers to compete for a place in the city tournament. Those designated to vie for the title of city champion were chosen from qualifying flights known as Medal Play, with the lowest 16 scorers going into what was known as the championship flight. The next lowest 16 scorers went into the first flight and the next group into the second flight, with a continuation down the line. The lowest 16 scorers were called The Sweet 16, and they moved into Match Play, where each golfer would play one opponent. The 16 were reduced to eight the first day, the eight cut in half the second day, the four being pared down to two the third day, and the main winner coming through on day four. Dottie made the Sweet Sixteen in 1958 and in every year thereafter in which she competed. Dottie shot in the 90s in her first match play, but by 1962 she was shooting in the 80s.

Prior to that, she made up part of the winning team at the Ladies-Pro Tournament at the Orchard Ridge Country Club in 1961, and she was an 18-hole medalist in the Ladies of Elks Golf Association Handicap Tournament in 1963. The following year, she reached a pinnacle in the Women's City Golf Tournament when she made it to the final round. Although she lost to three-time winner Pat McGary, she played well, with a two-over-par 41 on the front nine. According to Jim Costin of the *Fort Wayne News-Sentinel,* "Now Dottie Collins knows how Arnold Palmer felt after the PGA Tournament a few weeks ago. Palmer played as well as he is capable in that tourney and still lost to Bobby Nichols." Dottie proved to be a gracious loser, even quipping to McGary on the seventh tee, "You don't have to be so thorough about it, do you?" Florence Watson, the Ladies of the Elks publicity chairwoman, commented on Dottie's fine sense of competition, and the *Sentinel* noted that it was difficult to tell the winner from the loser by the smile on Dottie's face. This attitude most definitely stemmed from her days on the diamond, when she learned not only the art of baseball but the meaning of sportsmanship as well.

Of course, the concept of sportsmanship also embraced the adage "don't get mad, get even," which Dottie did in 1969 when she knocked out Pat McGary in the semifinals to qualify for the finals for the second time in her golfing career. In this tournament, Dottie met another of Fort Wayne's premier female golfers, Pat Wright. Wright had expected she would play a battle of the Pats with Pat McGary, but Dottie had come a long way in five years and she had another scenario mapped out. Wright, who had won the title eight times already, qualified with an 80 and Dottie shot 81. Par for women at that time at the Brookwood Golf Club was 79. As sports columnist Jim Costin mentioned, "Dottie Collins, the former pitcher, was not only pitching but also driving and putting quite well, too, yesterday."

Unfortunately, Dottie was not putting or driving quite enough. Wright won the championship, registering a 3 and 2 victory over Dottie on the sixteenth hole. Yet she emphasized what a tough and determined competitor Dottie was. One shot in particular she remembered from that tournament in 1969. "We were playing a par 3 hole about 140 yards long," Wright recalled. "Dottie's first shot was resting at the bottom of a hill and she could only see the tip of the flagpole. Still, she hit a 40-foot pitch shot right in the hole for a birdie two. She won that hole because I only had a par." Wright also talked about the two other times she played against Dottie in city tournament matches. "I won both matches by only 1 up, which meant we went the whole 18 holes. I was either 1 up going into 18, or we were even after 17 and I won in 18. Now that is pressure," she said. During one match there was a rain delay and both Dottie and Pat Wright were interviewed by Hilliard Gates, a radio and television sportscaster. Wright remembered that when Gates asked Dottie to compare the competition between baseball and golf, Dottie replied, "Well, in baseball it's more of a team effort, but in golf you are all on your own." And all alone she did just fine.

Just two years later, in 1971, the newspaper headlines declared, "Dottie Collins Captures Women's City Golf Title." Dottie posted a 2 and 1 victory over Barbara Banet at the Elks Country Club that year. Harvey had won the men's city golf tournament in 1958 at the Fort Wayne Country Club, making them the only husband and wife team to have won city golf championships in Fort Wayne. Dottie had to rally to seize the title, though, as Banet was one up at the turn. Dottie then won the next three holes, and Banet dropped a three-foot putt for a birdie on the twelfth. After Dottie went in front on a par at 14, Banet lost the sixteenth and Dottie managed a half on the seventeenth for the win. By now, Patty was married with her first child, David, so the newspaper headlines proclaimed Dottie the "Golfing Grandmother."

"Grandma" continued her fine golfing feats throughout the 1970s and into the 1980s. In 1980, she again made the final match in the city golf tournament. Dottie had not planned on playing in the city tournament that year, thinking she would sit out one summer of golf and instead work as a hostess at her brother-in-law's restaurant, The Pickle, located in downtown Fort Wayne. She had played just two eighteen-hole rounds of golf that summer, yet her 90 was the highest score to make the championship flight. "I just never thought I would make it to the final with all these young kids in the tournament," said Dottie, who was almost 57 years old at the time. "I didn't even intend to play in the city tournament, but since it was the fiftieth anniversary I figured what the heck," she said. Ever the warrior, she walked the entire 18 holes for the first time in five years, although by now she was having a problem with her legs. However, she claimed that her concentration on the game improved if she walked the course rather than take a cart, and of course it was the game that mattered most.

In 1999, Dottie reached the ultimate in golfing glory when she was honored as Celebrity of the Year at the Celebrity Golf Tournament sponsored by the Benevolent and Paternal Organization of Elks. She was the first woman to receive the award. Seated in the front of the audience with various other local celebrities, Dottie once again basked in the glow of athleticism well rewarded. A collective gasp went around the room when the master of ceremonies, citing Dottie's lifetime achievements in golf, announced that she had won the Elks Club Golf Championship nineteen years in a row. For that amazing record, she also received a standing ovation. It is a true measure of her skill as an athlete that she not only achieved competence in two different sports but excelled in them as well.

She also proved herself as a bowler, carrying an impressive 170 average at the end, darn good for a woman, or a man for that matter, according to Dottie's friend and bowling partner, Gert McAtee. Gert and Dottie took up the game at the suggestion of the women they golfed with at the Elks. After golf season it seemed everyone needed some physical activity in their lives, and with the inclement weather in the Midwest during the winter months, bowling seemed like the ideal choice. Dottie first joined a league at Scott's Bowling Lanes, named for former New York Yankees pitcher Everett Scott Senior, an appropriate place for Dottie to begin her newly chosen sport. Dottie and Harvey, along with Gert and Mac, later became good friends with Everett Scott Junior and his wife, Sally.

The decades of the 60s and 70s also were a time of mentoring for Dottie, a role she took on inadvertently when she played baseball and one she assumed voluntarily in the middle years of her life. Few opportunities existed for women in school sports during the 1950s and 1960s, so young girls relied on people like Dottie to cultivate their interests. Through her membership in the Elks, Dottie organized junior golf leagues. "We had three leagues," Dottie said, "and we used to fill the golf course." Children around six or seven years of age started with five-hole golf. Those children who were a little older played up to nine holes, while the teenagers took on the entire 18 holes. Every Monday the course was cleared for junior league play, and the women from the Elks' golf league accompanied the little ones on their rounds. Dottie related the story of a woman quite a bit older than she at the time, who took Dottie's daughter, Patty, and Patty's friend, Sue McAtee, Gert and Mac's daughter, out onto the course. "She came in and told me I would never believe what happened," Dottie said. "When I asked her what, she told me that they didn't play much golf but they had a wonderful time chasing the squirrels. I had a good laugh out of that. They went off to play golf and ended up chasing squirrels."

Aside from the initial organizing, Dottie's duties included handling the paperwork for the leagues, such as the scheduling and handicaps. Often she helped arrange tournaments so the various clubs could compete against each other. In addition, Dottie was involved with the Elks' junior bowling league. Whereas the original Elks Club had only a few lanes, the new one was quite a bit larger, so more children could take advantage of the sport. Dottie calculated the averages and did other paperwork, but more importantly she was the force behind getting the league started in the first place. Both boys and girls benefitted from Dottie's desire to open opportunities for others as they had been opened for her, as attested to by a letter from one young bowler. "Dear Mrs. Collins," he wrote, "Thank you for making a bowling league so my friends and my brother and I could bowl. Bowling is my favorite sport. I wish I could bowl every day. But I can't because my mother and father are too busy," he concluded.

Dottie's involvement in youth sports also allowed her quality time with her children. Patty remembered her parents as strict but involved. Patty and her mother often made up a golf foursome with Gert and Sue McAtee, going back to either Dottie's house or Gert's afterwards for Kentucky Fried Chicken and Dutch apple pie. Patty recalled how much fun she had on the golf course overall, especially the time she played in the Junior City Tournament. Dottie always chuckled over that story because Patty's second-place win was 24 strokes behind the first-place winner, although Dottie admitted the winner was one terrific golfer. Nevertheless, Dottie was pleased that Patty enjoyed the game so much and that she had reached her own personal milestone. Her son, Dan, however, was another story. While Patty could hold her own with golf and bowling, Dan was more of a natural, especially when it came to golf.

From the time he was a little boy, between five and seven years old, Dan spent whatever time he could at the putting green at the golf course. The hedge was so much higher than he was that no one could see him. Whenever Patty and Sue were asked to look after him while their parents played golf, they found their job an easy one, since all Dan wanted to do was putt the entire time. He even putted the men for money and often put a few coins in his pocket for his efforts. Dan also played baseball when he was young, but Dottie told him to choose either baseball or golf, and Dan chose golf. "I've always been one of those people to let their kids do their own thing and try to guide them instead. Harvey was the same way. He was close to his children, but they made their own decisions." Forcing Dan to focus on one sport ensured the singular devotion needed to excel at any serious endeavor, something Dottie had learned from her own father.

The effort paid off when Dan won a scholarship to Lake City Junior College in Florida in 1972 for golf course management. Jim Costin of the *News-Sentinel* had predicted such accolades would come for Dan in the column he wrote the year before when Dottie won the city championship title. In that article, Costin began by informing his audience that Dottie's city championship title came about partly because of a tip from her 17-year-old son. It seemed that the day before the final match, Dottie was having difficulty with her chipping. Dan told his mother to use a 9-iron instead of her wedge for short chips and she would have better luck. He turned out to be right. Later in the article, when Costin referred to Harvey's city title win in 1958, he went on to say "And the way son Dan has been playing, he's sure to be a serious city threat in the not too distant future."

Dan left for college in August 1972, with a friend of his from Fort Wayne. During his two years at Lake City College, he collected several golf trophies, including the most improved golfer award and the 1973 golf letterman award. Returning to his home town after he graduated from college, he found different jobs at several golf courses in the Fort Wayne area. Finally, in 1983, a wonderful opportunity opened for him when a friend from college offered him a job as an assistant pro at a golf course near New York City. Sadly, Dan never had the chance to take him up on the offer. Riding home as a passenger with one of his friends, Dan was the victim of a terrible car accident. He was just 29 years old. It was a tragedy no parent should have to endure, but Dottie called upon something inside herself, perhaps that fierce concentration she perfected on the mound, and battled her way through the most difficult trial of her life.

Many people recalled the way Dottie endured during that time, including her good friend, Gert McAtee. "I was surprised how strong she was, because she adored her kids," Gert said. "I guess she just wouldn't let down in public. Too strong," she concluded. Her childhood friend, Barbara Hoffman, also remembered that time well. "I always admired Dottie for the way she handled the death of their son," Barbara said. "I know it was an awful time in their lives when that happened. But she was able to go right on and keep up with her work and never let it get her down." Yet during times of difficulty providence often shows its hand, and we find revealed what we need just when we need it most. For Dottie, that meant baseball. In the years following Dan's death, Dottie's devotion to the game she loved led her not to the playing field but to reviving the memory of the feats performed on that field by a league that had been too long forgotten. That such positive results flowed from her efforts paid tribute to her son's life as well.

EIGHTH INNING

Home at Last:
The 1980s to the Present

Though Dottie thought she had put the game behind her, baseball always hovered somewhere on the perimeter of her life. Dottie worked several part-time jobs while her children were young, including two that involved her sports background. One was with the Baseball Blue Book, headquartered at that time in Fort Wayne. The Baseball Blue Book held the records for Major League Baseball, and if a team wanted to acquire a certain ballplayer, a representative of the team would call the office of the Blue Book and ask for that player's statistics. Dottie's job was to answer the telephone and look up the information the various officials requested. While Dottie found her work at the Blue Book interesting, she also enjoyed her tenure with Vim's Sporting Goods. This was the same business that had staunchly supported the Daisies during their years in Fort Wayne and where Daisy fans had sent their ballots to keep their team in town, in care of Dottie Collins. Dottie's main responsibility was selling sports equipment. However, one day her biggest sale resonated not at the cash register but in her heart.

"I remember a little kid that I waited on," Dottie said, "he couldn't have been over five or six. He came in with his parents, who were Amish, and he walked over and picked up a baseball glove. You could just tell he wanted that glove right from the beginning. Since his parents were Amish, I didn't know if they would buy him the glove, and I thought he would have his heart broken. But they bought him the glove, and to me that was something, because that kid went out of there on cloud nine." For Dottie, shades of another child holding her own first glove followed in his wake.

It was not until the early 1980s that baseball took root more firmly in Dottie's life. This happened through the auspices of Run, Jane,

Run, the annual women's sports festival in Fort Wayne. Sponsored by the Fort Wayne Women's Bureau, Inc., the purpose of the festival was to celebrate women's sports progress in the community and give women a chance to compete and have fun. An article in *Creative Sports* in November 1985, quoted Harriet Miller, the executive director of the Women's Bureau. "One thing we try to do with Run, Jane, Run is to give recognition to achieving women. It's the one way to overcome the invisibility of women. We find if you repeat the names of female athletes often enough they can become household words."

In 1981, one of the festival organizers decided to resurrect some names that had been household words, but which had long been silenced. Wanting more for Run, Jane, Run than amateur athletics, Monica Wehrle Pugh approached Dottie Collins about the possibility of a Daisy reunion as part of the weekend event. In this way, Run, Jane, Run would also acknowledge the contributions the Daisies made to the community in terms of women's sports. The idea was to have the former female Fort Wayne baseball stars play an exhibition game against the city girls' baseball league and some women who had played on the Junior Daisies baseball team. The Junior Daisy League had been formed during the league's heyday as a type of farm system from which new talent could be culled, with similar leagues existing in the other league cities. Most of these junior leagues dissolved after the league folded, but the Junior Daisies stayed around Fort Wayne through 1963. The girls played by AAGPBL rules and used their uniforms and equipment.

Dottie provided Monica with a list of players' names, but only a few women responded. However, on the day of the game, fifteen Daisies convened at the Tah-Cum-Wah Recreation Center Field, sporting new hairdos, polyester pants, and their gloves from their days on the field. Some of the players who returned included Vivian Kellogg, sisters Betty and Jo Weaver, Elizabeth (Lib) Mahon, Isabel (Lefty) Alverez, Jean Geissinger Hardy, Mary (Wimp) Baumgartner, and Dottie Wiltse Collins. Perhaps the hesitation some of them experienced over coming stemmed from the time that had elapsed since the last game had been played in Fort Wayne, 27 years ago, to be exact. Many of the players probably thought no one would remember them and that going back courted dashed expectations and deep disappointment.

They need not have worried. The bleachers at the recreation center were jam-packed with close to a thousand spectators, many of them fans who had followed the Daisies more than 30 years ago.

Much older now themselves, they came clutching program books, bats, and balls, all from the Daisy era and all autographed by their favorite stars. No matter how much time had passed, they still wanted to see their Daisies play, and play they did. In a wonderfully nostalgic three-inning game, the Fort Wayne darlings beat the opposing team 21–8. Although each run the Daisies scored counted as three runs, the girls of summer showed they could still perform. The game served as a fitting finale to that year's Run, Jane, Run event.

The Daisies were also feted that weekend with a reception at the YWCA, with author Sharon Taylor-Roepke showing a slide presen-

tation on the league. In 1986, Roepke would go on to produce her pamphlet, *Diamond Gals*, the first history of the league since Merrie Fidler's 1976 master's thesis, *The Development and Decline of the All-American Girls Baseball League, 1943–1954*. On Saturday and Sunday, the women mostly reminisced, catching up on each others' lives and establishing new ties after almost three decades of being apart. Dottie provided several oversized scrapbooks to get the conversations started and to keep them flowing. All in all, the weekend was such a decided success that the girls determined to repeat the performance the following year. No one ever imagined, though, that what started as a small gathering of players for a game of baseball would blossom into the long

Dottie shows she still has her stuff as she pitches for the Daisies during an exhibition game at Run, Jane, Run in 1984. (Courtesy of the Northern Indiana Center for History)

awaited recognition that this league of over 600 women so richly deserved.

The next year, about 25 Daisies participated in Run, Jane, Run, ten more than the year before. Community interest in the Daisies' involvement in the event was also picking up. While very little press coverage had occurred the year before, now the event was being reported almost daily, and Dottie had a 30-minute television spot lined up. During an interview by the *News-Sentinel* prior to the festival, Dottie predicted that each year even more Daisies would show up, considering the expected turnout for 1982. She was right. By 1987, almost double the number of players who had originally shown up in the fall of 1981 participated in the Daisy portion of Run, Jane, Run. Not only did Daisy involvement increase each year, the players' competence on the field grew as well. In 1983, for instance, the Daisies posted a 16–14 five-inning victory over an All-Star team made up of players from various teams in the AAGBPL, called the AAGPBL Ol Stars. Run, Jane, Run had evolved from a weekend event to a weeklong one by this time, with Dottie listed as a contact person for the Daisy exhibition game.

This organizational role within Run, Jane, Run served two important functions. Coming as it did around the time of her son's death, Dottie's involvement with Run, Jane, Run gave her a productive outlet for her grief and a means to help her heal. In addition, coordinating the logistics of that and other exhibition games prepared Dottie for the part she would play in forming the Players' Association four years down the road. Women's Bureau Director Harriet Miller often lauded the opportunity Run, Jane, Run gave women to exhibit their leadership skills and attributed the festival's success to the excellent way everything was orchestrated. While Dottie had assumed such leadership roles numerous times during her years with the Daisies and through her involvement with the Elks, she now had the chance to sharpen her skills for what lay ahead.

Another set of circumstances that occurred shortly before the 1981 mini-reunion took place in Fort Wayne helped bring that future closer to the fore. Former leaguer June Peppas, now residing in Allegan, Michigan, had been contacted by someone wanting to write a paper on the league, most probably Sharon Roepke, who was conducting extensive research on the league at that time. A Fort Wayne native, Peppas had begun her major league career with the Daisies, moved on to play for the Racine Belles, and ended her baseball days with the Kalamazoo Lassies. The left-handed pitcher, who also played first base, was a two time All-Star and collected two pitching victories to lead the Lassies to the league championship over the Fort Wayne Daisies in 1954. One of those wins happened in the series finale, the last game ever played in the All-American Girls Professional Baseball League.

At one point during the interview, the author asked June if she was at all curious about what had happened to the people she played with. June admitted she was but could do nothing about it. Later, though, she decided she could do something. She wrote a letter to some people she had kept in touch with and asked them for names and addresses of former players they had been in contact with. "And I didn't hear a word," June said. "Not a word from any of them. Well, after Thanksgiving and Christmas, all of a sudden I started getting replies, like 'I know where so and so is.' And I thought, hey, this is great! So, working in the printing business, I thought I'd put out another newsletter. That was in February, 1981. And all of a sudden the people were coming in like you wouldn't believe." Before long, June had heard from close to 200 people. More were yet to come.

During a break in the festivities during Run, Jane, Run that September of 1981, several former players sat around discussing the possibility of getting as many players together as possible at one time in one place. Most of the women agreed that the task was too tremendous even to consider. Never one to let such a minor matter get in her way, two time All-Star Elizabeth "Lib" Mahon threw out a challenge for someone to pick up the ball and run with it. Ruth Davis, a bat girl for the South Bend Blue Sox who had signed a contract for the 1955 season that never materialized, took Lib up on the challenge. Soon, under Ruth's guidance, the first national reunion of the All-American Girls Professional Baseball League became a reality.

Over three hundred former All-Americans convened in Chicago, Illinois, from July 8–11, 1982, coming together as a large group for the first time in almost 30 years. "It was just fantastic," Dottie recalled. "We had so much fun." Various events planned for the weekend included a golf tournament, a boat outing on the Chicago River, and a Cubs game at Wrigley Field. The Lettermen sang the national anthem and June Peppas had the privilege of throwing out the first ball. Before the game, the Cubs honored the women baseball players by recapping a brief history of the league and its achievements. The highlight of the reunion, however, was the Saturday night banquet, the culmination of a weekend meant to bridge the past and the present, with a small path curving outward towards the future.

In the next newsletter she put out after the reunion, June Peppas described what the evening meant to the women gathered there. "Whatever rewards we had desired were already ours in knowing the happiness and joy of all the people who were before us—a totally unique group of people who, because of time and circumstance, could never be duplicated in any possible way." Writing next about the women standing together and singing the league song during the evening, "...the room became electrified with a sense of history, both past history and history being made. You'll never know how thrilling it was to see you, joined hand in hand, joined heart to heart, joined in spirit, in time and in pride." As Dottie later wrote to Merrie Fidler in September, 1982, "...I can't help but think what a shame that so many years passed by that we had no contact. Now that the contact has been made I for one am going to hang onto it."

Dottie had kept in touch with some of her former teammates throughout the years, but not very often. Mostly, she exchanged Christmas cards and such with a few people she knew from the league, although she had stayed particularly close to both Helen Callaghan Candaele and her sister, Marg Callaghan Maxwell. The girls would write back and forth on a regular basis, and when Helen and her family moved from Canada to California, they stayed with Dottie and Harvey for a month. "I just adored Bobby Candaele," Dottie said, referring to Helen's first husband, whom she subsequently divorced. "He was quite a guy." At the time Helen and her family stopped in Fort Wayne, Dottie had two children and Helen had five, including Casey Candaele, the future major league ballplayer, and Kelly Candaele, who would go on to produce the documentary upon which the film *A League of Their Own* was based. What Dottie remembered most about that hectic but happy time was how each day began.

"Bobby was a beautiful singer," Dottie said, "and sometimes he would come with our team when we traveled and sing on the bus. That time they came to visit, he would always get up first to feed the children. I had a sort of circular area in the kitchen, and he would line up the younger kids in the high chairs and put the older ones around the kitchen table, and he would sing to them about eating." There they were, Patty and Dan Collins, along with Ricky, Rocky, Kelly, Kerry, and Casey Candaele, listening to "Ta ta ta da, eat it, ta ta ta da, eat it," as Bobby waved a spoon around in accompaniment to the words. "I don't know what the neighbors thought," Dottie said, shaking her head, "but we sure had a lot of fun when he was around."

Dottie and Helen remained close until Helen's death in 1992.

Dottie stood by her friend after Helen's divorce, even playing match-maker at one point by pairing Helen up with Harvey's childhood friend, Bud Offerle. That was not one of Dottie's better ideas. Helen and Bud mixed like the proverbial oil and water. "One time we were driving around Fort Wayne and Helen and Bud started arguing. I think Helen said something about his driving," Dottie remembered, "and Bud told her if she didn't like it he'd quit driving. And he took his hands off the wheel and got in the back. I had to jump over the seat and grab hold of the steering wheel and get the car over to the curb." Dottie probably thanked her baseball stars that day that she had learned to react quickly no matter what the situation.

Coming together as a group during that summer of 1982 bred more possibilities than had before seemed possible. That weekend awakened a desire to spread the recollections the players shared beyond their intimate circle into a wider realm. At the Run, Jane, Run festival in September 1982, the *News-Sentinel* reported that what Dottie Collins and other former AAGPBL players wanted now was a Hall of Fame. "At least a place we can put our memorabilia," Dottie told the newspaper. She had picked up on this idea after hearing Merrie Fidler speak at the reunion banquet about her hope that the league would somehow be revived. "Your dream [of a place for everyone's AAGPBL memorabilia] has become my obsession ... I really feel that the history of our league & the girls who played in it should be preserved," Dottie confided to Fidler in the same letter in which she expressed her joy at reestablishing old friendships. Dottie continued in this same vein when she told Fidler, "...and in talking to others they all want it so very bad." Dottie also mentioned that she had appeared on the sports segment of the local television news, asking fans to check basements and attics for anything they might have saved from the Daisies. This desire to preserve the history of the league was the first step towards gaining recognition. First, though, the players needed to continue the momentum that had belatedly begun.

Encouraged by the success of the national reunion and the growing enthusiasm for the get-togethers in Fort Wayne during Run, Jane, Run, June carried on with her newsletter through the end of 1982 before turning it over to Shirley Stovroff, who had a printing business in California. At the time she relinquished her job, June could not know what an abiding contribution she had made to the league, with her initial one- or two-page bulletins ultimately growing into the missive of over thirty pages it is today. Once Shirley took over she produced the newsletter for one year and then handed the reins to

Pepper Paire. By then the issues were being printed more sporadically. In 1983, for instance, Shirley Stovroff only put out three issues compared to June Peppas's nine issues that first year. Part of the problem was the cost. June had often asked for donations to cover expenses, such as stamps and paper. What was needed was someone who could devote more time and energy to the project, someone who could coordinate the financial aspect in addition to disseminating the actual news.

In 1986, that person showed up in the person of Dottie Collins. When she approached June Peppas and told her she was thinking about putting together the newsletter herself, June asked Dottie if she knew what she was getting into. "I don't think she realized what a big undertaking it was," June said. "A lot of times I got up and wrote half a dozen letters before I went to work." Perhaps Dottie truly did not realize the amount of work involved, but once she got started she tackled the situation just as efficiently as she mowed down batters at the plate. According to former leaguer Fran Janssen, "It wasn't until Dottie took it over that it became a real newsletter with more information from everyone."

Things really picked up momentum after that. A second national reunion was held in Fort Wayne in 1986 in conjunction with Run, Jane, Run, putting paid to Dottie's notion that Chicago was "for sure a one-shot deal," and as a result more discussions got under way about gaining recognition for the league. Actually, some of that recognition was already happening at that very reunion. Both Janis Taylor and Kelly Candaele and his partner, Kim Wilson, were interviewing players and gathering material for their respective documentaries, with Taylor's documentary, *When Diamonds Were a Girl's Best Friend,* due out the next year. As the reunion organizer, Dottie forewarned the women about their impending stardom in a letter included in an early 1986 newsletter. "Make sure you gals all have your hair done before you arrive," she wrote, "'cause there will be a lot of filming going on."

Among the women, talk centered on finding a place to house the league artifacts and the desire for some type of display in the Hall of Fame in Cooperstown, New York. Dottie Collins was asking for volunteers to get these and other events off the ground when a certain conversation with Karen Kunkel sent her down another avenue entirely. Kunkel, a former player for the Grand Rapids Chicks and now a teacher and administrator at Northern Michigan University, convinced Dottie of the need to organize officially as a group in order to accomplish any of their goals. "I told Dottie that with my background and the resources available to me at the University, we could put together a preliminary plan for a players' association, invite some interested people, form a committee, and proceed," Kunkel said. "I drew up an organizational plan, a few sample by-laws, and other items for discussion at our first meeting."

On May 23, 1987, the first Players Association meeting was held at the home of Fran Janssen in South Bend, Indiana. Along with Fran and Dottie Collins, Jean Harding, Lillian Jackson, Karen Kunkel, Earlene "Beans" Risinger, and author Sharon Taylor-Roepke also attended, with June Peppas backing up the endeavor from her home. Dottie chaired the event, but the group relied on Karen Kunkel for guidance. Dottie asserted that if it were not for Karen Kunkel there would have been no Players Association. "She knew everything that had to do with business," Dottie said. "She knew how to do it, where to go, and who to contact."

Karen was the director of the Great Lakes Sports and Olympic Academy at Northern Michigan University in Marquette, Michigan, and knew the ins and outs of organizing such a group. At that first meeting she suggested the need for by-laws and dues and emphasized the importance of incorporating under the name that had been selected, The All-American Girls Professional Baseball League Players Association, Inc., a nonprofit organization whose main focus was to preserve the league's place in baseball history.

The women also elected officers from those in attendance to form an executive board, with Fran Janssen as vice president, Jean Harding as secretary, and Dottie Collins as treasurer, since she had already been collecting money for the newsletter. They selected June Peppas as president by phone. "After we decided June would make a good president I called her up on the phone and told her, 'We just made you president,'" Dottie said, chuckling at the memory. "I told her I wasn't taking no for an answer, either." The former leaguers also assembled a list of players from across the United States and Canada who in the past had offered to serve on a general board of directors. It turned out that no one refused the call for help. The former players also considered the need for an attorney, a logo, and financial matters.

The next meeting took place during the Run, Jane, Run reunion in Fort Wayne on September 17, 1987. At this meeting, the players discussed and passed the by-laws, decided on an official logo, which would be trademarked, and formed committees to ensure the establishment of a lifetime roster and an official history of the league.

Further discussions took place on how to get the word out about the league, such as finding a place to house the archives, locating museums to display league memorabilia, and compiling media packets to be sure that what went out about the league and its history was accurate. A dominant topic of discussion, though, was the Hall of Fame. After the meeting, June Peppas sent a memo to players, managers, chaperones, and friends, in which she reiterated the main objectives of the league. "It is our belief that one of our prime responsibilities is our place in Cooperstown," she wrote. "Another goal is to perpetuate our league. We do not want our league and what it stands for to die in the women's world of sports. We want to continue being role models for our young women of the future. We want our history to be there for research in the archives and our artifacts to be exhibited in museums. And for the many young women and girls that go to Cooperstown Hall of Fame, we want them to know we were a part of the baseball world and maybe someday they too could be. We do not want to take a man's place. We want our own place."

One of those most instrumental in securing this privilege for the women of the AAGPBL was Dottie Collins. "Dottie was responsible for most of the organizing for the display at the Hall of Fame," said Fran Janssen. She first sent out a newsletter to see who would be willing to help with the various aspects of coordinating the display. Next, she arranged for the collection of items that would be shown in the exhibit, since the history of the league was currently scattered across the United States and Canada. The most difficult aspect of making all the arrangements was that few women lived close enough to the Hall of Fame to give much assistance to matters such as housing and transportation. However, Ruth Williams Heverly, a relief and starting pitcher in her eight years in the league, answered Dottie's plea for assistance and headed a committee to arrange motel accommodations and travel arrangements. Living in Pennsylvania at the time, Ruth was relatively close to Cooperstown in comparison to where most of the other players were located.

During each step of the planning, Dottie kept the former players up to date through newsletters and numerous telephone calls. Before she and the association could begin their task, though, they had to convince the Hall to give them their own display in the first place. Sometime during the 1986 national reunion in Fort Wayne, Dottie Collins and several other former players had formed a committee to see about Cooperstown opening its doors to the league. Aside from Dottie, the committee was composed of Lynn Haber, a writer from Boston, Massachusetts, Karen Kunkel, Sharon Taylor-Roepke, and Danielle Barber. The October 1986 newsletter reported on the formation of the committee and asked each member to indicate what she would be "willing to give to The Baseball Hall of Fame if we are able to achieve our goal" and to send the information to Dottie Collins. Tentative feelers had gone out to the Hall, but no definite response was forthcoming. After all, the Hall of Fame's main focus had always been on men's Major League Baseball. Convincing the powers that be that a women's league should also have its due was probably going to be as difficult as hitting for the cycle. However, an interesting set of circumstances converged to change the way the Hall, and countless others, viewed America's oldest sport.

It started in 1984 when Ted Spencer, now the vice president of the Hall of Fame, met Sharon Taylor-Roepke, who was doing research at the library in the Hall of Fame for her upcoming booklet, *Diamond Gals*. Roepke asked Spencer if he would ever consider doing an exhibit on women's baseball. Since he knew very little about the league, she handed him what she had written so far, along with a packet of about eighteen baseball cards she had designed of some of the players. Taylor-Roepke had first introduced the All-American Girls Baseball League Star Series Baseball Cards at "The New Agenda" Conference sponsored by the U.S. Olympic Committee, the purpose of which was to redefine women's participation in sports in the upcoming decade. Spencer wrapped an elastic band around the cards and stuck them in his drawer. Later, as he became immersed in the story Roepke had written, he realized that he had a personal connection to the women's league. Mary Pratt, a gym teacher in Spencer's grammar school system in Quincy, Massachusetts, had pitched for the Rockford Peaches and the Kenosha Comets from 1943–1947, hurling a no-hitter against Dottie Collins's Minneapolis Millerettes in 1944.

Intrigued, over the next two years Spencer often found himself taking the cards out of his desk drawer and reading the short biographies until he felt as if he really knew this group of women, one of whom was Dottie Collins. Then, in September of 1986, Ted Spencer got a telephone call from a reporter who was doing an article on the league for the *Los Angeles Times*. The reporter had heard about the league from Kelly Candaele, who was about to release his documentary. Like Sharon Roepke, she also wanted to know if the Hall of Fame planned on doing a women's baseball exhibit. Spencer and the Hall's publicity director, Bill Guilfoyle, had discussed the possibility, but the Hall of Fame was leery about moving away from its traditional stance. Both men, however, sensed the inherent draw of such a display, and perhaps, too, they realized the time for such recognition was now. Accordingly, Spencer indicated to the reporter that Cooperstown would love to do an exhibit, and his intention was announced when the article ran in December, 1986. Of course, Spencer had no idea what material was housed in the Hall's archives, if any, and he had absolutely no artifacts whatsoever, but he must have had some kind of blind faith that things would work out in the end.

About two weeks after the article appeared in the *Los Angeles Times*, Ted received a letter with Dottie Collins's name and return address. "And I knew exactly what it was," Spencer said. "And I got really excited and I opened the letter. I didn't even read it. I just saw her phone number and I called." Spencer told Dottie how thrilled he was to hear from her, because from reading the information on her card so many times he felt a special rapport with her. That bond would grow with time as Ted worked alongside Dottie to make the dream of the exhibit come true. Dottie served as Ted's number one contact person for the All-American League and its history. "She was the guiding light, the heart and soul of the whole operation from here on," Spencer said. "Because I really felt it was her drive that [made] it all came about in the time that it did. She wasn't pushy; she was never adversarial. She was always total cooperation, excitement, and positive thinking. She was the glue that held the whole thing together." The respect went both ways. "Without Ted Spencer we would never have made the Hall of Fame," Dottie stated matter-of-factly.

The first target date for the opening was 1990, because of renovations scheduled for 1989. Then, Spencer decided that the year before the renovations started would be even better. Dottie's first job was to have the reunion planned for Arizona in October 1988, changed to Cooperstown in November of that year. While she was unable to have the Arizona venue canceled, she managed to pull off two AAGPBL reunions for 1988. The main problem, though, was collecting the material to put on display in Cooperstown. Karen Kunkel had made it possible for the women to start collecting memorabilia by arranging to have it brought to Northern Michigan University, where she worked. She also found volunteers to catalog and store everything and later established a media center so if anyone wanted to do a story on the league, whether the press or freelancers, they could be referred to one central place.

After Karen's retirement, and at the time Cooperstown was

seeking materials, all the artifacts had been moved to the Northern Indiana Center for History, in South Bend, Indiana. Since the Historical Society had the rights to the material, they first had to agree to lend whatever the women had donated to the Hall of Fame. Dottie hooked up with the Northern Indiana Historical Society and developed a relationship with them so that Ted Spencer was able to work with a contact person at the society. Spencer then sent Dottie a list of the items he wanted. Fran Janssen was responsible for gathering those items, and Dottie took over from there, coordinating the myriad of details, making numerous phone calls, and herding off the outlaws among the former leaguers.

"There was one little group that gave us trouble all the time," said Dottie. "They wanted to be inducted into the Hall of Fame. Ted and I talked on the phone, and he said there was no way Major League Baseball would stand for it. I understood that and so did our board, but not that one little group." To be inducted into the Hall of Fame a player had to have played for twelve seasons, among other qualifications, and only one woman had played in all twelve seasons of the league, Dorothy "Dottie" Schroeder. Besides, the women were looking for recognition as a group, not fishing for individual kudos. Finally, Ted Spencer soothed the ruffled feathers and the plans continued for the big day.

November weather in upstate New York can be a big gamble, but the baseball gods must have smiled down upon Cooperstown on the day of the opening. The reunion ran from November 3 through November 6, 1988, with the unveiling of the women in baseball display planned for the fifth. As part of the activities the women played an exhibition game at Doubleday Field. That game was reenacted three years later for the movie *A League of Their Own,* and the game in the film was played in the same type of beautiful weather that had blessed the All-Americans. The film people also hired the same umpire to oversee the game in the movie who had worked the game during the exhibit weekend. Chet is the character at the end of the movie who says, "Yesterday it may have been a ball. Tomorrow it may be a ball. But today it's a strike."

The highlight of the four-day bonanza was of course the opening of the display itself. The exhibit was housed in a room that had been vacated expressly for that purpose, with the existing exhibits covered for the event. In the movie, that room appeared as a gallery. It would have been exciting if the Hall could have kept the display intact after the movie, so people could see the display as it appeared on the set, but the contract called for everything to be put back the way it was. The original 1988 exhibit was actually a tribute to all women in baseball throughout history, starting with an 1867 photograph of a Vassar girls' baseball team. "Many of the women who played before those who played in the league played against great social opposition," said Ted Spencer. "But, they loved the game so much they played as men or played against men and they were really known more as odd-ities than anything else. And that is part of our mission, to show just how strong the pull of the game is." However, the All-American Girls Baseball League is, as Spencer admitted, "head and shoulders the high-water mark, the apex of the whole story."

The program for the event announced that the "Baseball Hall of Fame Presents The All-American Girls Professional Baseball League of 1943–1954, Featured in the Display 'Women in Baseball,' November 5, 1988." A twelve-foot-long glass display case framed a plaque on which was etched the names of the 555 women who played in the league and which also included their hometown. Also numbered among the mementos of the league were uniforms, bats, balls, gloves, spikes, programs, and pictures. One photograph depicted a shot of a crowd at Peoria Stadium of over 10,000 fans. A three-by-four action picture showed Faye Dancer sliding into third base during a game. Serving as the centerpiece of the exhibit was a towering champi-onship trophy won by the Grand Rapids Chicks, one of two they won during their ten-year tenure in the league. Two-time Player of the Year, Doris "Sammy" Sams, donated one of her awards to the Hall of Fame and also demonstrated the essence of being an All-Ameri-can. "Doris asked us if we could take off the plate on her trophy and recreate it with the names of all the girls who had won for the vari-ous years," Ted Spencer remembered. "It was kind of funny," he said. "They were so aggressive on the field and so self-effacing off of it." Yet what the majority of these women truly desired was to be valued for their achievements as a whole. As the refrain of their victory song so proudly proclaims, "We're all for one, we're one for all, we're All-Americans."

Fittingly, the person who fought so diligently to bring recogni-tion for all was the one chosen to pull the curtain to officially open the display. "I'll never forget the moment when we had Dottie Collins pull the drape with Howard Talbot, the director of the Hall of Fame," said Ted Spencer. It was the first-ever curtain rising for a Hall of Fame display and the first-ever exhibition "event" in the Hall's his-tory. "From the first, I insisted that she alone with our director would be the one to unveil the exhibit." Dottie's grandson, John Gilbert, who was fourteen at the time, remembered it as the proudest moment of his life. "I thought, wow, that's my grandma up there," John said, as he recalled watching his grandmother take her place in baseball history. What Ted Spencer remembered was looking around and seeing 1200 people milling around, when on a normal Saturday in November they would have had about 400 people. "I realized then," Spencer said, "that we had just changed the whole direction of the museum. Because it really brought home to me how important the game is culturally. We always knew how important it was, but this really drove it home."

For the women it was a day of bittersweet moments. Each of them received a certificate presented by the National Baseball Hall of Fame in recognition of her contribution to women's baseball as a member of the All-American Girls Professional Baseball League. Later, in January, 1989, President Reagan followed up the general accolades with his personal congratulations, prodded in part by 21 notes sent to him from Wilma Briggs's third grade class and three letters sent to him by pitcher Lou Arnold, the last of which noted that if a men's league had received such recognition he would probably not only have written but called with his best wishes. Reagan's letter read in part, "As professionals in our national pastime of baseball, you were pioneers among women in the world of professional sports.... You can reflect and rejoice that the example you and others set is now depicted at Cooperstown to inspire and inform your fellow Americans and visitors from abroad for years to come." Even if he did have to be pushed a little, how appropriate it was that the man who started out announcing baseball games, and who had starred in the movie Dottie promoted as the "Million Dollar Baby" of softball, should be President of the United States at such a time and thus be the one to offer his commendations for the country as a whole.

The 147 former players also reunited with many people whom they thought had long ago faded into the past. From the cities where the girls played came fans who had not seen a game in over 30 or 40 years, and not just women. Ken Sells, the first president of the league under Phillip Wrigley from 1943–1944, and the man who had pulled the plug on Dottie's first team, the Millerettes, was in attendance, as were three chaperones: Dottie Hunter, Helen Hannah Campbell, and Lex McCutchen. A van full of softball players whom Wilma Briggs coached made the trip from Rhode Island to acknowledge the former Daisy and one of the league's career leaders in home runs. A busload of well-wishers from her home state of New Jersey came to greet Lois "Tommie" Barker, who was the oldest rookie in 1950 at the age of 27.

Perhaps the most touching moment at the reunion involved a man who came all the way from Calgary in Canada. He shuffled up to Ted Spencer on the day before the opening as Ted and his assistant were checking the last-minute details. Verifying that this was the women's exhibit, he asked Ted Spencer if any of the former players were around and if he could meet some of them. In talking with him further, Ted learned that his wife had been a player and that she had died four years ago. "This man told me that his wife always claimed that her years in the league were the best time of her life," Spencer said. "When he read about the opening in the paper," Spencer continued, "he decided to come in case he could meet any of the girls his wife played with." Spencer immediately herded him over to the registration site at Presbyterian Church Hall, and there the women of the AAGBPL gave him the welcome of his life. Later, at the banquet, the players presented him with a small gift as a token of their appreciation of what his wife had contributed to the league.

With the perpetual high the All-Americans rode on that day, the time passed quickly between the conclusion of the opening festivities and the dinner planned for that evening. They laughed and cried and savored the validation that should have been theirs all along. "It was the largest group they've ever had at Cooperstown at one time," Dottie said. "We took it over. All you could see when you were outside the Hall of Fame was a solid mass of people walking up and down the streets. We couldn't even walk on the sidewalk." The crowds were amazing, as Cooperstown typically slows down at that time of year. To accommodate all of the people who had converged on the tiny town, the players had to convince several establishments to stay open beyond the time they usually closed for the season.

What also struck Dottie that weekend besides the number of people was the reaction of the players' children, many of whom could not believe the enormity of what their mothers had done. Even if they knew their mothers had played baseball—and many of them assumed the game they played was softball—they had no inkling just how much their mothers had contributed to the world of sports. Naturally both of Dottie's children knew she had played for the Daisies, but Patty admitted that she never thought much about her mother as a professional baseball player. "I looked at her scrapbooks," she said, "but it didn't hit me what I was reading. Everything with mom was golf in those days."

Patty accompanied her mother on the seventeen-hour ride to Cooperstown, although at first she was unsure whether or not she would attend. Dottie and Harvey planned on taking their two grandsons, David and John, but left it up to Patty what she wanted to do. "We were ready to pull out the next morning," Dottie remembered, "and Patty called and said, 'Mom, can I go, too?' I'll never forget that. I thought it was great, because I didn't beg her to go. It was up to her." Patty made the right decision in the end. No one could have imagined just how big an affair the weekend would be, with some added surprises tucked into the package besides. John and David received one of the biggest thrills of their life when Ted Spencer took them on a special tour of the basement area of the National Hall of Fame, the repository for everything not on display. "They really thought they were big shots then," Dottie recalled, thinking also of their excitement at being made the first charter members of the Players Association.

The culmination of the opening day was the Saturday evening banquet, which was held at the Sportsman Tavern. Mistress of Ceremonies Karen Kunkel first thanked both June Peppas and Dottie Collins for their efforts in preserving the history of the league until the league's acceptance into the Hall of Fame. Former outfielder June Emerson then gave the invocation, during which she blessed the "lovely lady from Indiana" for her "vision, compassion, and devotion" in bringing the women together. After dinner, some of the former players got up and reflected on their days in the league, with Gloria Cordes Elliott giving the closing prayer. The grand finale to the evening was the women's rendition of the All-American Girls' Victory Song, a tune the women had been bellowing out with enthusiasm throughout the day. Ted Spencer mentioned this to some of the women he spoke with over the weekend. Spencer remembered telling them, "You've been singing that damn song all day long. And the museum has never had that much noise. It's been great."

One person who had planned to be at the banquet but was absent was Penny Marshall, of *Laverne and Shirley* fame. About a month before the opening, Marshall saw the press release announcing the scheduled events. She called the publicity director at the Hall of Fame and expressed her desire to attend the ceremony, since she suspected there might be a movie here. Wanting to mingle with the women as much as possible, she also purchased a ticket for the Saturday banquet. The only problem was that the Sportsman Tavern could not accommodate all of the players plus their families and friends. To allow the former leaguers to all be together, many friends and relatives, including the four members of Dottie's family, had given up their paid admission to the banquet. Now here Penny Marshall stood, ticket in hand.

"So we took it away from her," Dottie said. "Karen Kunkel came up and asked me why Penny Marshall should be at the dinner and not Harvey," Dottie said, "since Harvey was one of the ones we shoved downtown to eat at one of the restaurants there." Deciding to rectify the situation, Dottie and Karen found Penny Marshall and told her their concerns. "I let Karen do most of the talking because she was good at it," Dottie said. "We said that we were real happy that she came, but this [was] not right that she got to go to the dinner but not our families." Fortunately, Marshall understood and immediately gave up her ticket. Of course, being the resourceful women they were, Dottie and Karen had already gotten a refund from the restaurant before they met with Marshall and so were able to give her back what she had paid for her ticket. In addition, banquet or no banquet, Penny Marshall had a very good reason for sticking around.

The women suspected something was in the wind the minute they spotted Marshall in town. "We knew something was being planned," Dottie said, "because Penny was asking a lot of questions and taking a lot of notes. And she didn't get mad and leave when we wouldn't let her come to our banquet," Dottie said with a grin. Marshall genuinely seemed to enjoy being around the baseball women and was obviously inspired enough by the people she met to go through with her original idea. Ted Spencer remarked that due to her popularity at the time she seemed to be hiding in plain sight. "Penny Marshall was a chain smoker, so she was always sneaking into the merchandising guys' office to have a smoke, always with sunglasses on and a hat pulled down to hide her face. The only time she seemed really relaxed was when she was with the ladies at the private events and everything," he concluded.

The movie that evolved from Marshall's stay in Cooperstown, a film that moved the league beyond the sphere of sports into the hearts of filmgoers worldwide, did not happen for a couple of years due to several factors. Originally, LongBow Productions of Los Angeles signed a contract with the league through the Players Association. When Penny Marshall wanted to do the movie, she had to negotiate with LongBow Productions before everything could be ironed out. What held things up even more was that the right female lead could not be found. Debra Winger was first considered for the role, but that never materialized, with some sources citing problems between Winger and director Penny Marshall over the casting of Madonna as the reason. Unable to find anyone to replace Winger, tryouts in Evansville, Indiana, for about one hundred extras needed for the game scenes had to be postponed in June, 1990. Filming could not resume for at least nine months as the cast and crew were dependent on warm weather for most of the filming. Thankfully Geena Davis was soon cast for the top spot, or the movie could have been put on hold indefinitely.

Various locations were used to film the movie, including the town of Henderson, Kentucky, Chicago's Wrigley Field, and Dedeaux Field at the University of Southern California in Los Angeles. The opening scene of the movie, where the bus carries Dottie Henson past Otsego Lake to Doubleday Field, was shot in Cooperstown, as were the later reunion scenes, which were shot in the Hall of Fame. The crew took over an entire room in the Hall during their ten-day stay. Around forty All-Americans were on hand in Cooperstown for bit parts either in the Hall of Fame scenes or in those played out on Doubleday Field. Dottie stopped in Cooperstown after a baseball reunion in Clearwater, Florida to see how the women were doing. There she found some very tired ladies who had been putting in ten- to twenty-hour days on the set, but who were very much elated by the chance to be celebrities for a week.

Quite a bit of the filming was done in towns in Indiana, mainly at Evansville's Bosse Field, which saw over three weeks of filming. The *Evansville Courier* reported that the memories surrounding the making of the movie would linger for a very long time to come in Evansville and surrounding towns. First there was the calf born during the filming in Posey County near St Philip, named Penny after director Penny Marshall. Then, how could residents forget the swimming pool Geena Davis had installed at her rental house or the fluorescent signature Madonna left on the wall of her favorite bar in Evansville? Florists in particular would remember August 16, Madonna's birthday, when they sold out of the while lilies that are Madonna's signature flower. Finally, there were all the fledgling stars who experienced the thrill of fame when the call for extras rang out.

Director Marshall used 33,000 people as extras, many to pack the stands at Bosse Field for the World Series scene at Racine Field, home of the Belles. Discouraged at first by the poor turnout on many of the days when the crowd scenes were shot, Columbia Pictures agreed to raffle off $5000 if 5000 people showed up on the last Saturday in

September to fill the bleachers. Over 9000 people eager to pad their pockets poured onto the field that day, with corporate support for free movie passes, ice cream, and doughnuts bolstering the effort even more. In addition, the stars gave away autographed baseballs and personally appealed to area residents to come and do their part. Tom Hanks and Geena Davis, among others, spelled out Evansville in body language in the middle of the field as an added incentive, and Rosie O'Donnell sang the theme song from *The Brady Brunch* in a duet with Geena Davis.

Dottie visited the crew several times when they were on location in Evansville to see how the movie was shaping up. Although Karen Kunkel was in charge of making sure the baseball scenes were accurate, consulting with a number of players to do so, as a member of the board of directors Dottie was allowed to be on the set. "I mostly stayed out of the way," Dottie said. "I knew Karen was in charge, and I wasn't about to tell people what to do." Letting others have their share of the limelight was typical of Dottie. Ted Spencer also noticed this. "Dottie's always been 'share everything,'" Spencer said. "She always had a more feet-on-the-ground feeling about everything that came after the movie, too." No doubt the temptation existed for players to boast that a certain character represented themselves, when actually each character was a compilation of a number of players, but Dottie never gave into that type of self-promotion.

She kept a close eye on what was happening on the set, though. One of the players tended to embellish a bit, telling the producer, for instance, that the girls used to light bonfires in the dugout to keep warm. "Never did that," Dottie insisted. She also pointed out a part of the movie that was not authentic at all: Madonna catching the ball in her hat. "They would have thrown us out of the league if we ever did something like that," Dottie said. "We did some stupid things, but not when it came to baseball."

Whether or not Madonna's character committed a blooper, Dottie praised Madonna herself for the way she immersed herself in her role to reflect the true nature of an All-American ballplayer. "She was a good influence, and she worked her butt off," Dottie said. "We'd all be in the hotel—we were in Chicago at the time for the tryout scenes in the first part of the movie—and we'd all be in the shower cleaning up, and Madonna would still be at the ball diamond getting somebody to help her. She did a good job." Dottie also liked Rosie O'Donnell. "She was fun to be around," Dottie remembered. "She was just as common as an old shoe." Dottie particularly admired her skill in baseball. "Rosie was the only one that was a ballplayer," Dottie said. "She knew what she was doing. One of the girls in the league could throw a baseball to two people at the same time, and she taught Rosie how to do it. Rosie can still do it." Later, Rosie even performed the stunt on her daytime television program. One other "star" whom Dottie knew quite well was Karen Kunkel's husband, Jack. In the first part of the movie, Jack was cast as a member of the board of directors who met to decide how to go about organizing a women's baseball league.

A League of Their Own premiered in Fort Wayne, Indiana, on Thursday, June 25, 1992. A grandstand reception honoring the AAGPBL players, with ballpark food and beverages, took place before the screening at Bandido's Restaurant. The $25 admission would benefit the AAGPBL and also the Fort Wayne Women's Bureau, a fitting recipient as the Women's Bureau offered peer counseling, rape awareness programs, and career opportunities for women. Some of the players who attended the gala were Vivian Kellogg, Beans Risinger, Dottie Collins, and Lou Arnold, leaning on a walker emblazoned with the AAGPBL logo. Before entering the theater, the women wrapped their arms around each other, raised their faces to the stars, and sang their signature song. As they filed into the movie house, Ben Smith of the *Journal-Gazette* referred to them as "graying women who still moved with the eternal grace of ballplayers."

What Dottie and the other All-Americans could never have imagined was how far their influence would extend. While their inclusion in Cooperstown represented a turning point as far as sports were concerned, *A League of Their Own* drew in admirers from all walks of life, people who valued them as ballplayers, as women, and as the embodiment of what it means to realize a dream. Dottie, listed as the contact person at the Hall of Fame and in Columbia Pictures' press releases, received the brunt of the deluge that poured in after the movie came out, fielding hundreds of telephone calls from the media and a mailbox overflowing with letters. Right after the movie's premiere, Dottie often sat for four or five hours at a time with the phone glued to her ear. One of her more pleasant calls came from a former neighbor in California whom she had not heard from in almost 50 years. This man had been a little boy when his parents bought the vacant lot next door to Dottie's house in Inglewood, the same lot where Dottie's dad set up a backstop so they could play their nightly games of catch.

Dottie also had her six and a half minutes of fame shortly before

A League of Their Own opened in Fort Wayne. She, Betty Trezza, an outfielder for the Racine Bells, and Gloria Cordes Elliott, a pitcher for Racine and the Kalamazoo Lassies, appeared on *Good Morning America* with Charles Gibson on June 22, 1992. The women stayed at the Ritz Carlton and were whisked off to the studio by limousine for their early-morning appearance. After giving the viewers a brief history of the league and some news about the upcoming movie, Gibson interviewed the women about their playing days. Dottie was slightly more retiring than the other two players, but then she could let her record speak for her. One thing that Gibson remembered in particular was that one of the players had notched up 29 wins in one season. When he asked which of the women had done so, Dottie very quietly replied, "That was me," almost as if she would rather have let the matter slide. Dottie posted that record in 1945, her first year with the Fort Wayne Daisies. Gibson next asked Dottie if she had really pitched through her fifth month of pregnancy. Dottie's response typified her perspective on the game, "Well, when you're a ballplayer, you're a ballplayer," she said, "and you play the game."

All of this unexpected attention also meant that Dottie's involvement with the Players Association grew tremendously. Yet Dottie met the added challenges easily, and as June Peppas pointed out, she seemed to thrive on it. Jean Harding concurred. "If you had a wheel, rim, spokes, and then the hub, our hub was Dottie Collins," Jean said. "She was a tireless worker, making the Players Association her cub, and like a lioness, she fought and protected her cub." And of course, as June Peppas also noted, Harvey was behind Dottie every step of the way, fielding telephone calls, attending all the reunions, and helping in any way he could. Together, Dottie and Harvey made the Association what it is today. They balanced each other perfectly, with Dottie needing to take charge and Harvey being more laid back. "I'm going to take a nap; wake me in five minutes," Harvey was famous for saying. Or as their daughter Patty put it, "Mom made the house work; dad made it fun."

Just as Harvey's easy-going nature complemented Dottie's drive, her more insistent ways were a boon for him, too. At no time was this more evident than in the aftermath of Harvey's heart attack and series of strokes. After the last stroke, when Harvey was not expected to live long, Dottie first brought him to Florida to recuperate and then backed him when he insisted on returning to work selling cars, which he loved doing and which he had done most of his life. More importantly, Dottie forced him to depend upon himself. One time when

Harvey asked Dottie to get him a coke when he was still convalescing, Dottie told him if he wanted one to get it himself. "I almost cried because I had to say that to him," Dottie told June Peppas, "but I had to. I had to get him to do it himself." Harvey played golf afterwards, and the man who was not supposed to make it long in this world lived for almost fourteen more years.

Despite Harvey's health problems, Dottie undertook two major projects for the Players Association, both of which would perpetuate the league's accomplishments more fully. The first was truly a labor of love. Over months and then years Dottie compiled information on all of the players, such as the teams they played on, the years they were in the league, their birth dates and their hometowns. This information was later made into a database. Dottie used each player's stat sheet to organize the list of players, and Fran Janssen and other former players living in the South Bend area helped her check line-ups from newspaper articles and go over photographs. They listed any player who was in a team photo or who had a stat sheet as a member of the league, since it followed that if they were in a uniform they had signed a contract. The completed group of statistics went to Cooperstown and the Northern Indiana Center for History in 1994.

The other big undertaking was signing a contract in 1994 with the Fritsch Card Company in Wisconsin to prepare baseball cards for the former leaguers. Dottie took charge and contacted players for written permission to print the cards, along with a request for photographs. Each girl also agreed to pay for her own card. The Association then prepared all of the information that would appear on the cards. Using the stat sheets that Howe News Service had printed at the end of each season, Jean Harding and Fran Janssen prepared a sheet for each player, after which Dottie coordinated the information to give to the card company. It was here that some controversy arose among the players within the Association.

Since the sale of the cards would go back into the Association rather than to separate individuals, a small group of former players refused to have a card made up. This same group hired an agent and branched out on their own for publicity purposes, cashing in on their newfound glory to line their own pockets. Several players in the Association tried to reason with them, since their actions directly opposed the creed by which these women played and by which they hoped to preserve their unique heritage, that creed of all for one and one for all. Yet in any large group, philosophies are bound to differ. In the end, the majority of players left the others to their own devices and continued on with their quest.

While Dottie was busy generating national recognition for the league, some hometown laurels also came her way, both for her individually and for her beloved Daisies. The first Fort Wayne honor came when the large stone that serves as a commemorative marker was placed in Memorial Park, courtesy of an anonymous donor in the Fort Wayne Women's Softball Association. Dottie and several Daisies, including Isabel Alverez, Vivian Kellogg, and Jean Harding posed around the rock during the dedication ceremony. So widespread was the Daisies' influence in the community that it was only fitting they be so honored. Not only did the Junior Daisies survive longer than most other junior leagues, but once the Daisies folded a type of ball called Daisy Ball came into being through the auspices of the city leagues. Players used a ball smaller than a softball and larger than a hardball, but they played down and dirty baseball, even using recycled Daisy uniforms. Daisy Ball even found a permanent home when the man famous for making pianos specified that part of Packard Park be set aside for young women's sports.

Another tie-in to women and baseball occurred four years later. Diamond Number 2, traditionally called the "women's diamond," at the Tah-Cum-Wah Community Center was renamed Daisies Field in 1996 to honor the team which had graced the city from 1945 to 1954. During the dedication, Dottie Collins told the *News-Sentinel*, "I knew the movie was popular, but I thought that would be it. I figured this kind of stuff would be wrapped up a long time ago ... I can't believe this is still going on." Nor had it ended as yet, at least not for Dottie.

In 1999, Dottie was chosen as number 16 in the *News-Sentinel's* countdown of northeast Indiana's top 50 athletes. Dottie was cited as one of the AAGPBL's best pitchers, with her career record of 117–76 and her lifetime ERA of 1.83. That same year, Dottie was also one of the first women ever inducted into the Northeast Indiana Baseball Association's Hall of Fame. The Hall of Fame, started in 1961 and currently boasting 152 members, has a nine-person Hall of Fame Committee who research, suggest names, and then vote among themselves to choose four or five inductees a year. The other woman who joined Dottie in 1999 was fellow leaguer Joanne Weaver, three-time All-Star, three-time batting champion, and the 1954 AAGPBL Player of the Year. During the banquet at which the awards were conferred, Dottie was introduced as a four-time 20-game winner. Denver

Howard, a member of the selection committee, told *News-Sentinel* reporter Nate Trela that the lack of women in the hall of fame was a situation that should have been addressed long ago. How appropriate that two people who were pioneers in the world of women's baseball should blaze the way for women in this local shrine to achievements in sports. Since Dottie's induction, several other women, including Vivian Kellogg, Dottie Schroeder, Maxine Kline, and Wilma Briggs have been recognized by the Hall.

Yet the most satisfaction Dottie derives comes from interacting with the young people she comes across, sometimes through letters, like the one from the young boy who wrote, "The baseball card you sent me has left me speechless. Thank you!!! I'll keep the card right next to my heart," or the girl from Germany who wrote on behalf of her baseball club, "Many, many thanks for your packet. We were very happy to get it ... I still wear one of the AAGPBL buttons on my jacket," or perhaps meeting them in person. In 2003, Dottie, Isabel Alverez, and Mary "Wimp" Baumgartner spoke about their experiences in the league to a group of students at New Haven High School in Fort Wayne. Dottie also left a huge stack of signed baseball cards for the teacher to pass around. Later, the teacher called Dottie to thank her for her time and to tell her how ecstatic all the students were to receive the cards, both boys and girls. It is times like these that make all of Dottie's efforts worthwhile, knowing that the love and determination she poured into the game continues to flow into other hearts and other minds, the thrill of the sport ever present and ever alive. Perhaps someday another young girl may even say, "All I ever wanted to do was play baseball. Thank God I had the chance."

NINTH INNING

Epilogue

Dottie Collins turned eighty on September 23, 2003. Slowed down somewhat by open heart surgery in the winter of that year, Dottie nonetheless attended the 60th anniversary reunion of the All-American Girls Professional Baseball League in Cooperstown, New York, shortly before her birthday. How fortunate that she was able to attend. During the ceremony at the Hall of Fame, Mayor Carol Waller of Cooperstown honored the women of the AAGPBL by announcing, "Whereas their ability was a welcome respite during the War years; and whereas over six hundred women had the opportunity to play at a professional level never attained to; and whereas it is their 60th reunion; and whereas their story has motivated many new women athletes and inspired us all; therefore, as the Mayor of the Village of Cooperstown, I recognize their contribution to America and baseball and hereby proclaim today, September 12, 2003, the All-American Girls Professional Baseball League Day."

Coincidentally, a group of 24 navy men from World War II were on hand that day, independent of the women's group. These men had been together on the USS *Samuel Roberts* when the ship was sunk on October 25, 1944. As told by Hall of Fame president Dale Petroskey, the men spent three days in the water before being rescued, but an interesting baseball tie-in determined whether or not they would be saved. The question asked of each man to see if he was an American or a spy was which team had won the World Series a few weeks before. When Petroskey asked the men to identify themselves by raising their hands, since many of them were now in wheelchairs, the women of the AGGPBL gave them a standing ovation and a rousing rendition of *God Bless America* in acknowledgment of their service to their country. Yet, as Petroskey so aptly pointed out, the two groups were united in a common purpose during those years of turmoil, each in their own way doing the most important work of their lives.

The Hall of Fame had another surprise in store for the women. On the lawn to the east of the Hall of Fame Library, near the steps where the former players were grouped for the ceremony, two bronze statues of Johnny Podres and Roy Campanella, the battery of the world champion 1955 Brooklyn Dodgers, posed as if ready for action. The Hall had contacted the sculptor in Italy who had created the statues and commissioned him to do one commemorating the All-American Girls Professional Baseball League. Jane Moffett, Dottie's successor as AAGPBL treasurer, had presented a plan to the Hall of Fame that May for a life-sized statue of a player in an AAGBPL uniform swinging a bat. Her choice rested on the fact that while all the girls had played different positions in the league, every girl had stepped up to the plate. Thus, the statue represented each woman who had played in the All-American Girls Professional Baseball League. Originally planned for the spring of 2005, the statue's new target date is set for sometime around Memorial Day, 2006.

In addition, upon the conclusion of the current renovations being done at the Hall, which will add 30 percent more exhibition space to the existing area, the museum plans on expanding the Women in Baseball display. According to Ted Spencer, the exhibit will be three-dimensional and at least triple the size, with a space that museum-goers can walk through. Rather than merely showcasing the various memorabilia, the material will be arranged in such a way that the story of women's contributions to baseball will be revealed in the context of the times in which they played.

This growing relationship between the Hall of Fame and the AAGPBL can be directly attributed to that which Dottie Collins so purposefully began more than 16 years ago. As Dottie watched the seed of her efforts take root, with awareness of the league growing worldwide, she gradually lessened her involvement in league activities, although never severing herself entirely. Part of the reason Dottie stepped back somewhat was Harvey's death on February 13, 2000. Harvey had collapsed with another stroke about two weeks prior to that, but he worked up until the very last doing what he loved to do, selling cars. Dottie claimed he must have had a premonition that something was wrong, because before he left work that night he showed a co-worker all his files with his customers' names and telephone numbers, something not in character for him to have done.

At the time Harvey died, he and Dottie had been married just shy of 54 years. They had celebrated their 50th wedding anniversary on March 10, 1996 with a family dinner at Hall's Guesthouse in Fort

Wayne. The newspaper article announcing their anniversary informed readers that Dottie Collins was a member of the Fort Wayne Daisies Professional Baseball Team. The September after Harvey's death Dottie chose not to run for reelection as treasurer of the Players Association, staying mainly to herself in the months following Harvey's death. If she did not cope in the same way as she did when her son died, when she moved outward instead of inward, perhaps it is because she had Harvey to lean on then, and that extra hand was just what she needed to get by.

Dottie had also lost some close friends from the league by the time Harvey died, but the one that affected her most deeply was the sudden death of Dottie Schroeder in 1996. "I'll never forget that," Dottie told Ben Smith of the *Fort Wayne2* just before Dottie Schroeder's posthumous induction into the Fort Wayne Hall of Fame. "She was the most loved player in the league by both the players and the fans." Dottie Schroeder was buried in an old cemetery in the middle of the Illinois countryside, near her hometown of Sadorus, Illinois, population around 450. Towering over the grave is a huge tombstone etched with the AAGPBL logo. Dottie Collins brought a blanket with the same logo to put over Dottie's casket at the funeral. Since the coffin was already in the ground by the time she arrived, Dottie Schroeder's twin brother, Don, put the blanket across his sister's bed, where it still remains to this day.

As people left her life, so, too, did others enter it. Dottie's two grandsons blessed her with five great-grandchildren, four boys and a girl. The letters from young people also keep coming, including a recent request for information about the league from a girl in Hutchinson, Kansas, where Dottie's father, Dan Wiltse, was born more than one hundred years ago. Another letter from a budding art student included two sketches, one of Dottie in a Daisy uniform, pitcher's mitt in hand, and the words "My hero...Dottie Collins" to the left of her kneeling form, and another of Dottie Collins and Dottie Schroeder, which proclaimed them as "super role models." Additionally, Dottie continues to influence the younger generation by speaking at schools with Isabel Alverez and Wimp Baumgartner, their closeness solidified through having worked together on the Daisy part of Run, Jane, Run until 1999. Another new group of people joined her life in a different way, Dottie's allegiance having switched from the New York Yankees to the Chicago Cubs once she realized she was a Midwesterner by right of place if not by birth. If she is not meeting friends for lunch, Sunday afternoons during the baseball season find her in front of the television set hoping that this year is finally the year for her beloved Cubs.

Dottie can afford to sit back and bask in what she has accomplished. Her tireless efforts have paid off in untold dividends. Both in Cooperstown and in the Northern Indiana Center For History the All-American displays have become highly popular exhibits. Ted Spencer admitted that in his 22 years at the Hall of Fame, as of 2004, he had never gotten more than a few letters for any one exhibit. Yet in the first year alone of the Women In Baseball Exhibit Spencer said he "stopped counting at two hundred." The Hall of Fame also began establishing separate files for each player in the AAGPBL in 1995, "to honor and document the lives and careers of women who have played baseball." By 2004, Tim Wiles, the research librarian at the Hall of Fame, announced that most living players have a file as well as the more well-known deceased members.

The Northern Indiana Center for History has witnessed a similar surge of interest in the league. In 2000, Cheryl Taylor, the Center's executive director, told the Players Association Board that the All-American collection was the most popular exhibit and the one most requested by researchers. The spring of 2004 saw the Center fielding up to 25 calls about the league during the busy spring months. In addition to these two repositories for league material, the aagpbl.org, website illustrates the league's appeal to an unbelievable degree. The site averaged 350 hits daily in 2004, with the three-month period of June–August experiencing over 22,000 hits.

This rise of the league from virtual oblivion to the force it is today serves as a towering testimony that the talent, determination, and passion that Dottie Collins has shown for the game of baseball has been duly noted and registered. Fellow All-American Jean Hardy shared this thought: "Dottie had a rare insight and instinct that I came to trust. If anything needed doing she would do it. I am lucky she considers me a friend." Continuing along this line, Ted Spencer of the National Baseball Hall of Fame stated simply, "I consider her one of the best people I have ever met." All of this is high praise indeed and makes one thing abundantly clear. While the league is the legacy of all the women who played professional baseball during the war years and after, the fact that the league has a legacy at all is due in a large measure to Dottie Wiltse Collins.

Bibliography

Books

Browne, Lois, *Girls of Summer*. Toronto: HarperCollins Publishers Ltd., 1992.

Galt, Margot Fortunato, *Up to the Plate*. Minneapolis: Lerner Publications Company, 1995.

Gregorich, Barbara, *Women at Play: The Story of Women in Baseball*. San Diego, New York, London: Harcourt, Brace, & Company, 1993.

Hart, Jeffrey, *From This Moment On: America in 1940*. New York: Crown Publishers, 1987.

Hawfield, Michael C., *Here's Fort Wayne Past & Present*. Fort Wayne: SRS Publications, 1993.

Johnson, Susan, *When Women Played Hardball*. Seattle: Seal Press, 1994.

Kennedy, David M., *Freedom from Fear: The American People in Depression and War, 1929–1945*. New York: Oxford University Press, Inc., 1999.

Lingeman, Richard, *Don't You Know There's a War On? The American Home Front 1941–1945*. New York: Thunder's Mouth Press/Nation Books, 2003.

Macy, Sue, *A Whole New Ball Game*. New York: Penguin Books USA Inc., 1993.

Madden, W.C., *The Women of the All-American Girls Professional Baseball League: A Biographical Dictionary*. Jefferson, North Carolina: McFarland & Company, Inc., 1997.

May, Elaine Tyler, *Homeward Bound: American Families in the Cold War Era*. New York: BasicBooks, 1988.

Meyerowitz, Joanne, Editor, *Not June Cleaver: Women and Gender in Postwar America, 1945–1960*. Philadelphia: Temple University Press, 1994.

Waddingham, Gladys, *The History of Inglewood*. Los Angeles: The Historical Society of Centinela Valley, 1994.

Ward, Geoffrey C., and Burns, Ken, *Baseball: An Illustrated History*. New York: Alfred A. Knopf, 1994.

Wise, Nancy Baker, and Wise, Christy, *A Mouthful of Rivets: Women at Work in World War II*. San Francisco: Josey-Bass Publishers, 1994.

Interviews

Jeri Baldwin, personal correspondence with author, November, 2002.

Jacqueline Baumgart, personal correspondence with author, November, 2002.

Dottie Collins, personal interviews with author, June, September, 2002; August, 2004, Fort Wayne, Indiana.
Dottie Collins, personal correspondence with author, March, July, September, 2003; February, April, 2004.
David Gilbert, personal correspondence with author, October, 2002.
John Gilbert, personal correspondence with author, October, 2002.
Jim Glennie, personal correspondence with author, November, 2002.
Jean Harding, personal correspondence with author, February, 2004.
Barbara Hoffman, personal correspondence with author, October, 2003; March, 2004.
Frances Janssen, personal correspondence with author, February, 2004.
Vivian Kellogg, personal correspondence with author, October, 2003.
Virginia Larson, personal correspondence with author, October, 2003.
Margaret Maxwell, personal correspondence with author, February, 2004.
Gert McAtee, personal correspondence with author, March, 2004.
Carl Offerle, personal interview with author, Highland Beach, Florida, March, 2003.
June Peppas, personal interview with author, Hobe Sound, Florida, October, 2003.
Mary Rountree, personal interview with author, Highland Beach, Florida, October, 2002.
Carol Sheldon, personal correspondence with author, November, 2002.
Rich Sangillo, personal correspondence with author, October, 2002.
Ted Spencer, personal interview with author, Cooperstown, New York, February, 2004.
Patricia Tyler, personal correspondence with author, October, 2002; January, November, 2003; February, 2004.
Kathryn Vonderau, personal correspondence with author, October, 2003.
Judy Widen, personal correspondence with author, November, 2003.
Pat Wright, personal correspondence with author, March, 2004.

Newspapers

The Fort Wayne Journal-Gazette, 1945–1950.
The Fort Wayne News-Sentinel, 1945–1950.
The Los Angeles Examiner, 1936–1944.
The Los Angeles Times, 1936–1944.
The Minneapolis Daily Times, 1944.
The Minneapolis Daily Tribune/Sunday Tribune, The Minneapolis Evening Star Journal, 1944.

Thesis

Fidler, Merrie. *The Development and Decline of the All-American Girls Baseball League, 1943–1954.* Amherst: The University of Massachusetts, 1976.
Fidler, Merrie. *The Origins and History of the All-American Girls Professional*

Baseball League, 1943–1954. To be published by McFarland & Company, Inc., Publishers, 2005.

World Wide Web Sites

IMDB.com
MLB.com
www.springtrainingmagazine.com/history2.html. "Greetings from Catalina Island, Spring Training Home of the Cubs from 1921–1951."
www.cityofInglewood.org/depts/council/history.htm. "History of Inglewood."
www.baycities.org/history.htm. "History."

Index